SURFACE DESIGN
FOR FABRIC

FAIRCHILD BOOKS

SURFACE DESIGN
FOR FABRIC

KIMBERLY A. IRWIN

SAVANNAH COLLEGE OF ART AND DESIGN

Fairchild Books
An imprint of Bloomsbury Publishing Inc

BLOOMSBURY
NEW YORK · LONDON · NEW DELHI · SYDNEY

Fairchild Books
An imprint of Bloomsbury Publishing Inc

1385 Broadway   50 Bedford Square
New York   London
NY 10018   WC1B 3DP
USA   UK

www.bloomsbury.com

FAIRCHILD BOOKS, BLOOMSBURY and the Diana logo are trademarks of Bloomsbury Publishing Plc

First published in 2015

Library of Congress Cataloging-in-Publication Data
Irwin, Kimberly.
Surface design for fabric / Kimberly Irwin.
pages cm
Summary: "Surface Design for Fabric is a comprehensive, how-to guide to more than 60 surface design techniques for various fabrics and leather—ranging from traditional to experimental. Clear, step-by-step instructions and photographs demonstrate surface design techniques, allowing readers to quickly grasp the material and further explore and experiment on their own. Irwin covers a broad range of surface design techniques including: dyeing, staining, removing color, resists, printing and transfer, fiber manipulation, fabric manipulations, embroidery, and embellishments. Each chapter begins with a brief description and historical overview of the technique, and includes a fabric selection quick guide, tools and materials, how to set up your workspace, application methods and safety guidelines for each technique. Photographs and designer biographies showcase surface design techniques used in real-world designs. The final chapter offers advice on how to combine techniques to create commercial and avant-garde surface design. This modern studio resource clearly guides readers in the creation of beautiful, innovative, and professional surface designs"— Provided by publisher.
ISBN 978-1-60901-885-6 (hardback)
1. Textile design. 2. Textile printing. 3. Decoration and ornament. 4. Surfaces (Technology) I. Title.

TS1475.I79 2015
667'.38—dc23

2014020238

ISBN: HB: 978-1-609-01885-6
ePDF: 978-1-609-01936-5

Typeset by Precision Graphics, A Lachina Company
Cover Art Credit: Giannoni/WWD; © Conde Nast
Cover Design: Eleanor Rose
Printed and bound in China

This book is dedicated, in loving memory, to my brother Darrin Irwin.
I love you more.

CONTENTS

EXTENDED CONTENTS

5   FABRIC MANIPULATION

6   EMBROIDERY

PREFACE

Surface Design for Fabric is an instructional guide that details surface design techniques commonly used on fabric and leather. The text introduces more than fifty different techniques that aid in adding color, texture, and embellishment to fabric—transitioning it from simple, flat fabric to a unique creation. Each technique's step-by-step guide includes photographs, illustrations, material lists, and inspirational images. This comprehensive guide is invaluable to the fashion, interior, or textile design student because it:

+ provides a comprehensive guide to a wide range of techniques, each explained clearly, making it a useful reference guide for exploration of surface design
+ demonstrates how to complete each technique in a limited workspace, like a classroom or home studio
+ inspires students and gives them confidence to experiment

Once students realize how easy it is to transform simple fabric into extraordinary artwork, they discover that the imagination is the only limitation to beautiful surface design.

As a professor of fashion design, I encouraged my students to experiment with fabric manipulations. Teaching in an area of the country where high-end fabric stores are limited, the need to substitute or alter what materials were readily available was a necessity for students' visions to come to light; and because there was not a comprehensive book available that covered the wide range of surface techniques, I found myself accumulating countless texts and DIY books for the students to reference. Most of these books were either outdated or directed toward a novice and not the budding professional. So, I began collecting bits and pieces from across the surface design spectrum and compiled them into one step-by-step instructional guide. The intention is to appeal to creative students by offering clear visual explanations supported by text. I have found that this combination gives students the confidence to not only try new techniques but also to have successful outcomes without compromising creativity. The tools in this text give students the ability to create surface treatments on fabric that add depth to a portfolio or uniqueness to a collection.

This text is written for students at all levels of surface design although some basic sewing knowledge is required as well as access to a sewing machine for more advanced techniques. Fashion, interior, and textile design students will find it useful because it provides a comprehensive guide to a wide range of techniques, each explained clearly, making it a useful reference guide for early exploration of surface design. As students progress through each program, the need to demonstrate technical prowess and personal creativity becomes more important and, with most programs culminating in a final collection, the need to stand apart becomes more important. This text allows students who may not have access to designer fabrics commercially the ability to manipulate what is available into high-end fabric.

Surface Design for Fabric is organized as a user-friendly reference guide, allowing the student to select a technique and have all of the pertinent information compiled and accessible. Techniques are discussed individually within larger chapters divided by topic. They are arranged in a manner consistent with the order in which the techniques should be applied if creating multilayered surface design. Each chapter begins with a basic introduction, historical information, and an environmental impact statement along with supporting imagery. Then, each technique is explored in greater detail, including a more specific introduction, material lists, workspace recommendations, and safety precautions. This is followed by step-by-step instructions and examples of finished pieces. Select techniques also include designer profiles, which highlight professionals working in the fields of fashion or textile design, and collection spotlights that show how the technique can be applied to a garment for runway presentation.

In addition to clear instructions, each chapter includes pedagogical features including chapter objectives and key terms, which are defined within the text in bold and organized into a glossary at the end of the text. Additional resources are provided after each technique to aid students in finding materials and inspiration or sources for further explanation. Designer Profiles and Collection Spotlights show practical applications of each technique by working professionals. Hint boxes and quick reference guides throughout the text clarify important details and provide easy understanding. Student projects are presented at the end of each chapter to assist the student in understanding practical applications of the techniques.

The final chapter of the text focuses on combining any of the techniques covered in the text and provides a comprehensive flow chart that serves as a visual guide that breaks down the techniques based on fabric selection. This is followed by a gallery of artists and designers who combine and layer techniques, masterfully creating surface design for commercial and gallery use.

RESOURCES

Surface Design for Fabric STUDiO

Fairchild Books has a long history of excellence in textbook publishing for fashion education. Our new online STUDIOS are specially developed to complement this book with rich media ancillaries that students can adapt to their visual learning styles. STUDIO access is offered free with new book purchases and also sold separately through Bloomsbury Fashion Central (www.BloomsburyFashionCentral.com).

Features
+ Online self-quizzes with results and personalized study tips to help students master concepts
+ Flashcards with definitions and image identification to help students master terminology

Video Tutorials
+ Chapter 1: Dyeing Leather
+ Chapter 2: Discharge Paste Technique
+ Chapter 3: Part 1: Preparing a Screen and Part 2: Printing Using a Screen
+ Chapter 4: Part 1: Preparing Wool for Felting and Part 2: Wetting and Rolling Felt
+ Chapter 5: Direct Smocking
+ Chapter 6: Embroidery Stitches: Blanket Stitch, Chain Stitch, and French Knot
+ Chapter 7: Beading Techniques: Back Stitch, Dangle Stitch, and Sequins
+ Chapter 8: Combining Techniques: Vegetable-Tanned Leather with Mono Printing and Embroidery

Instructor's Guide

The Instructor's Guide provides sample syllabi adapted to course length, project ideas, grade sheets, quizzes, and ideas for integrating the video tutorials with at-home lessons to save valuable class time.

ACKNOWLEDGMENTS

This text could not have been written without the team at Bloomsbury Publishing, particularly Amanda Breccia, my Acquisitions Editor, who guided me from proposal to manuscript; Amy Butler, the Development Editor who kept me on track and responded to countless and sometimes silly emails; and Edie Weinberg, my Art Development Editor, for her ability to understand my vision.

The reviewers who took the time to provide valuable insight and recommendations that have made this text stronger: Melinda K. Adams, University of the Incarnate Word; Jason Bunin, SCAD Atlanta; Chrissy Day, Maryland Institute College of Art; Phyllis Fredendall, Finlandia University; Suzanne Goetz, Fashion Institute of Technology; Geetika Gupta, Art Institute, San Francisco; Mary Jane Matranga, Indiana University; Aaron McIntosh, Maryland Institute College of Art; Susan Strawn, Dominican University; Marcia Weiss, Philadelphia University.

Rafterman Photography for spending long days photographing samples and instructions all the while learning more about surface design than they ever cared to.

The countless artists and designers who allowed their spectacular work to be presented to the next generation of artists. In particular: Mary Edna Fraser, Eva Fulinova, India Flint, Dionne Swift, Julie Shackson, Karen Casper, and Irit Dulman for providing valuable insight into their processes and techniques.

Special thanks to those who have supported me academically and professionally particularly, Jonathan Kyle Farmer and John Bauernfeind who not only challenged me academically but also showed me what it means to be a teacher. Also, my colleagues at SCAD, especially Jason Bunin, Sarah Collins, and David Goodrowe for their understanding during life's many challenges.

Thank you to my friends and family whose support and encouragement knows no bounds, particularly Emily Colson for proofreading endlessly and not judging me for my inability to punctuate properly, and Sara Preville for her consistently positive attitude, which has kept me grounded and focused through our long friendship.

Special recognition is owed to my grandmother, Ruth Irwin, who patiently taught me many of the techniques in this text and instilled in me a love of surface design, for which I will always be grateful.

Complete gratitude is owed to my parents, David and Kathy Irwin, and brothers, Rich and Darrin Irwin, who gave me the strength and courage to follow a path toward my dreams, a path that often wandered off aimlessly.

SURFACE DESIGN
FOR FABRIC

chapter 1

DYEING AND STAINING FABRIC

OBJECTIVES:

+ Using dye to permanently change the color of protein-fiber fabric

+ Using dye to permanently change the color of synthetic fabric

+ Using household or organic methods to permanently change the color of natural fabric

+ Dyeing vegetable-tanned leather

+ Staining fabric with rust

+ Staining fabric with soil or clay

+ Staining fabric with grasses, leaves, or flowers

+ Using household materials to stain fabric

Chemical or organic methods can be used to add consistent color to an entire piece of fabric. Dyeing and staining permanently change the color of most fabrics, but the processes require some sort of chemical reaction to maintain the fabric's vibrancy, or **colorfastness**. These reactions can have a tremendous impact on the environment. See the box on page 3 for a discussion on how to limit the environmental impact of the techniques described in this chapter.

DYEING

To **dye** fabric means to create a chemical bath of a colorant dissolved into water. Fabric is submersed and agitated until the color is sufficiently absorbed—this is known as the **immersion technique**, or *tub dyeing method*, a reliable method for even distribution of dye. Often a **mordant**, or *dye carrier*, is needed to help the dye adhere to the fabric and to provide colorfastness. The dye binds with the fabric molecularly to create long-lasting, vibrant colors.

When thickened to the desired consistency using a dye thickener like Superclear or sodium alginate, dye can be applied to a fabric via **direct application**—applied directly to the surface of the fabric like paint (Figure 1.1).

Natural/organic methods are used on **protein** (animal) and **cellulose** (plant) **fibers**. These methods are often criticized for providing less consistent results when compared to chemical dye options, but consistency issues arise with chemical dyes too. Depending on the desired outcome, organic methods are sometimes the best option for natural color or an aged appearance.

The first recorded use of dye dates back thousands of years to ancient civilizations when people started using organic materials to create vibrant colors on clothing and other objects often found at burial sites.[1] Early humans used natural resources to create dyes, often discovering them accidently through the pounding, soaking, or boiling of flowers, trees, insects, minerals, and shellfish.[2] The most prominent ancient dyes were **indigo**, derived from the indigo plant to achieve blues; **cochineal**, an insect, which when crushed provides a crimson color; and **madder**, a plant root used to achieve reds, purples, violets, and browns. These organic dyes "originated from plants grown in hot climates where the sun's heat and rich vegetation contributed to strong vibrant colors in plants and animals."[3] Even the early process of dyeing leather was completely organic, using tree bark, roots, wood, alum, and salt. The **raw leather**, with all fats and oils removed, was placed into a large vat of water with the crushed ingredients sandwiched between the skins for six months or more.[4]

As humans' understanding of chemistry progressed, so did the ability to create more permanent and vibrant colors on fabric. In 1856, William Perkin accidently discovered synthetic dye when he was trying to make a drug from coal tar to control high fever. When he dissolved the compound into alcohol a mauve color emerged.[5] The year 1862 saw the development of **acid dyes** for use on animal protein fibers, and in 1922, A. G. Green and K. H. Sunders developed the first **disperse dyes** used on synthetic fibers and water-repellent **hydrophobic fabrics**.[6]

Today, the ability to create vibrant, long-lasting color is easier than ever, but because some dyes work better on certain fabrics, it is important to select the dye based upon the fabric choice. Consult Table 1.1 for quick reference.

1.1 Maison Martin Margiela RTW Fall 2013 collection showed bright pink oversized shirt cuffs, a look that can be done in a home studio with a paintbrush and thickened dye appropriate to the fiber content of the fabric.
Giannoni/WWD; ©Condé Nast

Table 1.1: Fibers and Appropriate Dyes

Fiber Choice	Dye Group	Types and Brands of Dye	Advantages	Disadvantages
protein (wool, mohair, silk, feathers, nylon, and some acrylic fabric)	acid dye	Dharma acid dyes, Jacquard acid dyes, PRO Washfast acid dye (Nylomine dye), PRO Sabraset dye (Lanaset dye)	bright colors, easy to use, low waste	streaks easily, some powders can be hard to dissolve
synthetic (polyester, acrylic, acetate, rayon, and nylon)	disperse dye	PROsperse disperse dyes, Aljo disperse dyes	light- and colorfast, easy to use	requires a mordant and high temperatures
cellulose or protein (cotton, silk, hemp, linen, rayon, wool)	natural dye	indigo, madder, cochineal, household spices, berries, vegetables	creates subtle color, environmentally friendly	requires a mordant and results are not consistent

ENVIRONMENTAL IMPACT: DYEING AND STAINING FABRIC

To limit dyes' and dye baths' impact on the environment, it is important to handle, store, and dispose of them properly. Great care should be taken when handling dyes; always wear gloves and protect your skin as much as possible. It is also important to wear protective eyewear and a dust mask while mixing dyes to guard against splashing and to avoid inhaling potentially toxic chemicals. All dyes should be stored in airtight glass or plastic containers to avoid unintentional spilling or inhalation of fumes or particles. Disposing of a dye bath down the drain is not considered hazardous when done only a few times a month. The large quantities of water dilute the chemicals enough to make them relatively harmless to a septic system. However, it is always best to neutralize any dye bath before pouring it down a drain. Acid dye can be neutralized by adding a couple of teaspoons of soda ash, while disperse dyes only require a splash of vinegar. Do not dump dye baths directly onto the ground or into a storm drain, even if they have been neutralized, because they could seep into the water supply or drain into a stream.[7]

Dyeing and staining using organic methods is the most eco-friendly option but should still be handled with care. Some natural materials may still cause skin irritation, so gloves should always be worn. A natural dye bath should only be disposed of down a sink drain; the alum used for a mordant makes it unsafe to be composted or disposed of directly onto the ground.

Leather tanning has a huge impact on the environment, but the leather dyes used on naturally tanned leathers are more eco-friendly. Some leather dyes are water based and can be diluted with water and simply washed down the drain. Others are alcohol based and release fumes, so they should always be used in well-ventilated areas. They are still safe to dispose of down the drain when diluted with water. Always wear gloves when working with any leather dye because it will stain skin and nails.

Acid dyes are used on protein fibers (wool, mohair, silk, feathers, nylon, and some acrylic fabric) and are powdered, economical, fast acting, and permanent. Primarily used for immersion or tub dyeing, acid dyes can be thickened with Superclear or sodium alginate and applied like paint to the surface of the fabric, but because it is a dye it will penetrate the fibers and become permanent. **Fiber reactive dyes** are another option for wool fibers and all cellulose fibers. (See the box on page 5 for further information.)

Although the word "acid" implies that these dyes are caustic, they are actually some of the safest dyes available. The acid refers to vinegar or citric acid added to a dye bath, which lowers the pH and helps the dye particles bind to fibers. This particular dye class is known to create consistent color because the molecules of the dye are so small and simple that they float through the water quickly and attach evenly to fibers.[8]

Before dyeing, all fabric must be **scoured**, meaning washed in very hot water (140 degrees) to remove any dirt, oil, or **sizing**, which is a chemical coating applied to fabric to repel stains or dirt, but which can also repel dye. **Synthrapol** is a commercial concentrated cleaner used to scour the fabric and to fix the dye in the final dye bath.

LOW-COST ALTERNATIVE TO SYNTHRAPOL

A common low-cost alternative is Dawn dish detergent, which is just as effective but less expensive.

Materials

Figure 1.2 shows some of the materials needed for acid dye.

+ Acid dye—almost any color can be purchased, but the dye powders can also be mixed (see Appendix B, Figure B.27).
+ Citric acid or vinegar (see Appendix B, Figure B.35)
+ Dust mask
+ Stainless steel or enamel pot (used only for dyeing)
+ Measuring spoons (used only for dyeing)
+ Protective eyewear
+ Protective gloves: rubber, vinyl, or latex depending on skin sensitivity
+ Protein-fiber fabrics: wool, mohair, silk, feathers, nylon. Cotton can also be used but results will be less vibrant. Fabric should always be scoured before use (see Step 2 in the instructions).
+ Scale for weighing fabric
+ Sodium alginate used for thickening (see Appendix B, Figure B.40)
+ Wooden spoon or fork (used only for dyeing)
+ Synthrapol or Dawn dish detergent
+ Urea used for thickening (see Appendix B, Figure B.38)

1.2 Materials needed to dye fabric using Jacquard acid dye.

Application Methods

+ Direct application (see Chapter 3, Printing on Natural Fabric, page 67)
+ Fluid application with thinned dye. Add 1 cup of hot water to 5 ounces of acid dye powder to create a very concentrated solution.
+ Stovetop method

Workspace

+ Cover surfaces to avoid cross contamination.
+ Sink
+ Stovetop

Fiber reactive dyes work best on cellulose fibers like cotton, rayon, hemp, and silk; the process is similar to acid dyeing. First, the fabric must be scoured in hot water using Synthrapol. Next, dissolve the dye in warm water in a separate container. (Follow the measurements provided by the dye manufacturer for precise color matching.) Add dissolved dye to dye bath and mix well; then carefully place wet fabric into the dye bath and begin agitating with a wooden spoon immediately, and continue for at least 20 minutes. Dye molecules will start binding as soon as the fabric touches the water, so constant movement of the fabric is essential. Next, prepare soda ash by dissolving it into warm water. Slowly add the soda ash to the dye bath (over a minimum of a 10-minute period of time). Never pour the soda ash directly onto the fabric or it could create blotching and freckling. Continue agitating the fabric for another 30 minutes for lighter colors and up to an hour for darker colors. Finally, rinse the fabric in cool running water until the water runs clear. A final wash in hot water and Synthrapol will set the dye into the fabric. For more in-depth instruction visit Dharma Trading Company (http://www.dharmatrading.com) or consult *The Surface Designer's Handbook* by Holly Brackmann.

Safety: With all dyes, be careful not to inhale powdered toxic chemicals by wearing a mask. Always wear gloves to avoid staining skin and nails, as well as protective eyewear in case of splashing.

Instructions for Immersion Dyeing on a Stovetop

1. Weigh dry fabric using a standard kitchen scale.
2. Scour fabric to remove any dirt, oils, or sizing. Add about one capful of Synthrapol to a washing machine and wash in very hot water. This can also be done on a stovetop. Fabric can be dried and stored for later use.
3. Evenly wet scoured fabric using regular tap water, and don't allow it to dry out.
4. Fill a stainless steel or enamel pot with enough hot water for the fabric to move freely, then turn heat on.
5. Apply dust mask and add dye powder, being careful not to inhale any dye particles. The general rule is to add 2 to 4 percent of the weight of the dry fabric. So, for one pound of dry fabric, use about 1/3 to 2/3 ounces of dye powder, depending on the desired intensity. More dye creates darker colors.
6. Stir until all of the dye powder is dissolved.
7. Add wet fabric to pot. Dry fabric will not soak up the dye evenly and can create spotting.
8. Raise the temperature to just under boiling.
9. Add one tablespoon of citric acid per pound of dry fabric.
10. Maintain a constant temperature and stir frequently for about 30 minutes.
11. Wash in Synthrapol to set the dye.

Troubleshooting

Freckling can be caused if the dye powder is not fully dissolved before adding the wet fabric. Some colors are harder to dissolve and may need to be predissolved in 1 cup hot water and strained through a nylon stocking. Always add the liquid to the powder, not the powder to the liquid.

Spotty or uneven color is often caused by overcrowding the fabric in the dye bath or not agitating the fabric well in the dye bath. Adding Glauber's salt with the citric acid in Step 9 can also help to level color.

Acid Dye | Color Chart

Color	Number	Color Name	C-M-Y-K	R-G-B	Web
	600	Ecru	0-10-20-6	239-216-191	#EFD8BF
	601	Yellow Sun	0-0-100-0	255-242-0	#FFF200
	602	Bright Yellow	0-5-100-5	247-218-0	#F7DA00
	603	Golden Yellow	0-5-100-5	247-148-30	#F7931E
	604	Burnt Orange	0-60-100-10	222-118-28	#DE761C
	605	Pumpkin Orange	0-60-100-5	232-123-30	#E87B1E
	606	Deep Orange	0-85-90-0	240-78-48	#F04E30
	607	Salmon	0-65-50-0	243-123-112	#F37B70
	608	Pink	10-100-0-0	216-11-140	#D70B8C
	609	Scarlet	0-100-90-0	237-27-47	#ED1B2E
	610	Burgundy	5-100-70-20	187-19-58	#BB133A
	611	Vermillion	20-100-50-20	166-22-76	#A6164C
	612	Lilac	45-50-0-0	146-131-190	#9283BD
	613	Purple	80-100-20-15	83-37-110	#53266E
	614	Violet	90-100-0-0	71-47-146	#472F92
	615	Periwinkle	60-50-0-10	104-115-173	#6873AC
	616	Russet	20-100-100-10	183-33-38	#B72026
	617	Cherry Red	0-100-60-0	237-22-81	#ED1651
	618	Fire Red	12-100-80-8	198-29-56	#C61D38
	619	Crimson	7-100-60-20	184-18-67	#B81243
	620	Hot Fuchsia	0-100-0-0	236-0-140	#EC008C

1.3a and b Jacquard acid dye color charts. ©JaquardProducts.com

Examples

Figures 1.3a and b are Jacquard acid dye color charts, and Figure 1.4 shows a variety of acid-dyed fabrics.

Additional Resources

Sourcing: Binders Art Store (www.bindersart.com), Dharma Trading Company (www.dharmatrading.com), PRO Chemical and Dye (www.prochemicalanddye.com), Jacquard (www.jacquardproducts.com)

Further Explanation: *The Surface Designer's Handbook* by Holly Brackmann

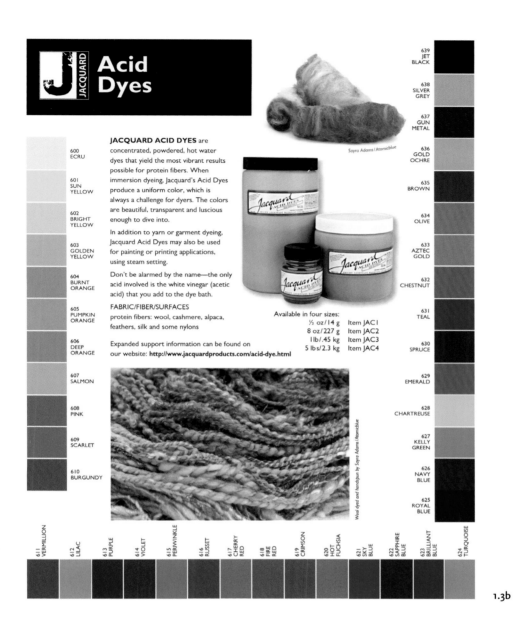

Acid Dyes

JACQUARD ACID DYES are concentrated, powdered, hot water dyes that yield the most vibrant results possible for protein fibers. When immersion dyeing, Jacquard's Acid Dyes produce a uniform color, which is always a challenge for dyers. The colors are beautiful, transparent and luscious enough to dive into.

In addition to yarn or garment dyeing, Jacquard Acid Dyes may also be used for painting or printing applications, using steam setting.

Don't be alarmed by the name—the only acid involved is the white vinegar (acetic acid) that you add to the dye bath.

FABRIC/FIBER/SURFACES
protein fibers: wool, cashmere, alpaca, feathers, silk and some nylons

Expanded support information can be found on our website: http://www.jacquardproducts.com/acid-dye.html

Sayra Adams/Atomicblue

Available in four sizes:
½ oz/14 g   Item JAC1
8 oz/227 g   Item JAC2
1 lb/.45 kg   Item JAC3
5 lbs/2.3 kg   Item JAC4

Wool dyed and handspun by Sayra Adams/Atomicblue

600 ECRU
601 SUN YELLOW
602 BRIGHT YELLOW
603 GOLDEN YELLOW
604 BURNT ORANGE
605 PUMPKIN ORANGE
606 DEEP ORANGE
607 SALMON
608 PINK
609 SCARLET
610 BURGUNDY

639 JET BLACK
638 SILVER GREY
637 GUN METAL
636 GOLD OCHRE
635 BROWN
634 OLIVE
633 AZTEC GOLD
632 CHESTNUT
631 TEAL
630 SPRUCE
629 EMERALD
628 CHARTREUSE
627 KELLY GREEN
626 NAVY BLUE
625 ROYAL BLUE

611 VERMILLION
612 LILAC
613 PURPLE
614 VIOLET
615 PERIWINKLE
616 RUSSET
617 CHERRY RED
618 FIRE RED
619 CRIMSON
620 HOT FUCHSIA
621 SKY BLUE
622 SAPPHIRE BLUE
623 BRILLIANT BLUE
624 TURQUOISE

1.3b

1.4 Left to right: silk chiffon, cotton broadcloth, silk gauze, cotton jersey, silk dupion. Royal blue created using 1/3 ounce red and 1/3 ounce blue acid dye. Chartreuse created using 1/3 ounce blue and 1/3 ounce yellow acid dye.

Disperse dyes are used on synthetic fabrics such as polyester, acrylic, acetate, rayon, and nylon. Unlike acid dyes, disperse dyes do not dissolve in water and may require a mordant to help suspend the chemicals in water. Note that mordant is essential with polyester.

Disperse dyes are made up of rather large molecules (when compared to acid dyes), which makes them suitable to use on synthetics and other hydrophobic fabrics that do not absorb dye quickly. The molecules of the dye don't dissolve into the water but are, instead, suspended in it with the aid of a dye carrier. The carrier also helps the dye to migrate to the fibers. Once the temperature of the dye bath is elevated, the dye penetrates the surface of the fiber to become permanent.

Disperse dyes are lightfast and colorfast and create brilliant, strong colors on synthetics. However, with this type of dye it is difficult to achieve a dark indigo color in a traditional studio space because of the extremely high water and dry heat temperatures required to set the color permanently into the fabric.

Materials

Figure 1.5 shows some of the materials needed for disperse dyeing.

+ Disperse dye (see Appendix B, Figure B.28)
+ Dust mask
+ Dye carrier (see Appendix B, Figure B.36)
+ Measuring spoons
+ Protective eyewear
+ Protective gloves: rubber, vinyl, or latex depending on skin sensitivity
+ Scale for weighing fabric

+ Stainless steel or enamel pots. Two are needed and should only be used for dyeing.
+ Synthetic fabric. Scour fabric; see Step 1 in the instructions.
+ Synthrapol or Dawn dish detergent
+ Two containers to mix dye
+ White distilled vinegar or citric acid (see Appendix B, Figure B.35)
+ Wooden spoon or fork (used only for dyeing)

Application Methods

+ Direct application (see Chapter 3, Printing on Synthetic Fabric, page 68)
+ Stovetop immersion dying
+ Transfer method (see Chapter 3, Transfer Printing with Thickened Disperse Dye, page 82)

Workspace

+ Cover surfaces with plastic to prevent cross contamination.
+ Sink
+ Stovetop or hot plate

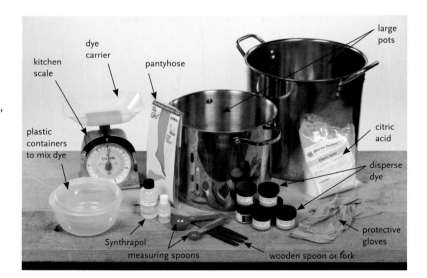

1.5 Materials needed for dyeing with disperse dye.

Safety: Always wear protective gloves and an apron. Be careful not to inhale dye powders, and never use any utensils for food use after they have been used to mix dyes.

Instructions for Stovetop Immersion Dyeing

1. Scour fabric in hot water and 1 teaspoon of Synthrapol. Fabric should be dampened before dyeing if it has been previously washed.
2. Apply dust mask and prepare dye by dissolving it in 1 cup boiling water. See Table 1.2 for general guidelines to achieve different shades. Be careful not to inhale any dye particles.
3. Strain the dissolved dye through nylon pantyhose to remove any left over particles. Strain a second time.
4. Dilute the dye carrier by mixing 2 tablespoons into 1 cup of boiling water.
5. Prepare dye bath in the following order stirring well between each ingredient:
   + 2 1/2 gallons hot water (140 degrees, almost boiling)
   + 1/2 teaspoon Synthrapol
   + 1 teaspoon citric acid or 11 teaspoons white distilled vinegar
   + Diluted dye carrier from Step 4
   + Strained dye solution
6. Stir well and add damp scoured fabric.
7. Bring the dye bath to a rapid boil while constantly stirring. Simmer for 30 minutes for lighter shades and 40 minutes for darker shades.
8. Bring a second pot of water to a boil.
9. Remove the fabric from the dye bath and place it into the second pot of hot water.
10. Remove the dye from the original dye pot and refill with hot water and 1/2 teaspoon of Synthrapol.
11. Rinse in hot water to remove any excess dye and allow to dry.

Troubleshooting

Freckling can be caused if the dye powder is not fully dissolved before adding the wet fabric. Some colors are harder to dissolve and may need to be predissolved in 1 cup hot water and strained through a nylon stocking. Always add the liquid to the powder, not the powder to the liquid.

Spotty or uneven color is often caused by overcrowding the fabric in the dye bath or not agitating the fabric well in the dye bath.

Examples

Figure 1.6 shows PRO Chemical and Dye's disperse dye color chart and Figure 1.7 demonstrates how the same color dye can produce various colors on different fabrics.

Additional Resources

Sourcing: PRO Chemical and Dye (www.prochemicalanddye.com/)

Further Explanation: *The Surface Designer's Handbook* by Holly Brackmann

Table 1.2: How to Achieve Various Color Shades

	Light	Medium	Dark	Black
Dye Powder	1/2 tsp.	1 1/2 tsp.	3 tsp.	6 tsp.

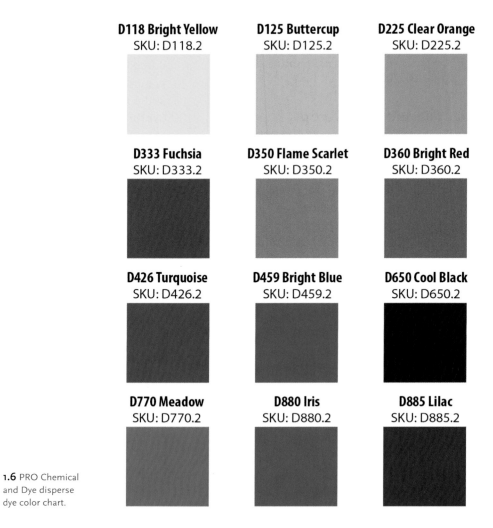

D118 Bright Yellow
SKU: D118.2

D125 Buttercup
SKU: D125.2

D225 Clear Orange
SKU: D225.2

D333 Fuchsia
SKU: D333.2

D350 Flame Scarlet
SKU: D350.2

D360 Bright Red
SKU: D360.2

D426 Turquoise
SKU: D426.2

D459 Bright Blue
SKU: D459.2

D650 Cool Black
SKU: D650.2

D770 Meadow
SKU: D770.2

D880 Iris
SKU: D880.2

D885 Lilac
SKU: D885.2

1.6 PRO Chemical and Dye disperse dye color chart.

1.7 Created using a single dye bath of 1 teaspoon red and 1 teaspoon yellow PROsperse disperse dye. Notice how differently each fabric reacts to the same dye combination. Left to right: polyester chiffon, polyester lining, rayon georgette, nylon, polyester satin, polyester mesh, and acetate lining.

The colors produced using natural elements tend to be slightly more subdued when compared to acid or disperse dyes. Intense dramatic color can be achieved with materials such as indigo or madder, but most of the organic methods will result in subtle hues or an aged look. But, the best part of natural dying is the experimentation. Cupboard staples like coffee, tea, wine, herbs, spices, fruits, beets, berries, and black grapes provide beautiful purples, pinks, and grays, while vegetables like onions create golden and yellow hues. With consistent agitation, an even color can be achieved using natural dyes.

Most natural dyes are not colorfast and therefore require the addition of a mordant to help the dye adhere to the fibers. Some natural dyes like indigo provide excellent colorfastness, while dyes like madder tend to fade over time. The most commonly used mordant is alum, and although it is relatively nontoxic, it should always be stored safely and handled with care. Other mordants like iron, tannic acid, and chrome can be used and will produce varying results.

Generally, natural dyes take longer to penetrate the fibers of natural fabrics and will need to be placed in the dye bath longer than chemical dyes. Heat and constant agitation are also required to create even color tone.

Natural dyes once thickened with sodium alginate can be applied using a direct application to create a painterly effect (see Chapter 3, Printing on Natural Fabric, page 67).

Materials

Figure 1.8 shows some of the materials needed for dyeing with household materials.

+ Alum (see Appendix B, Figure B.33)
+ Fabrics with natural fibers work best.
+ Household or organic materials such as spices, berries, madder, vegetables
+ Mesh strainer or pantyhose
+ Protective gloves: rubber, vinyl, or latex depending on skin sensitivity
+ Synthrapol for scouring fabric
+ Stainless steel or enamel pots that are used only for dyeing. Two pots will be needed, and each should be large enough to hold the fabric without overcrowding.

1.8 Materials needed to dye using household or organic materials.

Application Methods

+ Direct application (see Chapter 3, Printing on Natural Fabric)
+ Stovetop immersion dying

Workspace

+ Stovetop

Safety: Never use pot or strainer for food preparation after it has been used for dyeing. Always we ar protective gloves and a dust mask when working with powdered natural dyes.

Instructions

1. Scour fabric using a washing machine (hot water) and a capful of Synthrapolor on the stovetop with enough hot water to allow the fabric to move freely in the pot without overcrowding and 1 tablespoon of Synthrapol.

2. Soak fabric in alum solution (7 tablespoons for every gallon of water) for 20 minutes. Fabric can be soaked and stored for later but should be used within a month or it will begin to degrade.

3. Dampen dry fabric before adding to dye bath.

4. In a large stainless steel pot with enough water for the fabric to move freely, add any household ingredient such as spices, berries, vegetables, tree bark, or anything with strong color.

5. Bring pot to a boil and simmer for 1 hour.

6. Strain the water and ingredients through a mesh strainer or a pair of pantyhose (for ingredients like spices) into another stainless steel pot.

7. Add wet fabric and bring to a light boil.

8. Simmer for 1 hour, stirring occasionally.

9. Wash the fabric gently in Synthrapol to set the dye.

10. Allow to dry.

Examples

Figure 1.9 demonstrates various results of organic dyeing.

1.9 Left to right: henna-dyed silk chiffon, cotton broadcloth dyed with cherries, madder-dyed silk habotai, and silk twill dyed using red onions and green peppers.

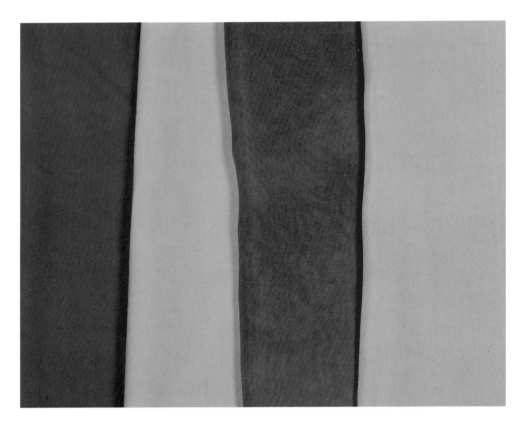

DESIGNER PROFILE: EVA FULINOVA

Tinctory's founder Eva Fulinova, resident of the Midlands, United Kingdom, always enjoyed creating small-scale objects. This fascination with all things miniature led her to creating jewelry. Combining that with her love of naturally dyed fabrics, Fulinova creates beautiful, tiny works of art. Using fine silk dyed from plants found on nature walks in her own backyard, she adds hand-pleating and smocking to create necklaces, bracelets, and earrings.

When in season, Fulinova collects goldenrod flowers to create yellow colors and hawthorn berries to achieve tans—but no palette is complete without blue, a hard color to achieve with natural dyes. Fulinova's solution is a combination of buying indigo from other dyers and experimenting with Japanese indigo and madder, grown in her own balcony garden. Fulinova has even created her own small indigo fermentation vat where she painstakingly maintains ideal conditions by keeping it warm and regularly adding bran to aid in the fermentation process.

Once the fabric is dyed, pleated, and smocked, she overdyes the fabric a number of times to give the tops of the pleats a different tone, and the new dyes blend with the background to create more complex colors. Once the ideal color is achieved, Fulinova transforms the piece from a textile to wearable art (Figures 1.10a and b).[9]

1.10a Pinwheel pleated and smocked necklaces paired with the seasonal leaves that created the dusty colors.
Eva Fulinova

1.10b Printed with autumn leaves and smocked to create a necklace concealing a tiny pocket.
Eva Fulinova

Additional Resources

Sourcing: A local grocery store can provide you with a variety of options, but flowers and tree bark collected from nature also work well.

Further Explanation: *Dyes From Kitchen Produce* by Setsuko Ishii, *The Complete Guide to Natural Dyeing* by Eva Lambert, www.prairiefibers.com

Leather dyeing is the process of applying a consistent color to the surface of leather. Leather dyeing, or **tanning**, is done in highly specialized facilities specific to the skin being used, and thus the process is difficult to generalize. It starts with the removal of all fats and oils from the skin and then replacing these oils with chemicals to prevent the skin from deteriorating. There are three main types of leather tanning, the first being **oil tanning**, or *latigo*. Latigo is water resistant, flexible, and strong and is often used for laces or products, such as shoes, that are consistently exposed to the elements. Next, **chrome tanning**, the most common type of tanning, uses a mixture of chromium sulfate and other chemicals. The process produces a water-resistant, long-wearing leather that is softer and more fluid than oil-tanned leather. The third tanning process, and the focus of this section, **vegetable tanning**, is done with a combination of oak bark and other chemicals.

Vegetable-tanned leather absorbs the water and dye quickly, creating an even distribution and providing an opportunity for a molded surface. It comes in a variety of thicknesses, making it suitable for almost any project. Vegetable-tanned leather will always need to be treated with a finish to protect it from oil, dirt, and water, and although vegetable-tanned leather can be made water repellent, it cannot be made water resistant when processed in a traditional studio space.

A variety of leather dyes are available and can be generalized into three basic categories: alcohol, spirit- or water-based, and oil-based dyes. **Alcohol-based leather dyes** are quickly absorbed into the surface of the leather and dry rapidly but they change the feel of the leather, leaving it tougher. This type of dye releases fumes, so be sure to work in a well-ventilated area. **Spirit-** or **water-based leather dye** retains the leather's natural properties but takes longer to dry and can be easily disrupted later by water, unless properly treated. **Oil-based leather dyes** penetrate the leather best and even soften the leather slightly. This type of dye takes much longer to dry and, because it is oil-based, the colors are limited.

APPLYING DYE TO LEATHER

All of these dyes can be applied the same way—choose the one most appropriate to your project. Leather dye can be mixed and layered to create deep, rich, varied colors, or it can be directly applied (Figure 1.11).

1.11 Felder-Felder RTW Winter 2011 collection created a dress that was likely created in a tannery, but the same results can be accomplished with a direct application of dye to the leather in a painterly fashion.
Giannoni/WWD; ©Condé Nast

Materials

Figure 1.12 shows some of the materials needed for dyeing vegetable-tanned leather.

+ Dust mask if using alcohol based dyes
+ Leather dye (see Appendix B, Figure B.29)
+ Protective gloves: rubber, vinyl, or latex depending on skin sensitivity
+ Vegetable-tanned leather
+ Wool pad or old cotton t-shirt cut into strips

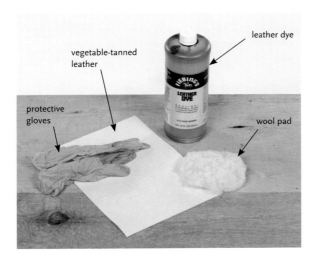

1.12 Materials needed to dye leather.

Application Methods

Direct application works best with dye straight from the bottle. Always apply in a circular motion.

Workspace

+ Cover workspace with newspaper or plastic to prevent cross contamination or unwanted staining of the work surface.

Safety: Always wear gloves when working with leather dye because it will stain and potentially irritate skin. When using alcohol-based dyes, a ventilation mask is recommended to avoid breathing any toxic fumes. Masks can be easily acquired at a local craft or hardware store.

Instructions

1. Cover work surface with newspaper and put on gloves.
2. Lay leather flat on work surface.
3. Pour dye into a small dish and lightly dip wool or rag into the dye. Try not to oversaturate the cloth or this could lead to streaking.
4. Lightly apply dye using a circular motion. Try to move the wool pad quickly to avoid oversaturation of dye in any particular area (Figure 1.13).

VIDEO

Go to Chapter 1 Video Tutorial: Leather Dye

1.13 Apply leather dye in a circular motion in thin layers.

5. Allow each layer to dry before applying a second or third coat.

1.14 Apply dye in circular motion until the desired color is achieved; allow to dry between each coat.

6. Continue applying dye until the desired color is achieved.

1.15 Leather dyed using dark brown Fiebings dye after four layers.

Examples

Figure 1.16 shows how darker shades can be achieved with the same dye color.

1.16 Light or heavy circular strokes create different depths of color. Notice how each successive coat becomes darker, and a light application achieves an aged look.

Additional Resources

Sourcing: Tandy Leather Factory (www.tandyleatherfactory.com), Zack White Leather (www.zackwhite.com)

Inspiration: *Leather: The New Frontier in Art* by J. Robert Buck

STAINING

Staining is adding pattern to fabric using a direct application of objects, dye, or paint to the surface of the fabric. Staining will create a pattern that penetrates into the fibers of the fabric and cannot easily be removed. Of course, commercial detergents and stain removers are designed to remove organic stains like grass, blood, and coffee, so pretreating fabrics with a mordant, like alum or vinegar, will help maintain the stain's vibrancy.

Staining fabric with grass, leaves, or soil was discovered accidently by ancient civilizations and is likely the precursor to actual fabric dyeing. But it wasn't until small pockets of the population, mostly nomads, began experimenting with the resources available that they found that muds, tree bark, flowers, and leaves could be used to decorate their skin and clothing. Consider the Australian Aborigines who use colored clay to decorate themselves, their homes, and ceremonial artifacts. They finely grind ochre (shades of yellow and red), charcoal (black), or gypsum (white) and then mix in water.[10] The result is a substance easily manipulated onto the surface of fabric, wood, or skin.

Although the materials are easy to manipulate, there isn't a lot of control over the results when staining with rust, earth, clay, grass, leaves, or household/organic methods, but the finished product can be extraordinary. Experimentation is vital, and fabric choice plays an important part in the results achieved. Generally, a tighter woven fabric, like linen, works best because the increased surface area gives the stain more opportunity to penetrate the fabric, resulting in more intense patterns.

Rusting is the creation of a pattern on fabric or leather with the help of any rusty metal object. The choice of object is what will create varying patterns; rusty nails create fine dots, as in Patrik Ervell's collection (see Collection Spotlight, page 20), whereas larger items create bold, dramatic patterns, as in Rio Wrenn's work using scissors (Figure 1.17).

Fabric is first soaked in either vinegar or saltwater (as Rio Wrenn does), which acts as a mordant, and then wrapped around, set on top of, or layered with rusty objects. Fabric and objects are then allowed to set for varying amounts of time depending on the results desired. The longer the rusty object is in contact with the fabric, the more dramatic the results. Vinegar should be added if the fabric begins to dry out during the process. The fabric is then washed in warm water and Synthrapol to remove any excess metal and to dispel the vinegar odor.

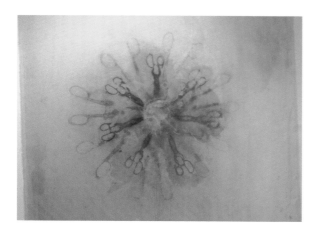

1.17 Rio Wrenn created *Blades In*, 2007. Wrenn uses saltwater, instead of vinegar, to first soak the fabric, and then places rusty metal scissors onto the fabric. She periodically rewets the fabric with saltwater until the desired results are achieved. This piece on silk was allowed to set for several days.
Rio Wrenn

Materials

Figure 1.18 shows some of the materials needed to rust fabric.

+ Fabric—almost any will do as long as there is no sizing, which can prevent the stain from penetrating into the fabric.
+ Plastic bags for storing rusted objects and fabric
+ Protective gloves: rubber, vinyl, or latex depending on skin sensitivity
+ Rusty objects
+ Spray bottle filled with vinegar
+ Vinegar

vinegar- or saltwater-soaked fabric

rusty objects

1.18 Materials needed to rust fabric.

Application Methods

+ A direct application is used—fabric is wrapped around rusty objects or placed in direct contact with them.

Workspace

+ Always cover work surface with newspaper or plastic.
+ Vinegar's strong odor usually makes this a process better completed in a well-ventilated area or outdoors.

Safety: Always protect yourself from small cuts and infection by wearing gloves when handling rusty objects and always work in a well-ventilated area.

Instructions

1. Briefly but thoroughly soak fabric in vinegar. Some fabrics can be damaged if soaked for too long.
2. Place rusty objects directly onto fabric, (Figure 1.19a) or wrap fabric around a rusty object (Figure 1.19b).

1.19a Rusty objects such as nails can be placed directly onto the surface of the fabric.

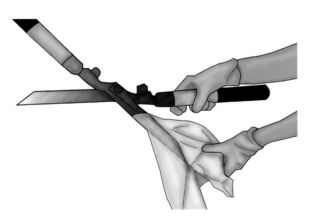

1.19b Vinegar-saturated fabric can be wrapped around a rusty object like a pair of garden shears.

3. Place into plastic bags and place outside. Rusting happens faster when heat and sunlight are involved. Objects can still be placed indoors, but it may take longer to achieve the desired results.
4. Check fabric regularly and spray with vinegar to keep the fabric and rusty objects moist.
5. Leave the fabric to rust until the desired results are achieved, though 24 hours is the minimum.
6. Rinse fabric with an outside hose to avoid creating rust in sinks.
7. Press samples with an iron used only with rusted fabrics.

Examples

Figures 1.20 and 1.21 show a variety of rusted fabrics.

1.20 Left to right: silk chiffon wrapped around metal rod, navy cow leather wrapped around metal rod, rayon georgette rusted with old garden shears, printed cotton stained using a rusty metal pail, blue satin rusted with nails, and printed upholstery cotton wrapped around garden shears.

1.21 Suede pigskin after being wrapped around a rusty rod for several days.

The spring of 2010 saw Patrik Ervell explore the use of rusting in his collection. His pieces created a stunning play on colors and textures when tiny, rusted dots intermingled with breezy blues and subtle khakis during his runway show. The use of rust on cleanly tailored suits (Figure 1.22) and buttoned-up shirts proves that rust does not always have to look rustic.

1.22 Patrik Ervell (left) with a model wearing a look from his RTW Spring 2010 collection at the CFDA/Vogue Fashion Fund Awards *Eichner/WWD; © Condé Nast*

Additional Resources

Sourcing: Rusty objects can be found almost anywhere, but local hardware stores are a great place to find metal objects like nails, washers, and aluminum sheeting that can be rusted quickly if sprayed with vinegar, water, or bleach and left in the sun to oxidize. All materials respond differently to rust, so experimentation is a must.

Inspiration: Bo Lundvang (www.rost.lundvang.se), Judy Loope (http://www.judyloope.com)

Using dirt, soil, or clay to create a pattern on fabric is known as **earth staining**. The chosen medium may be applied in various ways, but a direct application tends to work best. Earth staining is often used to create an aged, worn effect (Figure 1.23a), but because natural fibers have a tendency to simply rot away, small tears and holes may be present in the finished piece (Figure 1.23b).

Results differ depending on the choice of earth materials. Dirt and soils create browns, while clays can produce grays and reds. The fabric needs to be "buried" with the earth elements in order to fully saturate the fibers. This can be done outdoors by literally burying the fabric in the native soil or in a large pot filled with specific clay, soil, or compost if space is limited and geography does not allow access to native materials. The amount of time the fabric is buried has a significant effect on the results, so it is important to test the fabric and make sure to plan enough time to reach the desired outcome. Days or even weeks may be required to produce a saturated and striking pattern.

1.23a Silk buried in a compost pile containing carrots, grapefruit, orange, eucalyptus bark, kale, and coffee beans. Bundle was covered and left for a month. Created by Melinda Tai.
Melinda Tai, Obovate Designs, http://obovate.wordpress.com

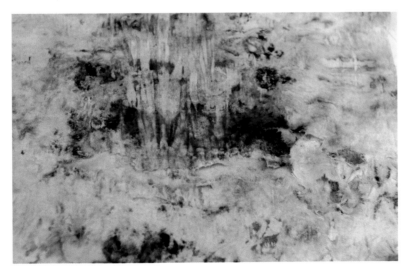

1.23b Some fabrics can rot and tear when buried for long periods of time. Melinda Tai embraces these sorts of accidents in her work.
Melinda Tai, Obovate Designs, http://obovate.wordpress.com

Materials

Figure 1.24 shows some of the materials needed for staining with earth materials.

+ Clay or soil
+ Dust mask
+ Natural fabrics, which have been scoured in hot water and Synthrapol
+ Plastic bags—large enough to hold the fabric. Planters also work well as long as they are big enough to hold the fabric and lots of dirt.
+ Plastic spray bottle to keep the fabric moist
+ Protective gloves: rubber, vinyl, or latex depending on skin sensitivity
+ Vinegar or soy milk

garden soil in a plastic bag

vinegar-, soy milk-, or water-soaked fabric

red clay

red clay mixed with soy milk in a plastic container

1.24 Materials needed to earth stain fabric.

Application Methods

+ Direct application
+ Immersion technique

Workspace

+ This process can be done anywhere, but working outdoors is always best because it can get messy.

Safety: Wear protective gloves when working with clay or soil to avoid skin irritation. Wearing a dust mask is also recommended to avoid inhaling any clay particles.

Instructions

1. Scour fabric and soak in vinegar, soymilk, or water. Each option produces slightly different results.
2. If using soil, bury the fabric so that it is completely covered or place it in a large plastic bag (Figure 1.25a). For clays, rub into the fabric, then place the clay and fabric into a plastic bag (Figure 1.25b). For an immersion technique, dissolve clay or soil into water, vinegar, or soymilk and immerse fabric completely in solution (Figure 1.25c).
3. Check the progress regularly and spray with water bottle to keep the fabric damp.
4. This process can take anywhere from a couple of days to a month in order to achieve the best results.

1.25a Fill a plastic bag with soil and add wet fabric, covering the fabric completely.

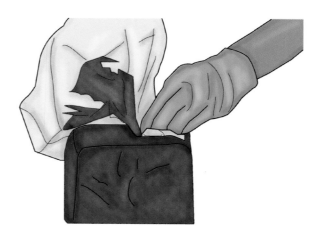

1.25b Fabric can be rubbed directly onto a piece of clay.

1.25c Fabric can be immersed in a clay and water mixture.

Examples

Figures 1.26 through 1.30 demonstrate the variations possible with earth staining.

1.26 Damp cotton fabric is wrapped into a small ball and rubbed directly onto a clump of red clay. Place fabric and bits of clay into a plastic bag and keep the fabric damp while it sets for 48 hours.

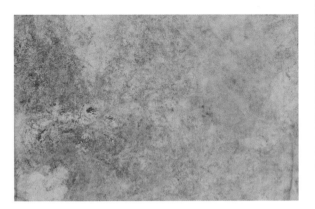

1.27 Cotton fabric immersed in a bath of vinegar and red clay and then allowed to set for 48 hours.

1.28 Cotton fabric immersed in a bath of red-clay mixed with soy milk and left for 48 hours.

1.29 Fabric buried under regular potting soil inside a large planter. From left to right respectively, the fabric was buried for three days, one week, and one month. The far right is a piece of vegetable-tanned leather buried for one month.

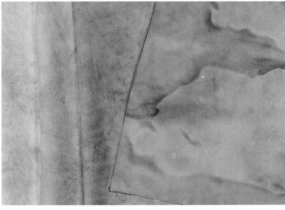

1.30 Fabric buried in red-clay soil and sealed in a large plastic bag. From left to right respectively, the fabric was buried for three days, one week, and one month. The far right is a piece of vegetable-tanned leather buried for one month.

Hussein Chalayan is a Turkish-born designer who in 1993 created his B.A. collection called "The Tangent Flows" for Central St. Martins in London. Chalayan constructed his collection, buried it in his backyard, and exhumed it just before the show. Although the results were unpredictable, the risk paid off and this collection ignited his career (Figure 1.31).

1.31 A garment from Hussein Chalayan's 1995 collection, created using the techniques developed for the 1993 collection. The top was created by burying cotton with rusty metal objects.
Chalayan, Hussein © V&A Images

Additional Resources

Sourcing: Hardware and garden stores offer a variety of soil options and clays can be found at most local art supply stores.

Inspiration: Lynn Krawczyk (www.fibraartysta.com), Francesca Owen (http://dancingwithdyes.wordpress.com), Kimberly Packwood (http://www.kbaxterpackwood.com)

Grass and leaf staining is the use of grasses and leaves to stain fibers, and can be manipulated to create ghostly, aged effects on fabric. Proper placement of the staining material in concert with a modern design can create intriguing, sophisticated garments as Irit Dulman demonstrates on a merino wool seamless felt coat stained with eucalyptus leaves, seen in Figure 1.32.

1.32 Felted merino wool seamless coat printed using eucalyptus leaves by Irit Dulman and Vilte Kazlauskaite.
Photography by Idan Levy

Materials

Figure 1.33 shows some of the materials needed for staining with grasses, leaves, and plants.

+ Alum solution: 7–8 tablespoons of alum per 1 gallon of warm water (see Appendix B, Figure B.33)
+ Leaves, flowers, grass
+ Jute to bind fabric
+ Two pieces of scoured natural fiber fabric or one piece large enough to fold onto itself
+ Protective gloves: rubber, vinyl, or latex depending on skin sensitivity

Application Method

+ Direct application of flowers, leaves, grasses to the surface of the natural fabric

1.33 Materials needed to stain with leaves, grasses, or flowers.

Workspace

+ Steamer (see Appendix A, Setting Up a Steamer, page 259)
+ Table to lay out fabric and organic materials

Safety: Always wear protective gloves to avoid skin irritation sometimes caused by grasses and leaves.

Instructions

1. Presoak fabric in an alum solution, but be careful not to soak too long or it will damage the fabric—20 minutes is usually enough.
2. Lay the fabric flat and add flowers, leaves, or grasses.

1.34 Lay fabric flat and apply grasses, leaves, and flowers in the desired pattern. Leave enough room along the edges to fold fabric over itself.

3. Place another piece of fabric to hold the leaves in place.

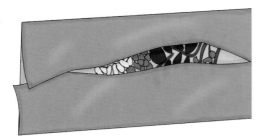

1.35 Cover organic materials with another piece of fabric or fold sides over to cover materials completely.

4. Roll fabric and bind with jute thread until it is a size that can fit into a steamer.

1.36 Roll fabric and bind bundle using jute rope.

5. Place into steamer and steam for about an hour. For further steaming, place the rolled fabric into a plastic bag and leave it until you see the desired results. A hot iron and lots of steam can work in place of a steamer but will require extensive ironing (about an hour).

6. Unroll fabric and rinse in an alum solution to set the stain.

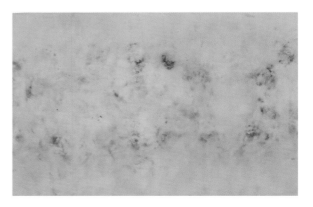

1.37 Completed sample of grass and leaf staining.

Examples

Figure 1.38 shows various fabrics stained with grasses, leaves, or flowers.

1.38 Left to right: silk chiffon stained with grasses and pine needles, silk habotai created using leaves from local trees, silk dupion stained with a mixture of leaves and grass, silk satin stained using pink and red carnations, and silk twill stained with eucalyptus leaves.

India Flint is an Australian artist who begins her creations with white, beige, or undyed cloth, which she transforms using regionally collected and ecologically sustainable dyes made of leaves (especially eucalyptus) (Figure 1.39), bark, or earth pigments. She then combines the new fabric with vintage materials found at thrift shops. Adding hand or machine stitching further evolves each one-of-a-kind piece, some of which are designed to be "second skins," objects meant to be worn but which can also be hung in a space or on a wall.

Flint uses a simple bundle dyeing process similar to shibori. Plant leaves are layered into the folds and the fabric is placed into a natural dye bath. The fabric is left to steep until the desired color is achieved. Like all natural dying processes, the outcome is unpredictable; artists who work in this medium must be willing to experiment and embrace the unexpected, because sometimes the unexpected creates extraordinary results (Figure 1.40).

1.39 A silk dupioni dress, bundle-dyed with eucalyptus.
Image by India Flint of work by India Flint using technique devised by India Flint

1.40 A eucalyptus eco-print, a process requiring only leaves and water.
Image by India Flint of work by India Flint using technique devised by India Flint

Additional Resources

Sourcing: Local garden stores and florists have a wide range of flowers and grasses that can stain fabric.

Inspiration: Deirdre Phillips (http://secretgardentextiles.wordpress.com), Constance Rose (http://constancerosedesigns.blogspot.com), Threadborne (www.wendyfe.wordpress.com)

Recall a time when a favorite garment fell victim to a rogue stain. Now consider the beauty that might be found in that stain, such as the captivating image Amelia Fais Harnas was able to create by stitching over a wine stain (Figure 1.41). Embracing accidents when working in this medium is crucial, as the results are often unpredictable. Spices, coffee grounds, and tea leaves can be easily manipulated to create stains, but so can wine, soda, and other liquids. Practicing the application is the best way to get controlled results.

1.41 Amelia Fais Harnas created this portrait by first applying a wax resist and then using red-wine as a stain to create the dark and light areas. Embroidery is added to define lines.
© Amelia Fais Harnas

Materials

Figure 1.42 shows some possible materials for staining with household items.

+ Alum solution—dissolve 7 tablespoons of alum into 1 gallon of warm water (see Appendix B, Figure B.33).
+ Household materials that cause stains. Anything that will stain fingertips will stain natural fabric.

+ Natural fabric, scoured in hot water and Synthrapol
+ Plastic bag or steamer
+ Protective gloves: rubber, vinyl, or latex depending on skin sensitivity

1.42 Possible household materials used to stain fabric.

Application Method

+ Apply materials directly to the fabric's surface.

Workspace

+ Any work surface is appropriate, just make sure to protect the surfaces from cross contamination.

Safety: Some household materials can create fumes. Always work in a ventilated area and never use materials for staining for any other purpose. Skin irritation can be avoided by always wearing protective gloves.

Instructions

1. Scour natural fabric in hot water and Synthrapol.
2. Soak natural fabric in an alum mixture of 7 tablespoons alum to 1 gallon warm water. Allow to soak for 20 minutes.
3. Lay damp fabric on a table and arrange any household materials that can stain skin (coffee, tea, cherries, pureed tomatoes).

1.43 Apply household materials to the surface of alum-soaked fabric in the desired pattern.

4. Fold fabric to secure all of the materials into a bundle.

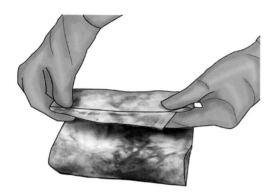

1.44 Fold fabric into a small bundle before placing into a plastic bag.

5. Place into a plastic bag and allow to sit overnight for lighter colors. To achieve more dramatic results place into a steamer for one hour (see staining with grasses and leaves).
6. Carefully unwrap fabric and discard any loose materials.
7. Rinse fabric in Synthrapol to set the stains, and allow to dry.

1.45 Completed sample of household staining on cotton.

Examples

Figure 1.46 demonstrates the results achievable with household staining methods.

1.46 Top to bottom: silk chiffon stained with red onion and green peppers, blueberry-stained cotton broadcloth, silk habotai stained with coffee and pomegranate tea, and silk dupion stained with curry and other spices.

Additional Resources

Sourcing: Local grocery stores have the materials needed for staining. Alum can be purchased through Dharma Trading Company, Sam Flax, Binders, or some local art stores.

Inspiration: Eric Meuring and Marjolein Wintjes (www.mocoloco.com/archives/023836.php), Judy Coates Perez (www.judycoatesperez.com)

STUDENT PROJECTS

1. *Sample Book:* Create pages for a reference sample book. First, select a colorway (reds, blues, greens, purples, etc.) and select a minimum of five techniques from Chapter 1 that include both dyeing and staining. For each technique create a 1/2-yard sample in the chosen colorway. Be sure to select fabric appropriate to the dye choice. For example, using purple as a color way, the combination could be using acid dye on wool to create purple, using disperse dye on polyester in a purple color, using blueberries to dye cotton, staining hemp using leaves from a purple flower, and burying silk in a compost pile of soil and eggplant. Present each sample on an 8 1/2" × 11" paper and include a brief description of the process, what can be done to achieve better/ different results, and how this sample could be used in a garment, accessory, or fine art.

2. *Record keeping to achieve consistent results:* Choose a dyeing technique (acid, disperse, or natural/ household method) and select at least five different pieces of fabric, no smaller then 10" × 10" square. Cut each square in half, creating two identical groups of fabric swatches. Make sure to select fabric with fiber content appropriate to dye choice. When in doubt, do a burn test (see Appendix A, Burn Test, page 252). Dye one group of fabric according to the dye choice. Take thorough notes of the process, paying close attention to the amount of dye used and the time the fabric spent in the dye bath. Record results. Notice how differently each fabric reacts. Now try to repeat the results another time using the second group of swatches.

3. *Layering:* Select a 1-yard piece of white fabric and choose a dye appropriate to fabric content. Next, choose two staining techniques and layer them onto the dyed fabric. Allow fabric to dry between dye and each layer of staining to ensure color-fastness. Record results and suggest three uses for the finished piece.

KEY TERMS

+ acid dyes
+ alcohol-based leather dyes
+ cellulose fibers
+ chrome tanning
+ cochineal
+ colorfastness
+ direct application
+ disperse dyes

+ dye
+ earth staining
+ fiber reactive dyes
+ grass and leaf staining
+ hydrophobic fabrics
+ immersion technique

+ indigo
+ leather dyeing
+ madder
+ mordant
+ oil-based leather dyes
+ oil tanning
+ protein fibers
+ raw leather

+ rusting
+ scoured
+ sizing
+ spirit- or water-based leather dye
+ staining
+ Synthrapol
+ tanning
+ vegetable tanning

ENDNOTES

1. Duerr, Sasha. *The Handbook of Natural Plant Dyes*. Portland, OR: Timber Press, 2011.

2. Bosence, Susan. *Hand Block Printing and Resist Dyeing*. Newton Abbot, Devon, UK: David and Charles, 1985.

3. Ibid.

4. Buck, J. Robert. *Leather: The New Frontier in Art*. Fort Worth, TX: Tandy Leather Company, 1992.

5. Brackmann, Holly. *The Surface Designer's Handbook*. Loveland, CO: Interweave Press LLC, 2006.

6. Ibid.

7. Ibid.

8. "Did You Know . . . How Acid Dye Works." Accessed April 29, 2014. http://www.dharmatrading.com/home/did-you-know-how-acid-dye-works.html.

9. Crabtree, Amanda. "Time with Tinctory." *Bella Armoire,* September/October, 2010.

10. McPherson, Di. "Mud and Dirt: Australian Soil as Self-Expression." *Textile Society of America Symposium Readings* 225 (2008). Accessed May 1, 2014. http://digitalcommons.unl.edu/tsaconf/255.

chapter 2
DISCHARGING COLOR AND USING RESISTS

OBJECTIVES:

+ Removing color from fabric using discharge paste

+ Using RIT color remover to remove color from fabric and leather

+ Using gutta resist on silk

+ Using wax resist

+ Using binding and folding as a resist

+ Applying resists to vegetable-tanned leather

+ Using potato dextrin as a resist

Color can be removed, or discharged, from most commercially dyed fabric using specially formulated materials like discharge paste or RIT color remover. It can be removed in a pattern, like shibori, or as an overall fabric lightener. Resists are used to create a negative design on fabric with products like gutta, wax, or leather resist, and are drawn onto the fabric before dyeing. Once the dye has been applied the gutta or wax is removed to reveal the design. Any time a dye is used, environmental concerns arise. See the box on page 34 for further discussion of the impact discharging color and resists can have on the environment.

DISCHARGING COLOR

A negative image or pattern on a dark-colored fabric or leather can be created by removing color (Figure 2.1). Color removal can also be beneficial as an all-over lightener or used before applying other dyes or prints to provide a lighter base, thus creating more vibrant results.

Chlorine is the predominate chemical in discharge and was originally discovered in 1774 by Carl Wilhelm Scheele when he found that it rapidly increased the bleaching of cotton.[1] Previously, common practice required cotton to be spread across large amounts of land until the sun naturally bleached the cotton, a process that could take months. By 1799, Scottish chemist Charles Tennant created a bleaching powder made of chlorine and slaked lime that could be produced in large quantities and was easily handled.[2] It remained the standard until the 1920s when liquid chlorine was introduced to the textile industry.

All fabrics respond differently to discharge; some colors, like black, can take on a variety of other colors ranging from orange to yellow to green. This is because black is generally made up of a combination of different colors, so the only way to know for certain how the fabric will respond is to test a sample. It is important to note that not all fabrics will discharge to white; some will take on various shades lighter than the original color. Acid dyes tend to discharge very well, whereas disperse dyes do not. Some commercial dyes are so colorfast that discharging will have very little effect on the fabric.

ENVIRONMENTAL IMPACT: DISCHARGING COLOR AND USING RESISTS

Discharging color removes dye from the fabric, so the remaining dye will become part of the dye bath. Because of this, the dye bath should always be disposed of with care. Wash it down the drain with plenty of running water to dilute the bath and limit environmental impact. Discharge paste or thickened bleach creates very little dye waste, but the chemicals in the products create toxic fumes when heated, so wearing a dust mask and working in a well-ventilated area are suggested. Discharge paste and RIT color remover can cause skin irritation so always wear gloves.

Most resists are nontoxic and are often water or heat soluble. The environmental impact stems from dyeing the fabric after the resist is applied. Most acid dyes are relatively eco-friendly as long as they are disposed of down a drain and never into the ground or storm drain where they could pollute the water supply. Techniques like potato dextrin are also eco-friendly because the resist is created using organic materials; although it could be ingested, it should not be. Some commercial dextrins contain chlorines that can bleach fabric and cause skin irritation. Wearing protective gloves is recommended.

Always store leftover dyes and discharges in airtight plastic containers to avoid the release of unwanted fumes and eliminate the possibility of spilling or leakage, which can contaminate a work area. If large quantities are spilled, try to contain the spill, and immediately clean up using paper towels or old rags. Place towels into a plastic container and contact your local department of public works for a licensed disposal site.

2.1 Maria Grachvogel's RTW Fall 2012 uses a print that highlights the dramatic results that could be achieved with discharge paste. All black fabrics react differently to discharge paste: some will turn orange, some green, and some yellow. Experimentation is vital, but similar results can be achieved with some practice.
Giannoni/WWD; © Condé Nast

Discharge paste can be purchased to remove, discharge, or extract color from a previously dyed fabric leaving a range of colors from white to a pale orange. The color remaining depends on the dye originally used on the fabric. Predicting the results without first testing the chosen fabric is not possible. Discharge paste works best on natural fibers and is thick enough to be used in many printing techniques (see Chapter 3: Printing and Transfer) such as screen printing or stamping or applied by hand to create ghostly streaks (Figure 2.2).

Discharge paste is activated with the use of steam either from an iron or a commercial steamer. The addition of heat activates the molecules in the paste, causing them to bind to dye. When this reaction takes place a strong ammonia odor is released, so it should be completed in a well-ventilated area. The longer the discharge is exposed to steam and heat, the lighter the color will become. Once the desired results are achieved the fabric is thoroughly rinsed and washed in Synthrapol to restore its original hand.

2.2 Brandon Sun created a streaking effect on his gowns for his RTW Fall 2013 collection.
Eichner/WWD; © Condé Nast

Materials

Figure 2.3 shows some of the materials needed for direct application of discharge paste.

✦ Brushes—paint and foam
✦ Discharge paste (see Appendix B, Figure B.26) or bleach thickened with sodium alginate (see Chapter 3: Printing and Transfer)
✦ Fabric—this technique works best on natural fabrics such as cotton or wool and does work on most synthetics: Experiment!
✦ Protective gloves: rubber, vinyl, or latex depending on skin sensitivity
✦ T-pins to secure fabric to work surface

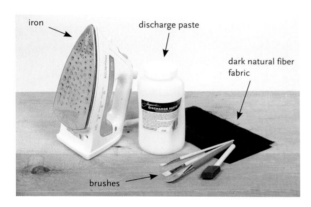

2.3 Materials needed for direct application of discharge paste.

Application Methods

✦ Direct application with paintbrushes
✦ Potato dextrin (see page 58)
✦ Screen printed (see Chapter 3: Printing and Transfer)
✦ Stamped (see Chapter 3: Printing and Transfer)

Workspace

✦ Foam-core board or padded table will be necessary to secure fabric that will be printed.

Safety: Always wear protective gloves to protect skin from discharge pastes, which can be a skin irritant. Avoid breathing in any fumes released during the ironing process, as they can be toxic.

Instructions

1. Secure fabric to a padded table (see Appendix A, Creating a Padded Work Surface, page 254) using T-pins.
2. Apply discharge paste in any of the applications mentioned above. This example shows a dripping technique. Apply paste thickly at one end of the fabric, then carefully hold the fabric up and allow the paste to slide down the fabric until the desired look is achieved.

VIDEO

Go to Chapter 2 Video Tutorial: Discharge Paste Technique

STUDIO:

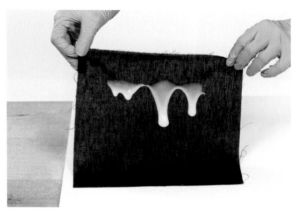

2.4 Hold fabric by one side and allow the discharge paste to slowly move down the fabric.

3. Blot off excess paste with a paper towel.
4. Allow to dry.
5. Sandwich fabric between two pieces of muslin; then iron from the back side of the printed fabric using very hot, dry heat.

2.5 Place fabric, discharge-paste side down, between two pieces of muslin and iron on high heat.

6. The color change can take a few minutes or happen very rapidly and varies depending on the fabric choice. Some fabrics will turn orange, green, or gray. Check the fabric regularly so that it does not burn. If using thickened bleach, ironing is not necessary; simply allow it to dry completely before rinsing off.

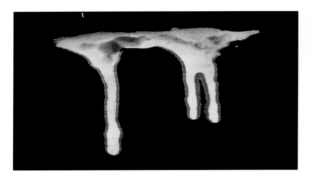

2.6 The color change achieved after a few minutes of ironing.

7. Rinse fabric to remove excess discharge and to restore the hand of the fabric.
8. Allow to air dry.

2.7 An example of how different fabric can create different color reactions.

Examples

Figures 2.8 through 2.11 demonstrate the versatility of discharge paste and potential results.

2.8 This look from "of the dark star" by Lisa Robin Design uses bleach to remove color from garments.
of the dark star by Lisa Robin Design

2.9 This look from Hussein Chalayan's RTW Spring 2013 collection can be achieved by applying discharge paste in a variety of thicknesses with different sized paintbrushes, using free and easy strokes to create a vein pattern.
Giannoni/WWD; ©Condé Nast

2.10 Discharge paste is applied with a stamp onto black cotton broadcloth.

2.11 Discharge paste applied with a screen onto red cotton.

Additional Resources

Sourcing: PRO Chemical and Dye (www.prochemicalanddye.com), Binders Art Store (www.bindersart.com), Dharma Trading Company (www.dharmatrading.com)

Inspiration: Becky Earley (www.beckyearley.com), Cedar Canyon Textiles (www.cedarcanyontextiles .com/discharge-with-stencils-playing-with-stencils-4/), And Then We Set it On Fire (www.andthenwesetitonfire.blogspot.com/2012/02 /discharge-past-decolourant.html)

RIT color remover is safe to use on almost any fabric, including leather. It is generally used to brighten whites or to remove some color from predyed fabrics. It will not remove all color from all fabrics; in the case of most prints it will simply lighten them. Because color remover is a powder activated by the addition of water, it is very thin, and a direct application does not work very well. **Vat discharging**—removing color in a large tub or washing machine—works best with color remover.

The easiest and most effective way to used RIT color remover is to bind or tie fabric and leather before placing it in the vat. See Shibori on page 52 for ideas. The tight binding prohibits the color remover from seeping into certain areas of the fabric; when unbound, the resist pattern emerges. Other resists can be used, but note that whichever resist is chosen, be sure that it is NOT water soluble; otherwise, it will dissolve in the vat and be ineffective.

Materials

Figure 2.12 shows some of the materials needed for RIT color remover.

+ Enamel or stainless steel pot used only for dyeing (not aluminum or nonstick)
+ Fabric or leather
+ Protective gloves: rubber, vinyl, or latex depending on skin sensitivity
+ RIT color remover (see Appendix B, Figure B.25)
+ Wooden spoon used only for dyeing
+ Rubber bands or string (to bind fabric for a shibori effect)

2.12 Color removal materials.

Application Methods
+ Stovetop
+ Washing machine (follow instructions provided by manufacturer)

Workspace
+ Hot plate or stovetop
+ Rack to dry fabric after application
+ Sink

Safety: Always wear rubber gloves and avoid inhaling any fumes from the discharge vat. Never leave the vat unattended; heating fabric can be dangerous and cause a fire.

Instructions

1. Prepare fabric for color removal by washing in Synthrapol. DO NOT DRY. To prepare leather, soak in cool water until fully saturated.

2. For an even color removal, make sure the fabric is thoroughly wet and free from any folds. For a shibori effect, bind the fabric using rubber bands or string. (See Figures 2.40 through 2.45 on page 54 for further clarification.)

3. Add water to pot and bring to a simmer.

4. Carefully add color remover powder, being careful not to breathe in any dust.

5. Stir to dissolve.

6. Carefully add wet items to vat. DO NOT add leather items at this time. See the box below for instructions on working with leather.

7. Maintain a simmer while stirring continually for 10 to 30 minutes or until the desired color is achieved. Do not let the vat boil.

8. Carefully remove items, rinse under warm water, and allow to dry.

INSTRUCTIONS FOR USING COLOR REMOVER ON LEATHER

When using color remover on leather follow Steps 2 through 5 in the Color Remover section. Allow the dye bath to cool substantially; it should be warm, not hot. Then add leather items and agitate for up to 40 minutes, depending on the desired color. See Figure 2.13 for an example.

Examples

Figures 2.13 through 2.16 show a variety of results using color remover.

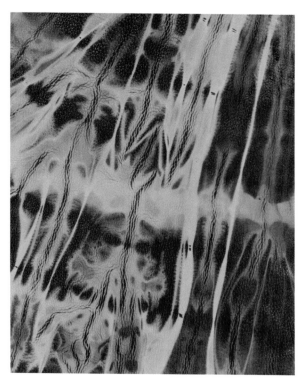

2.13 Deer leather accordion pleated and left in a cool vat for 20 minutes.

2.14 Blue cotton broadcloth. Far left: original color; center: all-over color removal; right: fabric bound with rubber bands in the manner shown at bottom right.

2.15 Printed cotton. Far left, original color; center: all-over color removal; right: fabric bound with rubber bands in the manner shown at top right.

2.16 Printed upholstery-weight cotton. Far left: original color; center: all-over color removal; right: fabric bound with rubber bands in the manner shown at top right.

Additional Resources

Sourcing: Local grocery stores often carry RIT products, as do many large craft stores.

Inspiration: Ayn Hanna (www.aynhanna.com), Tangerine Key (www.tangerinekey.wordpress.com)

RESISTS

A **resist** is a chemical medium used to block the penetration of dye, stain, or paint on a fabric's surface. A resist will prevent dye or stain from penetrating the areas to which it is applied.

A variety of resists are available to suit any application. **Gutta** is a thick latex resist used almost exclusively on silk to create intricate details. **Batik** is a hot wax that is applied to the surface of almost any scoured fabric as a resist to any dye that does not require a hot bath to fix the color, as the wax will melt. **Shibori**, also known as *tie-dyeing,* is a simple technique of binding or folding of fabric before it is placed into a dye bath. This technique is most valuable when using high temperatures to set the dye, because the strings or bands can hold up to high temperature dye baths. **Leather resists** can be applied to vegetable tanned leather to eliminate the full penetration of water-based leather stains. **Potato dextrin** is an organic method using actual potatoes to create a crackled appearance on fabric.

The use of resists can be traced back thousands of years thanks to a small fragment of cloth discovered in China in a tomb that dates from 683 AD. Stitching was used in the cloth to create a resist; needle holes were still present on the fabric.[3] By 756, Japanese textile artists had mastered the use of resists and were able to create intricate patterns using wax, fabric binding, and a technique that clamped folded fabric between carved wooden blocks.[4] Although resist techniques originated in China and Japan, they quickly spread to other cultures along the **Silk Road**, a trade route that connected Asia to the western civilizations of Europe. In the 12th century, Indonesia became known for batik with the invention of the **tjanting**, a penlike tool that keeps the wax hot so that it slowly drains toward the tip during application.[5] The complexity of resist patterns intensified, with some taking days or even weeks to complete, as is likely with the complex print shown in Figure 2.17.

2.17 A 20th-century interpretation of a forest design known as "Kain Fantasi Tulis" from Central Java, created on cotton. *Fulvio Zanettini fotographie*

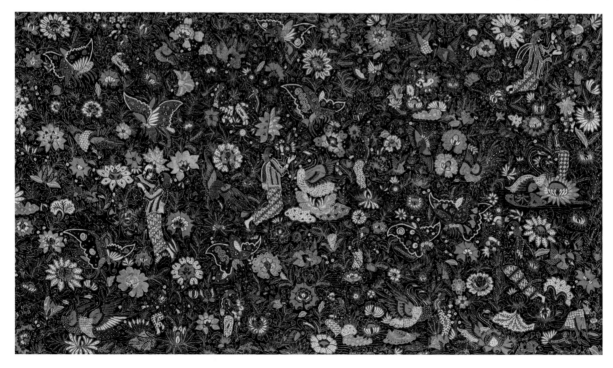

Gutta is a thick, clear liquid similar to white glue used as a resist on silk. After the gutta has been applied and allowed to dry thoroughly, it will create a bond with the fabric that doesn't allow dye to penetrate the treated areas. Gutta is a desirable resist because it presents few health hazards and has the ability to create clean, crisp designs when applied using a small plastic bottle and a variety of applicator tips. Although easy to use, gutta does take some time to master—the application process is not foolproof and air bubbles can create splatters on the fabric. It is important to be sure that all of the gutta lines are connected or the dye will migrate to unintended areas. Hold the fabric up to the light to see if any lines are incomplete.

Gutta comes in a variety of colors, including metallic, black (Figure 2.18), clear, and white. A white gutta is especially versatile because it can be dyed any color and, once removed, the dye color will remain.

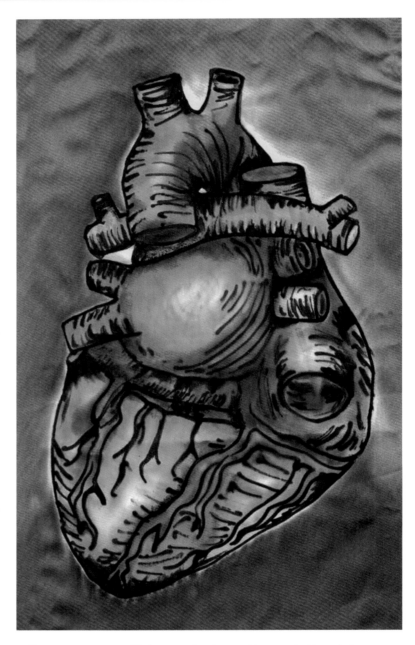

2.18 Victoria Varona uses a black gutta to draw lines in this anatomical heart design.
© *Victoria Varona*

Materials

Figure 2.19 shows some of the materials needed for painting on silk using a gutta resist.

+ Brushes
+ Dyes formulated for silk (see Appendix B, Figure B.32)
+ Dye set if appropriate to dye choice (see Appendix B, Figure B.39)
+ Gutta and applicator bottle (see Appendix B, Figure B.57)
+ Protective gloves: rubber, vinyl, or latex depending on skin sensitivity
+ Silk fabric that has been scoured in hot water and Synthrapol
+ Stretcher bars appropriate to the size of the project
+ Synthrapol
+ Tacks

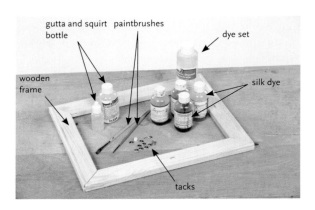

2.19 Materials needed for applying silk paints and gutta to silk fabric.

Application Method

+ Direct application of paints onto the surface of stretched fabric

Workspace

+ Any studio space is appropriate for gutta on silk.
+ Cover workspace when working with dyes.

Safety: Always wear gloves when working with dyes to protect against skin irritation.

Instructions

1. Fill plastic applicator with gutta or purchase a prefilled tube of gutta, sometimes easier for beginners.
2. Stretch one piece of silk fabric or attach to freezer paper. Create a grid using the gutta: this will serve as an area to test colors. Gutta turns white when dried but goes on clear.

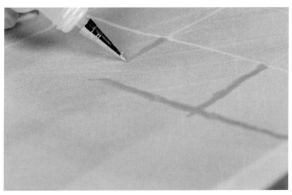

2.20 Apply gutta in a grid pattern using a squeeze bottle with a small metal tip. This will serve as an area to test colors.

3. Stretch fabric that will be painted following instruction in Appendix A, Stretching Fabric, page 254.
4. Trace design or draw freehand onto stretched silk fabric.
5. Using a small bottle and applicator, apply gutta to the lines of the design.

2.21 Gutta being applied to a pencil traced design.

6. Allow the gutta to dry thoroughly and make sure that all lines are connected, otherwise the dye will bleed. It is often helpful to create a gutta outline along the edge of the stretcher to prevent unwanted color contamination.

7. Apply dye to dried gutta design by dipping a paintbrush into dye and carefully placing it in the center of the area to be painted. The dye will move toward the edges on its own so do not over-saturate the area.

2.22 Dip paintbrush in dye and place in the center of the area that is to be painted; the dye will migrate to the edges on its own.

8. Experiment by sprinkling salt and sugar crystals onto wet dye to create sunburst effects.

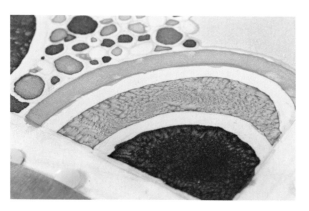

2.23 Experiment by applying salt or sugar to wet dye to create this starburst effect.

9. Glide a wet paintbrush over an area to create a highlight, or allow two colors to blend together by placing them side-by-side and adding a brush stroke of water to force them to run together.

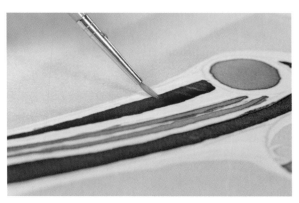

2.24 To add shading, dip a paintbrush in water and go back over the dye. This will dilute the dye slightly and lighten the color.

10. Continue painting until the piece is complete.

2.25 Fully painted sample.

Set dye according to the manufacturer's instructions. Jacquard silk dyes can be set at the same time the gutta is being removed. Using a liquid dye set mixed with water, soak the painted piece of fabric in the solution for 5 minutes, agitating frequently. Change the water and repeat. Note that color will often come out slightly lighter after the dye is set.

Examples

Figure 2.27 shows an example created by Diane Rogers.

2.27 Diane Rogers *Channel* is hand-painted onto silk and then quilted and embroidered to add dimension, resulting in stunning pieces of work that are visually and tactilely impressive. *Diane Rogers*

Additional Resources

Sourcing: Dharma Trading Company (www.dharmatrading.com)

Inspiration: Zhang Daqian (www.chinaonlinemuseum.com/ painting-zhang-daqian.php), Diane Rogers (http://www.dianerogers.co.uk)

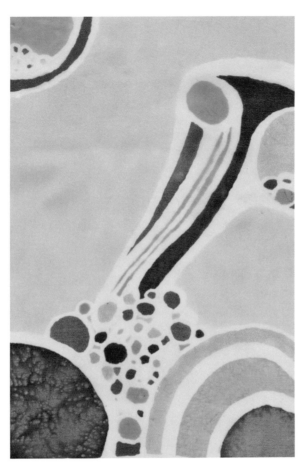

2.26 After the dye has been set, the colors may lighten slightly.

Batik is the act of using hot wax to draw on the fabric using a penlike tool called a *tjanting*. A small dish at the top of the tjanting holds the hot wax and maintains its liquidity. From the dish, wax drains down a narrow channel into a small spout, where it can be precisely laid onto the fabric. Once the wax has dried, a seal is formed on the fabric that will not allow dye to penetrate the treated area. The resisted fabric can then be painted by hand or immersion dyed in a cold-water dye bath (indigo dyeing works very well), as the wax will melt off in a hot water bath.

Batik wax is relatively easy to remove using steam, newspaper, and an iron. Sometimes the wax can create a halo effect using this method of removal, so another option is to slowly simmer the fabric in hot water until the wax is removed. Sometimes this can help with the hand of the final piece, too. Once the wax is removed, it reveals a design or pattern created by the undyed areas (Figure 2.28).

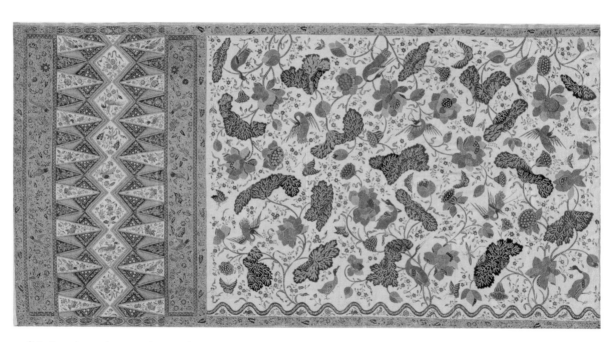

2.28 Batik can be used to create large predictable patterns similar to this woman's hip wrapper from Indonesia, circa 1880. *Courtesy of LACMA*

Materials

See Figure 2.29 for some of the materials needed to batik.

+ Batik wax
+ Dyes appropriate to the fabric
+ Iron
+ Newspaper
+ Protective gloves: rubber, vinyl, or latex depending on skin sensitivity.
+ Stretched fabric (see Appendix A, Stretching Fabric, page 254)
+ Synthrapol
+ Tjanting (see Appendix B, Figure B.59)

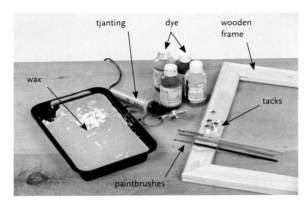

2.29 Materials needed to batik on silk.

Application Methods

+ Color is added with paintbrush or immersion in a cold-water dye bath.
+ Direct application of wax using a tjantung

Workspace

+ Any studio space is appropriate for batik. You will need a power source to plug in an electric tjanting.
+ Cover workspace when working with dyes.

Safety: Batik wax is very hot and so is the tjanting. Never touch the tip or liquid wax. Always wear gloves and an apron when applying dye. Cover workspace to avoid cross contamination.

Instructions

1. Stretch fabric over frame large enough to fit the project (see Appendix A, Stretching Fabric, page 254). Fabric must be stretched in order to allow the wax to penetrate through the surface of the fabric. Create a second stretcher for testing colors (see Figure 2.20 on page 45 for further clarification).

2. Break off small pieces of wax and place them into the dish at the top of the tjantung. Small pieces work best because large ones can cause a clog.

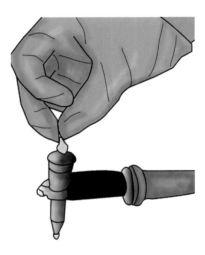

2.30 Break off small pieces of wax and insert them into the cup at the top of the tjanting.

3. Apply wax using a tjanting. Use slow steady motions. The more vertical the pen is, the faster wax will flow producing a thicker line.

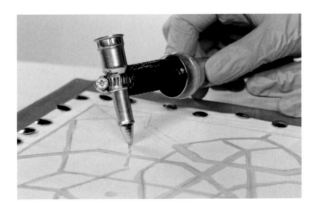

2.31 Carefully move the wax-filled tjanting over the lines of the design to apply the resist. The more vertical the tjanting is held the thicker the line of wax will be.

4. Allow wax to dry.

5. Paint in areas with dye appropriate to the fabric. Acid and disperse dyes will also work when thinned.

6. Dip paintbrush in dye, then place in the center of the area that is to be painted and allow the dye to drift to the edges. See Figure 2.22 on page 46 for further clarification.

7. Continue to fill in design, washing paintbrush thoroughly between color changes.

2.32 Completed and dried sample.

8. Allow to dry.

9. Remove fabric from stretcher. Pad an ironing board or table with sheets of newsprint, sandwich the fabric between two plain white paper towels or newsprint, and iron until the wax begins to melt and comes off on the paper towel or newsprint. Change towels frequently.

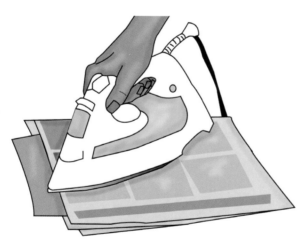

2.33 To remove wax, place it between a few pages of newspaper or newsprint and iron until the wax melts off. Change the paper frequently to absorb the wax quickly.

10. Set dye according to manufacturer's instructions.

11. Wash fabric in Synthrapol to set further, and allow to dry.

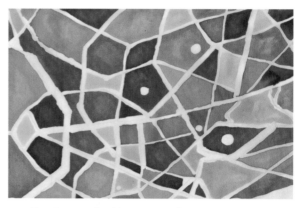

2.34 Complete sample with wax removed.

Example

Figure 2.35 shows an example of how wax can be applied in a splatter pattern to create abstract results.

2.35 An example of an abstract method of wax application.

DESIGNER PROFILE: MARY EDNA FRASER

Mary Edna Fraser is an American artist who uses traditional batik methods to create large-scale silk paintings so large that sawhorses are required to thoroughly stretch the fabric.

Some of her most notable batiks are taken from an aerial perspective, stemming from flights with her father and brother in their family's vintage plane. She will take as many as 500 photos on a single excursion. Once an image is selected and she becomes familiar with it, "the colors are chosen and the idea formulated." This ancient process of resist dyeing is organic and the results painterly.

Fraser enjoys researching site-specific locations and explores these areas by hiking, flying, or painting on location. She appreciates the process of collaboration with a scientist or fellow artist, which influences the content of her work (Figure 2.36).

2.36 Entitled *Bangladesh*, this large-scale batik highlights the use of a resist to create a pattern. Mary Edna Fraser uses Proceon dyes, beeswax, and paraffin on silk to show distinct features in this abstracted aerial image.
Photograph by Rick Rhodes/ © Mary Edna Fraser

Additional Resources

Sourcing: Most local art stores carry the materials to batik, but they can also be ordered through Dharma Trading Company (www.dharmatrading.com).

Inspiration: Robin Paris (www.robinparis.co.uk), Mary Edna Fraser (www.maryedna.com), Jonathan Evans (www.jonathanevans-batikart.com)

Shibori, referred to as **plangi** in Indonesia and **bandhani** in India, is a resist technique in which fabric is bound, pleated, or stitched to create a pattern that will then be immersed into a dye bath or saturated using a paintbrush for more control and color variation. The dye will penetrate only the areas that are not bound, leaving the other areas free of dye. Simple circular patterns can be achieved by tying off tiny segments of fabric, while folding and clamping fabric can create complicated patterns. It is also a great way to achieve big bold patterns on large pieces of fabric. A look similar to shibori can be achieved by hand painting thin, diluted dyes directly onto the fabric's surface using a heavily saturated paintbrush.

The Japanese developed a wide range of techniques to decorate kimono fabrics. The designs were built in stages: dyed, bound, and dyed again until an intricate pattern emerged, and it wasn't uncommon for a kimono to take a year to create.[1] Simple shibori patterns can take on even more dimension with the addition of other techniques, as Yohji Yamamoto employed in his Spring 1995 collection by combining smocking (see Chapter 5, page 175) and shibori (Figure 2.37).

Materials

Figure 2.38 shows some of the materials needed to shibori dye, including a variety of dye options depending on the fabric selection.

+ Dye appropriate to the fiber content of chosen fabric
+ Fabric
+ Rubber bands, clamps, or thin rope for binding

Application Methods

+ Immersion dyeing
+ Foam brush application
+ Squirt bottle
+ Dipping

Workspace

+ Will depend on what type of dye is chosen. Follow manufacturers' instructions.
+ Always cover work surfaces with plastic.

2.37 Yohji Yamamoto created this purple and blue coatdress by combining shibori and smocking techniques in his Spring 1995 collection.
Digital Image © 1996 Museum Associates / LACMA. Licensed by Art Resource, NY / © Artres

Safety: Shibori is a safe technique, but always work wearing gloves and take appropriate precautions depending on dye selection.

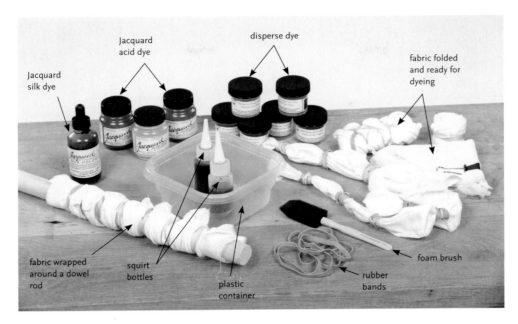

2.38 Materials needed to shibori fabric, including various dye options.

Labels on figure:
- Jacquard silk dye
- Jacquard acid dye
- disperse dye
- fabric folded and ready for dyeing
- fabric wrapped around a dowel rod
- squirt bottles
- plastic container
- foam brush
- rubber bands

Instructions

1. Scour fabric in Synthrapol and hot water.
2. Bind or fold fabric and maintain shape with rubber bands or thin rope (see Figures 2.40 through 2.45 on page 54).
3. Apply dye with a foam brush (Figure 2.39a), squirt bottle (Figure 2.39b), dipping (Figure 2.39c), or with an immersion bath.
4. Allow dye to dry for about 30 minutes.
5. Rinse in Synthrapol, while still bound.
6. Remove bindings, rinse in warm water, and allow to dry.

2.39b A squirt bottle can be used to apply dye to bound fabric.

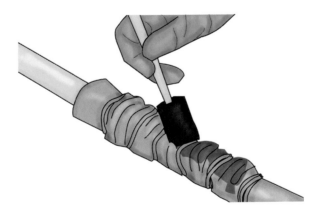

2.39a Dye can be applied using a foam brush.

2.39c Folded fabric can be dipped into a dish filled with dye.

Examples

Figures 2.40 through 2.45 show the results achieved with various binding techniques.

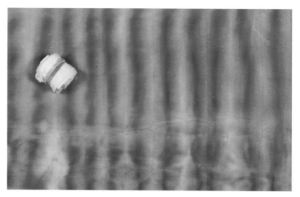

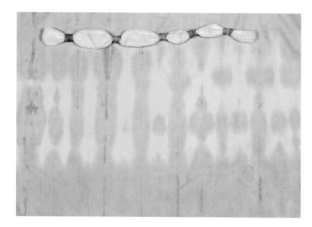

2.40 Nylon fabric folded like an accordion and bound with parallel rubber bands. Thinned disperse dye was applied with a squirt bottle.

2.43 Cotton broadcloth was accordion-pleated and then rolled before thinned acid dye was applied using a squirt bottle.

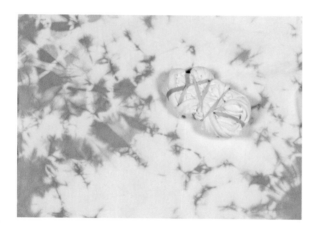

2.41 Cotton Lycra is bound randomly and tightly using rubber bands and immersed in acid dye.

2.44 Polyester satin was gathered at the center and smoothed to edges before rubber bands were applied (resembling a badminton shuttlecock) and then immersed in a disperse dye.

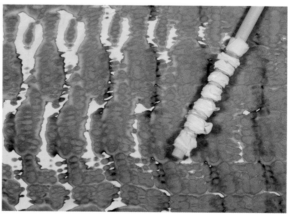

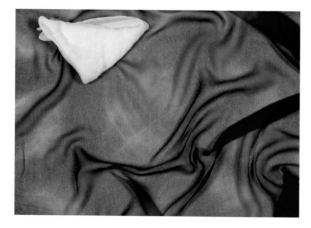

2.45 Silk georgette is wrapped around a dowel rod and bound with rubber bands before acid dye is applied with a foam brush.

2.42 Silk chiffon was folded into a triangular shape and dipped into silk dye.

Additional Resources

Sourcing: Most local art stores carry the materials to shibori, but they can also be ordered through Dharma Trading Company (www.dharmatrading.com).

Rodarte used shibori-inspired prints in its Fall 2013 collection. Similar results can be achieved by first choosing an appropriate background color—generally the lightest color in the palette unless a discharge technique is used. Working in large pieces, the fabric is twisted and bound to create a spiral or circular pattern (see Figure 2.44 in the Examples section) and dye is applied. Direct application of the dye using a saturated paintbrush works well on larger pieces because it is easier to control than trying to fit yards of fabric into a pot. Direct application also helps to add the streaking effect (Figures 2.46a and b) by allowing for some color contamination during the application.

2.46a Shibori featured in the Rodarte RTW Fall 2013 collection. *Giannoni/WWD; ©Condé Nast*

2.46b Shibori featured in the Rodarte RTW Fall 2013 collection. *Giannoni/WWD; ©Condé Nast*

Leather resist is applied to the surface of vegetable-tanned leather to eliminate the full penetration of water-based stains and antique finishes in the area where the resist is applied. Leather resist has a similar consistency to white glue and can be printed (see Chapter 3: Printing and Transfer) or applied directly with a paintbrush, sheep's wool, or a damp sponge. Two layers should be applied, allowing for each layer to thoroughly dry between applications before dye is applied. Leather resist doesn't completely block out color; instead a lighter version of the original dye will appear.

It is important to note that leather resist will only work on vegetable-tanned leather; commercially tanned leathers will not accept the resist because it has been treated to repel stains and water and will repel the resist as well.

Materials

Figure 2.47 shows some of the materials needed for applying resist and dye to vegetable-tanned leather.

+ Cotton rag or wool pad
+ Foam brush
+ Leather dye (see Appendix B, Figure B.29)
+ Leather resist, sometimes called "block out" (see Appendix B, Figure B.58)
+ Protective gloves: rubber, vinyl, or latex depending on skin sensitivity
+ Vegetable-tanned leather

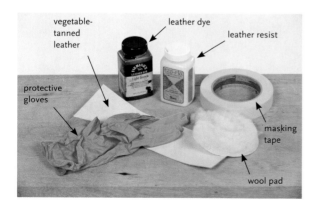

2.47 Materials needed to add a resist and dye to vegetable-tanned leather.

Application Methods

+ Materials to create a pattern for the resist (tape, stencil, stamp)
+ Direct application of dye (see Chapter 1, Leather Dye, page 14)

Workspace

+ Cover surfaces with newspaper because it absorbs some of the dye. Using plastic as a drop cloth isn't as effective because the dye will sit on the surface of the plastic and can cross contaminate projects.
+ Work in a well-ventilated area.

Safety: Alcohol-based dyes can release fumes, so work in a well-ventilated area and wear protective gloves to avoid skin irritation.

Instructions

1. Create a pattern with masking tape (Figure 2.48), paint freehand with a paintbrush, or apply with a stamp.
2. Apply a thin, even coat of leather resist, or *block out*, to the surface of the leather and allow to dry.

2.48 Once the masking tape is in place, use a foam brush to apply the resist. Apply a couple of coats, letting each layer dry between applications.

3. Apply alcohol- or water-based leather dye in circular motions, and allow to dry (see Chapter 1, Leather Dye, page 14). Notice that the leather resist does not completely block out the dye, but allows for some penetration.

2.49 Apply dye in a circular motion over the dried resist. Notice that the resist does not completely block out the dye, but allows some color to penetrate.

4. Apply additional layers of resist to add shine and create depth within a design.

2.50 Additional layers of resist can be applied to add shine and dimension to a design.

Examples

Figures 2.51 and 2.52 show various results with leather resist.

2.51 Vegetable-tanned leather dyed with purple Feibing's dye over resist applied with a paintbrush.

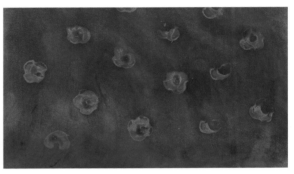

2.52 Eco-flo leather resist applied using a stamp and then dyed with Feibing's leather dye.

Additional Resources

Sourcing: Tandy Leather Factory (www.tandyleatherfactory.com), Zack White Leather (www.zackwhite.com)

Inspiration: *Leather: The New Frontier in Art* by J. Robert Buck

Potato dextrin is a water-soluble, organic resist made of instant mashed potato flakes and starch water. It can be made as thick or thin as needed with the addition of water. The mixture is applied directly to the surface of the fabric, manipulated using a paintbrush, squeegee, or even a fork, and then allowed to dry. As it dries the mixture cracks leaving areas of the fabric exposed. When applied thinly, it will produce fine lines and cracks where the dye can penetrate. A thick application produces wide, deep cracks. Because dextrin is thick, it can be applied to some areas of the fabric without too much fear of migration. If unintentional spreading occurs the dextrin can be easily scraped off with a plastic knife and paper towels while still wet.

Potato dextrin works well with paints, dyes, and discharge techniques, but make sure not to oversaturate the project or it will begin to dissolve. After the dye has dried, the dextrin can be easily removed with water. Potato dextrin is versatile and easy to use—it can even be used on leather, but it does have a hard time sticking to synthetic fabrics, so experimentation is necessary.

Materials

Figure 2.53 shows some of the materials needed for working with potato dextrin.

+ Dye appropriate to fabric (Fiber Etch, as described in Chapter 4, page 97, and discharge paste, described earlier in this chapter, can also be used.)
+ Paintbrushes or foam brushes to apply dye
+ Plastic spoon and fork
+ Potato dextrin made according to package instructions (It can be bought in a powder form; see the additional resources section or see the box on page 59 for a recipe.)
+ Scoured fabric. Natural fabrics work best because some synthetics have a protective coating that will not allow the dextrin to stick properly.

Application Method

+ Direct application with spoons or measuring cups. Once applied, the dextrin can be manipulated to create a variety of patterns.

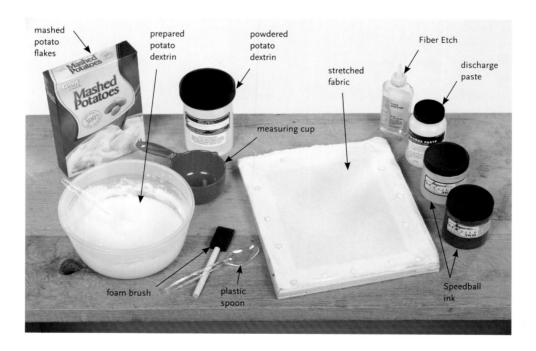

2.53 Materials needed to apply and dye using potato dextrin.

mashed potato flakes · prepared potato dextrin · powdered potato dextrin · Fiber Etch · stretched fabric · discharge paste · measuring cup · foam brush · plastic spoon · Speedball ink

MAKING POTATO DEXTRIN

To create potato dextrin:

▶ 2 3/4 cups water

▶ 1 cup instant mashed potato flakes

▶ 1 1/2 tablespoon of liquid starch

Instructions:

Bring the water to a boil and add potato flakes.
Turn the heat to low and allow to cook for 5
minutes, stirring regularly. Remove from heat
and transfer to an airtight container; then add
liquid starch and mix until smooth, using a whisk.
Allow mixture to cool before adding to fabric.
Store remaining mixture in airtight container in a
refrigerator for up to a month.

Workspace

✚ Allow adequate room for the pieces to dry
overnight.

✚ Cover all surfaces, as potato dextrin is very
sticky.

✚ Wooden stretcher and tacks or freezer paper
large enough to hold entire project flat.

Safety: Potato dextrin is nontoxic and even
considered to be food grade but should never be
ingested. Any tools that are used to mix or apply
the substance should not be used for anything
other than fabric manipulations.

Instructions

1. Scour fabric in hot water and Synthrapol to
prepare for dyeing.

2. Create dextrin following manufacturer's recipe
or reference the box above.

3. Stretch fabric on a stretcher or iron onto freezer
paper. Fabric can also be taped to a foam-core
board covered in plastic.

4. Spoon the potato dextrin onto the fabric and
spread it around until it reaches the desired
thickness.

2.54 Apply potato dextrin to fabric using a spoon and manipulate
using a foam brush or fork.

5. Applying the dextrin in a thin coat will create
small hairline cracks (Figure 2.55a). Thicker
application will create deep, thick cracks
(Figure 2.55b). The combination of thin and

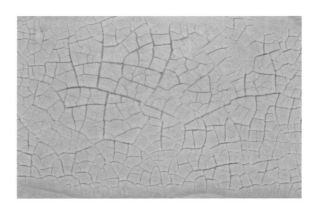

2.55a Thinly applied potato dextrin.

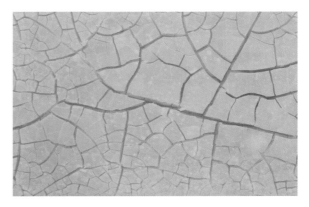

2.55b Thickly applied potato dextrin.

thick application crates a random crackle pattern (Figure 2.55c).

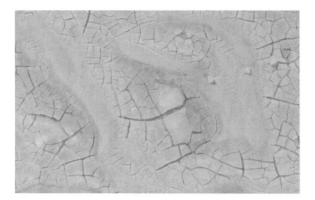

2.55c Potato dextrin manipulated with the edge of a spoon is applied thinly and thickly to fabric.

6. Allow to dry overnight. Once dried, the dextrin will begin to crackle. If a more crackled look is desired, flex the fabric to further break up the dextrin.
7. Apply dye onto dextrin and press into the cracks to make sure the dye reaches the fabric.

2.56 Once the dextrin has dried, apply the dye, being sure to press it deep into the cracks.

8. Once the dye has dried, flake off excess potato dextrin and lightly iron the fabric from the back side on a low setting to help set the dye or other medium.
9. Rinse off remaining dextrin with warm—not hot—water, and allow to dry.

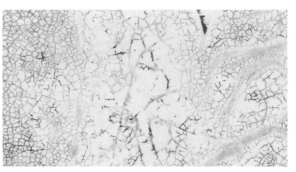

2.57 Completed sample demonstrating the results produced by applying varying thicknesses of potato dextrin. Left: thin application; center: thick application; right: varied application.

Examples

Figures 2.58 through 2.61 show potato dextrin on a variety of fabrics.

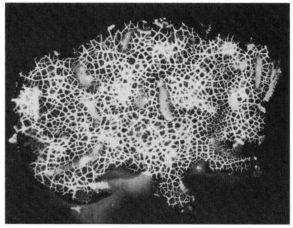

2.58 Discharge paste applied over potato dextrin on a blue cotton broad cloth.

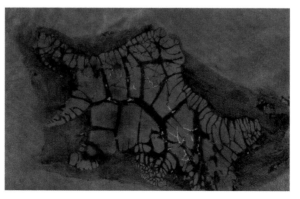

2.59 Dextrin on leather, dyed using speedball screen-printing ink.

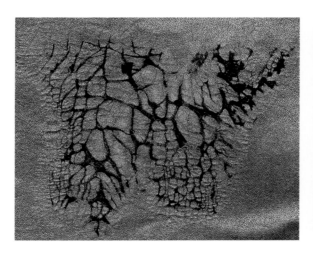

2.60 Dextrin on gray silk satin, dyed using speedball ink.

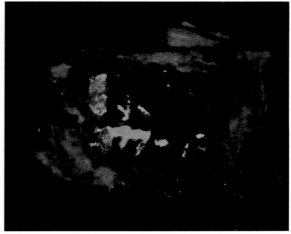

2.61 Potato dextrin on blended velvet—Fiber Etch and discharge paste create the color and texture variation.

Additional Resources

Sourcing: Dharma Trading Company (www.dharmatrading.com), PRO Chemical and Dye (www.prochemicalanddye.com)

Inspiration: *Complex Cloth* by Jane Dunnewold, Lisa Kerpoe (www.lisakerpoe.com)

STUDENT PROJECTS

1. *Discharging black fabric:* All colors of fabric will react differently to discharge paste, especially black. Select five different black natural fabrics and cut into 10" × 10" squares. Select one method to apply discharge paste, for example, with a paintbrush, household utensils, stamps, etc. (See Chapter 3: Printing and Transfer for ideas.) Remain consistent with each sample. Follow the instructions in this chapter (see Discharge Paste Technique, page 36). When the samples are dry, record your results.

   + How did each fabric react?
   + What colors appeared in each?
   + Which fabrics worked best?
   + After completing your analysis, sketch out three ways that this technique can be incorporated into a product or garment.

2. *Layering resists:* Some very interesting results can be achieved by using resists in layers. Choose a 1-yard piece of fabric composed of a natural fiber. Select one method of resist and follow instructions in this chapter; add dye by painting or immersion. Once the fabric has dried, observe the results and think critically about the pattern that has emerged.

   By adding another layer of resist and dye, what sort of results can be achieved?

   Make an educated decision and choose a second resist technique. Apply that to the 1-yard piece of fabric following the instructions provided and apply dye. Once the fabric is dry, record your results and describe three potential applications in fashion, fine art, fiber art, or interior design.

3. *Discharge over a resist:* Dyes aren't the only thing that can be applied over a resist. Why not try using discharge paste? Select three resist methods and three dark-colored fabrics (natural fiber fabrics work best), each about 24" × 24". Test a separate swatch of each fabric to make sure that the discharge paste will work. Apply the resist and then the discharge paste following the instructions in this chapter (see page 36). When fabric is dry, record your results. For each sample, answer the following questions:

   + How did each resist react to the discharge paste?
   + Were there unexpected outcomes?
   + What could be done to improve the results?
   + What are some practical applications for the resulting fabric?

KEY TERMS

+ bandhani
+ batik
+ discharge paste

+ gutta
+ leather resists
+ plangi

+ potato dextrin
+ resists
+ shibori

+ Silk Road
+ tjanting
+ vat discharging

ENDNOTES

1. "Timeline of Fabric History." Threads in Tyme LTD. Accessed May 5, 2014. http://threadsintyme.tripod.com/timelineoffabrichistory.htm.

2. Ibid.

3. Barton, Jane, Mary Kellogg Rice, and Yoshiko Iwamoto Wada. *Shibori: The Inventive Art of Japanese Shaped Resist Dyeing.* Tokyo, Japan: Kodansha International Ltd., 1999.

4. Ibid.

5. Kerlogue, Fiona. *Batik: Design, Style, and History.* New York: Thames and Hudson, 2004.

6. Singer, Margo. *Textile Surface Decoration: Silk and Velvet.* Philadelphia: University of Pennsylvania Press, 2007.

chapter 3

PRINTING AND TRANSFER

Printing and transfer refers to the application of an image directly onto the surface of the fabric. Transfer images cannot easily be reproduced except in the case of some photo transfer techniques, while printing creates predictable, repetitive results. Stunning, bold patterns can be created with either of these techniques, and results similar to Halston's dress from 1969 can be achieved with a little creativity and practice (Figure 3.1).

Printing or transfer techniques can be done with either a thickened dye or printing inks. Each will provide a slightly different result. Thickened dye will penetrate into the fabric's surface as it dries, and in most cases the fabric weave will still be visible. Printing ink will rest on top of the fabric and adhere as it dries, the design will be opaque, and the fabric's weave will not be visible. Both dyes and inks create environmental concerns; see the box on page 77 for further discussion.

PRINTING

Printing is the act of applying an easily repeatable pattern to fabric. It can be done on any fabric or leather as long as the dye or paint is appropriate to the fiber content of that fabric (see Appendix A, Burn Test, page 252). A wide range of printing techniques have been in practice for much of human existence. Simple repeatable images can be created using blocks or stamps, while screen printing achieves clean crisp lines on a larger surface area.

Simple stamps have been used to press color into fabric and leather all over the world, dating so far back the origins cannot be pinpointed. In Japan, stamps were used for printing kimono fabric. In India, wooden blocks were engineered with two or three holes to allow air and excess dye to escape, while in Africa, the use of stamps to print a starch resist on fabric was widely practiced. As the technical process of printing on fabric evolved, screen printing became the dominant method because larger areas could be completed more quickly and with less error. In commercial settings, a flatbed screen-printing process is used. It was invented in Lyon, France, in the 1930s using fine mesh silk as a screen.[1] The introduction of screens made of synthetic materials allowed them to last longer and maintain tension—thus keeping the design flat against the fabric. Metal frames added to the screen's stability, and by the 1950s the process was mechanized with an automated production technique.

Although much of this process has been mechanized since the industrial revolution, professional-grade results can be achieved in a small studio with a little practice.

3.1 Halston creates a Jackson Pollack–like pattern on this tricot evening dress from 1969, a look that can be achieved with a monoprinting technique. *Collection of the Goldstein Museum of Design, Gift of Mrs. Harvey Werner. Photo credit: Petronella Ytsma*

Printing on fabrics woven out of natural fibers is easy and permanent with dye or ink specifically designed for use on natural fibers. Most dyes need to be set with an iron at a temperature as hot as the fabric can tolerate. To determine fiber content, always do a burn test (see Appendix A, Burn Test, page 252), which is useful to determine natural and synthetic fibers.

Before printing begins, select whether to print with a thickened dye to achieve a more translucent look or printing ink for an opaque finish. Experiment by printing with a variety of dyes and inks to add depth to the finished product.

Dye/Ink Choices

+ Jacquard fabric paints, such as Lumiere, Neopaque, and Dye-Na-Flow
+ Jacquard screen-printing inks
+ Jacquard Textile Color
+ Speedball screen-printing ink
+ Thickened acid dye (see below)
+ Versatex screen-printing ink

Materials to Thicken Acid Dye

Figure 3.2 shows some of the materials needed to thicken acid dye.

+ Dust mask
+ Jacquard acid dye (see Appendix B, Figure B.27)
+ Plastic container with lid
+ Protective gloves: rubber, vinyl, or latex depending on skin sensitivity

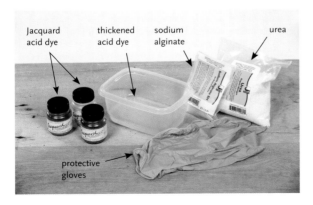

3.2 Materials needed to thicken acid dye.

+ Sodium alginate (see Appendix B, Figure B.40)
+ Spoon for mixing
+ Urea (see Appendix B, Figure B.38)

Safety: When working with dye powder, be careful not to inhale any of the powder, and always wear gloves and a mask.

Instructions

1. Mix chemical water by adding 1/2 cup urea to 1 tablespoon of vinegar in 1 quart of water.

2. Sprinkle sodium alginate (4 teaspoons for printing or 2 teaspoons for hand painting) over chemical water and stir constantly for 10 minutes.

3. Set aside for 1 hour and then stir again. Let the mixture rest overnight before mixing in dye. It should be the consistency of thick syrup.

4. Add dye powder or dye solution to thickener. Start with a 1/2 teaspoon and continue to add until the desired color is achieved.

3.3 Thickener should be the consistency of thick syrup.

Additional Resources

Sourcing: Dharma Trading Company (www.dharmatrading.com), PRO Chemical and Dye (www.prochemicalanddye.com), Binders Art Store (www.bindersart.com)

Printing on synthetics is trickier than on natural fabrics because they are sometimes coated with a substance that does not allow the dye or paint to adhere to the fabric's surface. Specific dyes or paints are needed when working with synthetics and can be harder to set because of the fiber's intolerance to high iron temperatures, which cause synthetic fibers to melt.

Synthetic printing inks tend be opaque and sit on top of the fabric, almost like a sticker, while synthetic printing dyes are translucent and get absorbed into the fabric. Decide what the project calls for before selecting whether to use dye or ink.

Dye/Ink Choices

+ Jacquard screen printing inks
+ Jacquard Textile Color
+ Jacquard fabric paints, such as Lumiere, Neopaque, and Dye-Na-Flow
+ Speedball screen printing ink
+ Thickened disperse dye (see below)
+ Versatex screen-printing ink

Materials to Thicken Disperse Dye

Figure 3.4 shows some of the materials needed to thicken disperse dyes.

+ Calgon or metephos (see Appendix B, Figure B.34)
+ Dust mask
+ Measuring spoons
+ Powdered disperse dye (see Appendix B, Figure B.28)
+ Protective gloves: rubber, vinyl, or latex depending on skin sensitivity

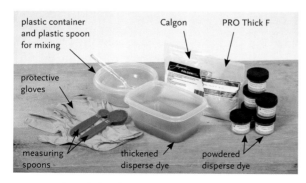

3.4 Materials needed to thicken disperse dye.

+ PRO Thick F
+ Spoon for mixing dye
+ Two plastic containers

Safety: When working with dye powder, be careful not to inhale any of the powder. Always wear gloves and a mask for safety.

Instructions

1. Measure 2 cups of warm water and put into a plastic container.
2. Add Calgon or metephos (1 1/2 teaspoons for hand painting or 2 tablespoons for printing) slowly while stirring. Stir until well mixed.
3. Add PRO Thick F slowly while stirring (7 1/2 teaspoons for hand painting or 7 1/2 tablespoons for printing). Stir occasionally until thoroughly mixed, usually about 45 to 60 minutes.

3.5 Thickener for disperse dye should be the consistency of rubber cement.

4. Store in a closed container overnight. The thickener should be the consistency of rubber cement.
5. Dissolve dye into 1 cup of warm water. Use 1/2 teaspoon for paler shades and up to 4 teaspoons for a darker color.
6. Combine 1/2 cup of dye to 1/2 cup of paste and mix well.

Additional Resources

Sourcing: PRO Chemical and Dye (www.prochemicalanddye.com)

Block printing, or *stamping*, is the process of carving an image or motif into the surface of a block in a relief by cutting away the unwanted areas; ink is applied to the block using a roller, sponge, or brush to ensure even coverage, and the block is pressed into the surface of the fabric. Almost any household item can be turned into a stamp for print purposes: metal hardware items, bubble wrap, coins, buttons, and keys can be attached to wooden dowels for easy handling. Shapes can be carved into sponges, wood blocks, erasers, or a special stamp-carving block. Even nature provides stamps in the form of leaves, flower petals, and grass or straw.

The design options are limitless, but consider that the final product will be a little rough and remember that you will have to carve the stamp yourself, so consider your abilities before taking on a complicated design. But, try to remember that the roughness of stamping is one of its most endearing qualities. See Figure 3.6 to see how much impact a simple design can have. Color variations within a stamp can be achieved by applying the chosen color to the area of the stamp you wish to use to print that color. After each use the stamp must be recoated with dye or paint or the image will become fainter with each consecutive print.

Materials

Figure 3.7 shows some of the materials needed for stamping on fabric.

+ Dust mask
+ Dyes, inks, or paints appropriate to fiber content of fabric. Acid and disperse dyes can be thickened; see Printing on Natural Fabric, page 67, and Printing on Synthetic Fabric, page 68, for directions.
+ Fabric
+ Stamps or blocks (see Appendix A, Making a Stamp, page 253)
+ Protective gloves: rubber, vinyl, or latex depending on skin sensitivity
+ T-pins

Application Method

+ Direct application with dye, discharge paste, or Fiber Etch

3.6 Stamps and a resist were used to create this consistent pattern. *Seydou Keïta Untitled, 1959/60, gelatin silver print, courtesy CAAC - The Pigozzi Collection, Geneva , © Keïta / SKPEAC*

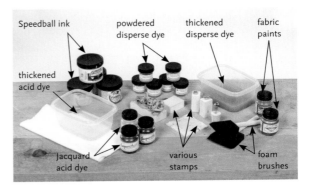

3.7 Materials needed for block printing/stamping on fabric.

Workspace

+ Padded work table (see Appendix A, Creating a Padded Work Surface, page 254)

Safety: When working with dyes, be sure not to inhale any particles by wearing a dust mask. Always wear gloves to protect skin from dye irritants.

Instructions

1. Scour fabric by washing with 1 tablespoon Synthrapol and hot water.

2. Working on a padded table (see Appendix A, Creating a Padded Work Surface, page 254), pin the fabric to the surface using T-pins. T-pins are best because they lay flat against the fabric and will not inhibit the placement of the stamp.

3. Apply dye to stamp with a foam brush, or roller, or simply place the stamp in the dye for a random look.

3.8 Use a foam brush or roller to apply dye to the stamp.

4. Place the dye-covered stamp onto the fabric and apply even pressure.

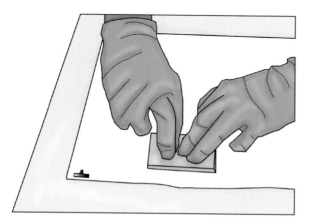

3.9 Press the dye-covered stamp onto the fabric.

5. Remove stamp slowly and evenly.

6. Apply more dye and continue applying stamp. After the design is complete or when a color change is desired, rinse stamp in cool water.

3.10 Continue to apply dye to the stamp and press it into the fabric.

7. Allow dye to dry or use a hair dryer to expedite the process. Some dye will seep onto the padded table, but as long as it fully dries before the next fabric piece is laid onto it, there should not be any cross contamination of dyes. Layering another piece of muslin under each project will also help to protect the work surface and will allow for faster movement between projects.

8. Iron fabric from the back side to set the dye.

Examples

Figures 3.11 through 3.13 demonstrate a variety of stamping options.

3.11 Thickened acid dye stamped onto silk chiffon.

3.12 Copper-colored Lumiere paint on red cotton—created with a stamp that was made by gluing rubber bands to a small block.

3.13 Acrylic paint stamped onto glittered cow leather using wooden blocks and metal washers.
Commissioned photo

DESIGNER PROFILE: SONIA ROMERO

Sonia Romero is a full-time artist living in Los Angeles and a teacher at the Los Angeles High School for the Arts in printmaking and public art. She is a graduate of Rhode Island School of Design with an emphasis in printmaking. Romero has created murals commissioned by the Los Angeles County Arts Commission, the Los Angeles Metro, and the Community Redevelopment Agency. In 2011, her debut solo show was held at Avenue 50 Studio, and she participated in a printmaking retrospective at Self Help Graphics. Romero is a frequent guest lecturer and presenter at southern California schools and sits on the board at the Craft and Folk Art Museum.[2] Romero works with linocuts, a variation of woodcutting in which a sheet of linoleum is used to create the relief. Linocuts are easier to carve than wood and tend to hold up longer, but because the linoleum is often heated before it is carved it's difficult to achieve large-scale prints (Figure 3.14).

3.14 A linocut, created by Sonia Romero called *She Plays Jarna Jarocho (Willow Tree)* measuring 13.5" × 17.5", edition 10, 2012 *Courtesy Sonia Romero*

Additional Resources

Sourcing: Dharma Trading Company (www.dharmatrading.com), PRO Chemical and Dye (www.prochemicalanddye.com), Binders Art Store (www.bindersart.com)

Inspiration: Katsushika Hokusai (www.katsushikahokusai.org), Wassily Kandinsky (www.wassilykandinsky.net), M.C. Escher (www.mcescher.com)

Screen printing is a method of printing that allows for an exact repeat of a clean, crisp image by pressing dye through a thin mesh screen wrapped around a wooden frame. The screen is coated with screen filler that will prevent the dye from reaching the fabric in the areas where the filler is applied. Dye is applied to fabric with a **squeegee**—a tool that forces the dye over the screen and through the mesh. The fabric is then allowed to dry completely before another color is applied.

Almost any design is appropriate for screen printing, but in the beginning start with very graphic, clean-line designs until you are comfortable enough with the process to attempt more complicated designs. Screen printing provides the most consistent results of the printing techniques discussed in this text—the design edges are crisp and the dye coverage is even.

This section discusses how to create a screen by hand drawing an image using a specially formulated drawing fluid. The screen is then filled in around the image, using screen filler, and the drawing fluid is rinsed away. Other options for creating prints on screens that allow for even more control require access to a darkroom. The screen is created using a photo emulsion solution and developed much like a photograph. This material choice will aid in creating complex designs because the images are transferred, or burned, on the screen. Some low-cost options are available too but don't last very long. Stickers or masking tape can be applied to a screen, or a stenciled piece of freezer paper can be attached, sometimes briefly, to a stretched screen with a warm iron.

LAYERING SCREEN PRINTS

If layering screens for part of the design, remember that only one color can be applied at a time, so plan for drying time. Each screen should represent one color.

3.15 Jane Foster's white cotton shopping bags demonstrate the repletion of design that can be achieved using screen prints. *Jane Foster, www.janefoster.co.uk*

Screens can be virtually any size—space is the only limitation—so before planning a design make sure there is a large enough surface area to work upon (see Appendix A, Creating a Padded Work Surface, page 254). Screen printing is also a relatively quick process once the screen is made. Designs can be quickly printed and screens only need to be washed and dried before changing colors (Figure 3.15).

Materials

Figure 3.16 shows some of the materials needed for screen printing.

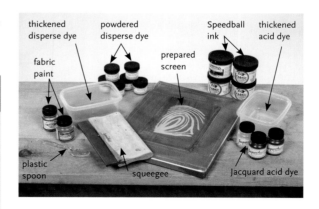

3.16 Materials needed to screen print on fabric.

- Dust mask
- Fabric
- Plastic spoons
- Prepared screen (see Appendix A, Creating a Screen, page 256, and Appendix B, Figure B.51)
- Protective gloves: rubber, vinyl, or latex depending on skin sensitivity
- Squeegee (see Appendix B, Figure B.52)
- Thickened dye or Speedball screen printing ink, discharge paste, or Fiber Etch

Workspace

- Padded surface
- Sink access

Safety: When handling any dye, use gloves and try to avoid inhaling fumes by wearing a dust mask. Store unused dye or ink in sealed containers to avoid spilling and cross contamination.

STUDIO:

VIDEO
Go to Chapter 3 Video Tutorial Part 1: Preparing a Screen and Part 2: Printing Using a Screen

3.17 Spoon dye onto the "lip" of the screen that is created with duct tape (see Appendix A, Creating a Screen, page 256).

6. Hold screen steady using your forearm as leverage, and draw ink across the screen slowly and evenly with the squeegee.

3.18 Using the forearm for leverage, hold the screen flat against the fabric and use the squeegee to drag the dye across the screen.

Instructions

1. Create screen for printing (see Appendix A, Creating a Screen, page 256).
2. Mix dye appropriate to fiber content of fabric. See Printing on Natural Fabric, page 67, and Printing on Synthetic Fabric, page 68.
3. Working on a padded table (see Appendix A, Creating a Padded Work Surface, page 254), use T-pins to secure fabric to table. When printing on a sheer or open-weave fabric, it is helpful to place a piece of freezer paper or palette paper under the design to avoid dye leaking onto the padded table and sticking to the fabric.
4. Lay screen flush against the fabric. There should be no room between the screen and fabric.
5. Spoon dye onto the lip of screen (created with duct tape, see Appendix A, Creating a Screen, page 256). The dye should be the consistency of pudding—dye that is too thin will cause shadowing.
7. More than one swipe with the squeegee may be necessary.
8. Carefully lift away screen.
9. Excess dye can be spooned back into a container and saved for later.
10. Rinse squeegee and screen with water; a soft toothbrush can be used to help clean the screen. If dye dries on the screen it can cause clogging, and subsequent images will be distorted.

11. Allow dye to dry thoroughly—a hair dryer can be used to expedite the process. Try not to move the fabric until it is dry.

3.19 Completed print using a silkscreen and Speedball screen-printing ink.

12. Allow for ample drying time between each print. If the dye is still wet when the next screen is applied, it will smudge the design. Check to ensure that the screen and squeegee are totally dry before proceeding, as water droplets can create a mess on a final project.

Examples

Figures 3.20 through 3.22 show different screen prints.

3.20 Thickened disperse dye, screen printed on nylon. Each color is allowed to dry between applications to avoid smearing. Notice some color spreading; this is common on slippery fabric like nylon.

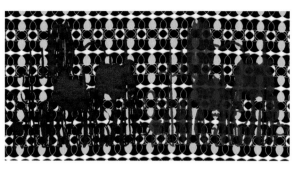

3.21 Screen printing on a printed fabric can be challenging, as some colors will completely block out the print while others will not. This sample was created using Speedball screen-printing ink on commercially printed cotton.

3.22 Shadowing of the image can be caused if the dye is too thin.

Additional Resources

Sourcing: Binders Art Store (www.bindersart.com), Dharma Trading Company (www.dharmatrading.com), Michael's Arts and Crafts (www.michaels.com)

Inspiration: Dan McCarthy (danmccarthy.org), Shepard Fairey (www.obeygiant.com), David Weidman (www.weidmansart.com)

Printing on leather can be done to achieve a wide variety of results, depending on the chosen printing method. Simple designs can be achieved with a stamp (Figure 3.23) or more complex, crisp, lined images with a screen print.

Paint and dye choice should be appropriate to the kind of leather that will be printed. Vegetable-tanned leather can be printed with any natural fiber ink or designated leather ink. If however, tanned and/or finished leather is to be printed, a water-based acrylic paint is necessary, and the image will sit on top of the leather instead of penetrating the surface. Very reliable and durable results can also be achieved by printing fabric screen-print ink onto leather and heat setting it with an iron on low heat.

3.23 Undercover RTW Fall 2013 print on leather. *Maître/WWD; ©Condé Nast*

Materials

Figure 3.24 shows some of the materials needed to print on vegetable-tanned leather.

+ Dust mask
+ Inks and dyes appropriate to leather choice (Table 3.1)
+ Items for printing (screen, stamp, brushes)
+ Masking tape
+ Protective gloves: rubber, vinyl, or latex depending on skin sensitivity
+ Vegetable- or chrome-tanned leather

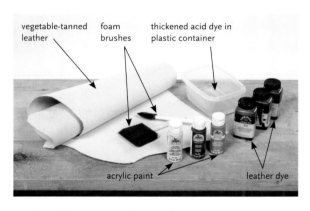

3.24 Materials needed to print on leather.

Table 3.1: Leather Dyes Appropriate to Vegetable- or Chrome-Tanned Leather

Vegetable-Tanned Leather	Chrome-Tanned Leather
Thickened acid dye (see Printing on Natural Fabric, on page 67)	**Acrylic paint**
Leather dye thickened with sodium alginate (create a sodium alginate base following manufacturer's instructions and add water-based leather dye until the desired color is achieved)	**Speedball screen-printing ink**
Acrylic paint	**Jacquard printing inks**
Speedball screen-printing ink	**Versatex screen-printing ink**
Jacquard printing inks	
Versatex screen-printing ink	

Application Methods

+ Painted with brush
+ Stamped (see page 69)
+ Screen printed (see page 72)
+ Monoprinted (see page 79)

Workspace

+ Padded work surface (see Appendix A, Creating a Padded Work Surface, page 254)
+ Sink to clean materials used for printing

Safety: Always wear gloves when handling dyes and wear a dust mask to avoid inhaling any fumes released by dyes.

Instructions

1. Secure leather to padded table using masking tape.
2. Select appropriate paint or dye for the type of leather chosen. See Table 3.1.
3. Apply dye or paint in a manner appropriate to application method (see above). This example demonstrates the use of a stamp carved to resemble a shoe print (Figure 3.26).
4. Apply thickened leather dye to the stamp and press evenly onto leather surface.
5. Allow each layer to dry.

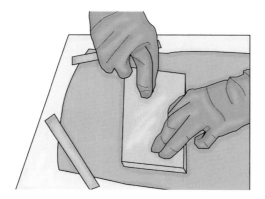

3.25 Using a stamp coated in sodium alginate-thickened leather dye, carefully press it onto the surface of the leather.

6. Once dry, additional layers can be added in another color.

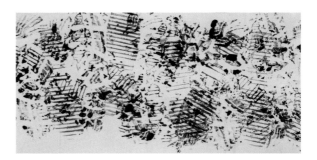

3.26 Stamps can be overlapped as long as each layer dries completely between applications.

Examples

Figures 3.27 through 3.29 show various prints on leather.

3.27 Chrome-tanned leather hand-painted with acrylic paints.

3.28 Screen-printed chrome-tanned leather using acrylic paint.

3.29 Thin acid dye, monoprinted vegetable-tanned leather.

Additional Resources

Sourcing: Tandy Leather Factory
(www.tandyleatherfactory.com), Zack White
Leather (www.zackwhite.com)

Inspiration: Kindah Khalidy
(www.kindahkhalidy.com), Dionne Marshall
(www.punctured-artefact.deviantart.com)

ENVIRONMENTAL IMPACT: PRINTING AND TRANSFER

Dye used in printing and transferring is often thickened using starch, flour, or gum—relatively harmless, but if disposed of improperly, they tend to linger and can be attractive to animals. Never dispose of dyes outside, and thin with water before washing down the drain.

The best way to limit the environmental impact is to reuse materials as much as possible. Stamps and screens can be recycled a number of times, until they begin to warp or deteriorate. Screen filler, used in screen printing, can be removed with Greased Lightning, a concentrated commercial cleaner available at most hardware stores, and a toothbrush. Like any concentrated cleaner, it should be diluted with water and handled with care. Always wear gloves when using, and keep properly stored.

Products used in marbling and sun printing are sold at most local craft stores and are safe,

even for children. Leftover dyes and pigments should be stored in containers with tight-fitting lids and placed in areas where accidental spillage is unlikely.

Cyanotype fabrics pose the most environmental concern when being created in a home studio, which is why websites like www.blueprintsonfabric .com are so helpful. The fabric arrives pretreated and possesses very little environmental concern. Amateurs should avoid creating cyanotype fabric in a home studio unless all safety precautions are met. The chemical that creates the deep blue color can be very toxic over time and when heated can break down into a very harmful gas. Dispose of all chemicals in accordance with local and federal practices. Contact your local department of public works for a licensed disposal site.

TRANSFER

Transfer printing is the act of applying a pattern to fabric or leather using dye, paint, ink, or stain. The fabric is laid directly onto the image that is to be transferred. Some transfer techniques, like sun printing and salt printing, can be duplicated as long as the process is precisely controlled. However, techniques such as marbling and monoprinting are one of a kind and cannot be accurately duplicated, but a little experimentation can create astounding results (Figure 3.30).

The practice of transferring designs onto fabric and leather has been around since the advent of dyes. Cultures across the globe began experimenting with transfer techniques leading to the development of practices still in use today. The development of marbling began at least as far back as 12th-century Japan. According to legend, knowledge of the art was given as a divine gift to a man named Jiyemon Hiroba in 1151.[3] Original marbling designs were mostly fluid, subtle designs until a more controlled process called **ebru** emerged from Turkey. This version introduced chemicals that allowed the paint to float on the surface of the water and eliminate some of the dye wandering associated with the traditional Japanese approach.

Chemically based transfer techniques like cyanotype, which is traditionally a brightly colored blue known as **Prussian blue**, do not exist naturally. A Berlin-based artist and color maker named Heinrich Diesbach first compounded Prussian blue accidently in 1704.[4] He found the substance created a brilliant blue when exposed to sunlight. Prussian blue began to be used for photography in 1842 when Fredrick William Herschel began looking for alternative photographic processes and turned his attention to inorganic photosensitive compounds. He began using Prussian blue for the photographic processes and called it "cyanotype."[5] Cyanotype is still used as a photographic method by many photographers.

Transferring images to fabric is all about experimentation and embracing the unexpected. Because most of these techniques make it difficult to reproduce past results, it is very important to take good notes of your process.

3.30 Giambattista Valli Fall Couture 2012 could be created with simple eyedroppers filled with dye and then transferred to white fabric following the instruction in the Monoprinting section of this chapter. *Giannoni/WWD; ©Condé Nast*

Monoprinting is a combination of printmaking and painting that will create a single image that can be transferred onto fabric. An image is painted or drawn onto a slick surface—freezer paper or a sheet of glass—by layering dyes or paints, then manipulating them with various tools to create patterns. The fabric is laid directly onto the painted surface until the dye is sufficiently absorbed. The fabric is then carefully removed and allowed to dry.

The patterns achieved by manipulating the dye can vary greatly depending on the choice of tools but often tend to produce images that are abstract in nature. Forks, straw, string, eyedroppers, bubble wrap, and paintbrushes can all create very different outcomes (Figure 3.31).

Materials

Figure 3.32 shows some of the materials needed to monoprint.

+ Dust mask
+ Dyes appropriate to fabric type; discharge paste or Fiber Etch can also be used. Experiment with thin and thick dyes.
+ Fabric
+ Freezer paper (see Appendix B, Figure B.50)
+ Items for application (see Application Method, below)
+ Protective gloves: rubber, vinyl, or latex depending on skin sensitivity

Application Method

+ Direct application with spoons, eye droppers, squirt bottles, paintbrushes, fork, and bubble wrap

Workspace

+ Workspace should be covered with plastic to avoid cross contamination of surfaces.
+ Foam boards and flat pushpins work well to hold the freezer paper flat during dye application.

Safety: Always wear gloves when working with dyes and avoid inhaling any fumes by wearing a dust mask.

3.31 Cedric Charlier used a print in his RTW Spring 2013 collection that can be easily created using a monoprinting method. Simply draw the dye across a slick surface with a fork to achieve thin irregular lines. *Giannoni/WWD;* © *Condé Nast*

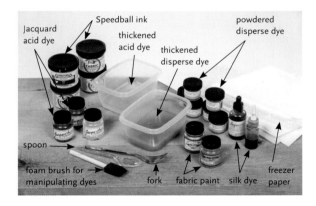

3.32 Materials needed to monoprint.

Instructions

1. Secure freezer paper (shiny side up) to foam-core board using flat pushpins.
2. Apply dye directly to the freezer paper using a spoon, eye dropper, paintbrush, or squirt bottle.

3. Manipulate the dye on the surface of the freezer paper using a fork (Figure 3.33a), toothpick, hair comb, or bubble wrap (Figure 3.33b).

3.33a Thickened dye can be manipulated with a fork, toothpick, or hair comb.

3.33b When bubble wrap is pressed into the surface of dye, it creates a dotted print.

4. Carefully lay fabric directly onto freezer paper and lightly press into the back of the fabric to aid in dye absorption.
5. Slowly pull fabric off to reveal the print on fabric.

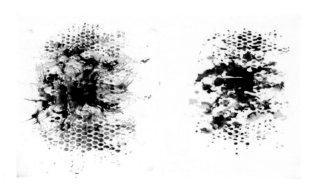

3.34 Left: manipulated dye on freezer paper; right: white cotton fabric after being laid onto dye.

Examples

Figures 3.35 through 3.37 show examples of monoprinting.

3.35 Speedball screen-printing ink applied to freezer paper and then folded to create an inkblot effect; silk chiffon was laid onto the freezer paper and the design was transferred.

3.36 Thickened acid dye applied using an eyedropper to freezer paper and manipulated with a fork. White cotton Lycra was then laid onto the dye, and the design was transferred.

3.37 Monoprint using discharge paste and Speedball screen-printing dye on a blue cotton. Once dried, the piece was ironed to cause the discharge paste to remove color and set the dye.

Additional Resources

Sourcing: Binders Art Store (www.bindersart.com), Dharma Trading Company (www.dharmatrading.com)

Inspiration: Jackson Pollack (www.jacksonpollock.org), Michael Keck (www. michelkeck.com), Vassil Stoyev (www. stoyev.com)

COLLECTION SPOTLIGHT: DRIES VAN NOTEN SPRING/SUMMER 2011

For his Spring 2011 menswear collection, Dries Van Noten created a splatter print that can be achieved using eyedroppers filled with dye and placed directly onto the surface of the fabric allowing the blues, blacks, and purples to mingle and create an ink-blot print (see Figures 3.38a and b). Monoprinting is another option and would start with the application of dye droplets to a slick surface. The color combinations can be manipulated with a paintbrush or by blowing onto the dye with a straw.

3.38a A look similar to Dries Van Noten Men's RTW Spring 2011 men's button-up shirt can be achieved by monoprinting. Using an eyedropper, apply large dots of thinned dye to a piece of freezer paper until a pattern reminiscent of an ink blot emerges. Carefully lay fabric onto dye and slowly remove. Set dye according to instructions.
Giannoni/WWD; ©Condé Nast

3.38b Monoprinting in Dries Van Noten Men's RTW Spring 2011 collection.
Giannoni/WWD; ©Condé Nast

Transfer prints can be created using thickened disperse dye (see Printing on Synthetic Fabric on page 68 in this chapter). The images are often abstract in nature and similar to monoprinting in that the dye is applied directly to a slick surface like freezer paper or parchment paper. The dye is left to dry, and as it dries the dyes begin to mingle to create swirls of color. Synthetic fabric is then carefully laid onto the dried dye and ironed using a high heat. The dye will begin to transfer by melting into the fabric after a few minutes. The longer the piece is ironed, the darker the color will become.

Make sure to determine fiber content before choosing a final fabric because disperse dyes will not transfer vibrant colors to natural fibers. It will result in muted colors, and the vibrant color swirls created by the dye will be unrecognizable.

Materials

Figure 3.39 shows some of the materials needed to transfer thickened disperse dye.

+ Brushes or spoons to apply color
+ Dust mask
+ Fabric
+ Iron
+ Parchment paper
+ Powdered disperse dye (see Appendix B, Figure B.28)
+ Protective gloves: rubber, vinyl, or latex depending on skin sensitivity
+ Thickener (see Printing on Synthetic Fabric, page 68)

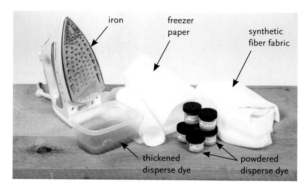

3.39 Materials needed to create a transfer using thickened disperse dye.

Workspace

+ Any workspace is appropriate—just have access to an iron and space to allow the dye to dry undisturbed.

Safety: Always wear gloves when handling dye and try not to breathe any fumes released during the ironing process.

Instructions

1. Secure a piece of parchment paper to a work surface using pushpins on a foam board.
2. Mix thickened dye according to instructions in Printing on Synthetic Fabric earlier in the chapter (see page 68).
3. Apply dye with a plastic spoon or paintbrush. Be sure that the dye is applied thickly.
4. As the dye dries, the colors will begin to mingle.
5. When the dye has fully dried, it will start to pull away from the parchment paper and resemble a fruit roll-up.

3.40 Left: wet dye on parchment paper; right: once dry, the dye will begin to roll away from the parchment paper.

6. Lay synthetic fabric onto the dried dye.
7. Apply light pressure with the iron first to get the dye clump to lay flat.
8. Continue to apply even pressure using a high setting on the iron until the color begins to transfer onto the fabric. Carefully pull up dye to see how the transfer is working. But be careful, as it will be VERY HOT.

3.41 Once ironed, the dried dye can be peeled off of the fabric, but be careful, as it will be VERY HOT.

9. Continue ironing the fabric and dye until the desired color is achieved.

3.43 Thickened disperse dye on a white polyester satin.

ACHIEVING VIBRANT COLOR

The longer the thickened disperse dye is ironed the more intense the color.

3.42 The longer the piece is ironed the more intense the color will become, as seen on this sample created on nylon.

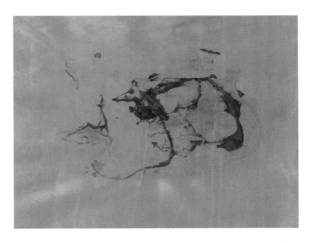

3.44 White polyester lining with a thickened disperse dye transfer.

Examples

Figures 3.43 through 3.45 demonstrate the results possible by transferring thickened disperse dyes.

3.45 Disperse-dyed polyester with a thickened disperse dye transfer.

Additional Resources

Sourcing: PRO Chemical and Dye (www.prochemicalanddye.com)

Marbling is sometimes called *Suminagashi,* a Japanese word meaning "ink floating," and is created by placing dye upon a treated water bath. The dye becomes suspended on the water and can be manipulated into brilliant swirling, fluid colors with a stylus or comb. The design can be transferred onto fabric or paper by placing the chosen medium onto the water and lifting away a diluted version of the marbled pattern. As fun as it is to create patterns in the water, the trickiest part is laying large pieces of fabric onto the solution, which might require an extra set of hands.

Marbling kits are readily available at craft stores and online retailers and are simple to create at home in a large tray or bathtub. The design results are generally highly graphic, fluid designs with repetitive color. The impact is dramatic and with some practice, very controlled designs are possible (Figure 3.46).

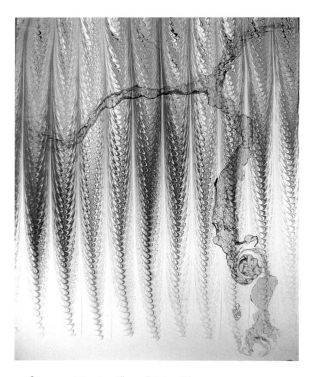

3.46 *Japanese Wisteria,* 18" × 24" Robert Wu.

Materials

Figure 3.47 shows some of the materials needed to marble small pieces of fabric.

+ Alum and methocel—small packages are available in a marbling kit (see Appendix B, Figure B.37).
+ Ammonia
+ Dust mask
+ Fabric scoured and soaked in an alum solution. Natural fabrics work best.
+ Newspaper
+ Marbling dyes (see Appendix B, Figure B.30)
+ Protective gloves: rubber, vinyl, or latex depending on skin sensitivity
+ Various items for making designs (hair pick, comb, toothpicks, skewers)

3.47 Materials needed to marble fabric.

Application Method

+ Dyes are made into a design on the methocel solution and the fabric is laid directly onto the dye. When the fabric is removed, the design lifts away.

Workspace

+ Shallow tray about 2 inches deep, or bathtub
+ Bucket for mixing alum and methocel solutions

Safety: Marbling is a safe process, but as with any dye, always wear gloves and avoid inhaling any fumes created while mixing alum or methocel solutions by wearing a dust mask.

Instructions

1. Dissolve 7 tablespoons of alum into 1 gallon of warm water. Soak fabric for 20 minutes and then allow it to dry. Press fabric to remove any wrinkles.

2. Create methocel solution by adding 4 tablespoons to every 1 gallon of warm tap water. Add 1 tablespoon of ammonia to aid in dissolving the methocel. Stir for approximately 5 minutes.

3. Pour methocel solution into a tray or bathtub and allow to rest for 30 minutes.

4. Just before beginning, drag a piece of newspaper over the methocel solution to remove dust particles and air bubbles.

5. Add dye one drop at a time to determine how each spreads. Some dyes spread more than others and ideally the ones that disperse the most should be applied first. The last color added is usually the most dominant.

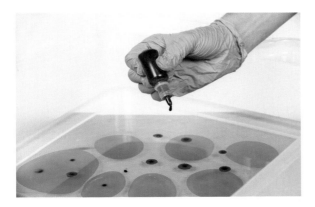

3.48 Using a small squirt bottle, drop dye, one droplet at a time, onto the methocel solutions. The dyes will naturally spread across the surface.

6. Once the dye is dropped on the methocel, patterns can be created with a comb, hair pick (Figure 3.49a), toothpicks, and skewers (Figure 3.49b).

3.49a A hair pick can be used to manipulate the dye.

3.49b Skewers and toothpicks can also be used to mingle dyes.

7. Once the desired pattern is achieved, carefully lay the fabric onto the dye. Hold the fabric at opposite ends. The middle of the fabric should touch first followed by the ends to prevent any air pockets.

3.50 Carefully lay fabric onto the dye being careful to avoid folding the fabric, as that will create lines in the design.

8. After a few seconds, lift off the fabric and lay it onto a flat surface. If the fabric is laid with any folds, lines will be created. Depending on desired results, folds or creases can be used intentionally.

9. The solution can be prepped for another design by dragging a piece of newspaper across the surface to pick up any remaining dye. Anything not collected by the paper will sink to the bottom of the tub after a few minutes.

10. Rinse under warm water to remove the methocel.

11. Allow fabric to dry flat and use a hot iron to set the dye.

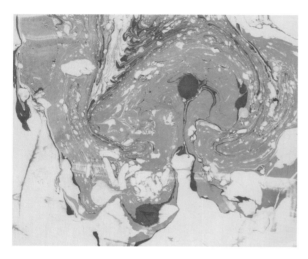

3.51 Once dried and pressed, the design will become permanent.

12. When finished, discard the methocel solution down the drain while running warm water.

Examples

Figures 3.52 through 3.54 show a variety of marbling results.

3.52 White cotton Lycra marbled with blue and yellow dye that has been manipulated using a skewer to create swirled patterns.

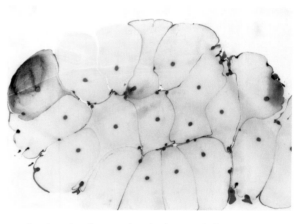

3.53 Droplets placed into methocel solution and allowed to spread across the methocel surface slightly before silk georgette is applied.

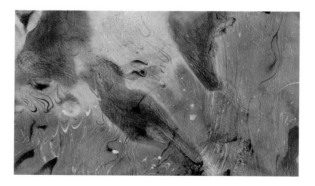

3.54 Marbling can be done on vegetable-tanned leather, but the results are unpredictable.

Patricia Garcia, a recent graduate of the Savannah College of Art and Design, used marbling in her senior collection (BFA, Fashion Design, 2012) (Figure 3.55). She was inspired by the swirling thoughts and brush strokes that Vincent Van Gogh is so well known for, which pair perfectly with the nature of marbling. She truly embraced this technique's beauty with bold combinations of striking colors, and the silhouettes remained feminine and body-conscious so that the prints could take center stage.

3.55 Patricia Garcia's marbled senior collection at SCAD.
Photography by David Goddard; designs by Patricia Garcia

Additional Resources

Sourcing: Binders Art Store (www.bindersart.com), Dharma Trading Company (www.dharmatrading.com)

Inspiration: *The Ultimate Marbling Handbook* by Diane Maurer-Mathison, Grace Yin Ping Lung (www.saatchiart.com/account/artworks/373466), Robert Wu (www.studiorobertwu.blogspot.com)

Sun-printed and cyanotype images can be created using the sun to "develop" a transfer pattern onto fabric. A solution is applied to the fabric, and an object (plants, cut-outs, or even an evening gown, as in Figure 3.56) or a photonegative is secured to the fabric and exposed to sunlight or an ultraviolet source. The light causes the solution to darken in the exposed areas of fabric, resulting in a negative image print.

3.57 "Pillow for Wet Dreams," created by Nancy Breslin demonstrates cyanotype's ability to cleanly and crisply reproduce photo negatives onto fabric.
©*Nancy Breslin*

3.56 Jennifer Glass creates large-scale artwork using cyanotype-treated fabric and evening gowns from her own collection to produce beautiful and dramatic results.
Jennifer Glass

Traditional cyanotype fabric can be ordered online and developed using light from the sun. Once the cyanotype print is properly **fixed**—made permanent—the fabric can withstand normal wear conditions without fading, making it a great option for interior decor, as Nancy Breslin demonstrates in Figure 3.57.

Sun printing is slightly different than cyanotype in that it is possible to procure a wide range of colors, using special sunlight reactive dyes called **Setacolor**, which are readily available at online retailers and some craft stores. This chapter will focus on the use of Setacolor because it is easy to use, does not require a darkroom, and offers more color options than a traditional cyanotype.

All sun printing and cyanotype processes are completed in the same manner, and the following instructions can work for either process—just be sure to read the manufacturer's instructions for preparing any photosensitive solution.

Materials for Setacolor Sun Printing

Figure 3.58 shows some of the materials needed to sun print using Setacolor dyes.

+ Fabric—cotton works best.
+ Foam brushes
+ Plastic container to hold water
+ Protective gloves: rubber, vinyl, or latex depending on skin sensitivity
+ Setacolor dye (see Appendix B, Figure B.31)
+ Sheet of glass or pushpins to secure objects
+ Transfer materials (images printed on a transparency, leaves, fabric, paper cut-outs)

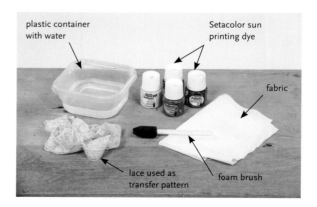

plastic container with water

Setacolor sun printing dye

fabric

lace used as transfer pattern

foam brush

3.58 Materials for sun printing using Setacolor dye.

Application Methods

+ Direct application of dye to fabric with a foam brush
+ Direct application of materials (resists) that will be used for printing

Workspace

+ Foam-core board covered with a plastic bag and pushpins to secure the fabric during dye application
+ Any workspace is appropriate as long as there is a sunny window or access to direct sunlight where the images can lay undisturbed.

Instructions Using Setacolor Dye

1. Gather resist items (leaves, cut-out shapes, printed transparencies, anything that will block out light penetration)
2. Mix Setacolors—one part dye to two parts water. Make sure to mix enough for the whole project.
3. Lay a plastic sheet or garbage bag onto foam-core board to use as a work surface.
4. Secure fabric to board using T-pins, tacks, or pushpins.
5. Wet fabric with a foam brush or paintbrush.
6. Apply dye using a foam brush or paintbrush to wet fabric.

7. Adding more water once the colors have been applied will create a watercolor effect.
8. Quickly place materials onto wet dye and press them into the surface. A sheet of glass or rocks will help to keep the items in place.

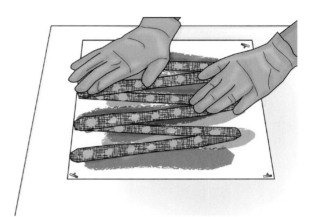

3.60 Press transfer materials into the wet fabric and secure.

9. Set outside in the sunlight, next to a bright window, or use a UV light source.
10. The fabric will begin to darken as it dries, leaving lighter the areas where the items were applied.
11. Once the piece has dried, remove the resists and iron gently for 2 to 3 minutes to set the dye.

3.61 Areas exposed to sun will darken as it dries.

3.59 Apply diluted Setacolor dye to wet fabric in the desired pattern using a foam brush or paintbrush. Once dye is applied, more water can be added for a watercolor effect.

Materials for Transferring Designs to a Pretreated Cyanotype Fabric

Figure 3.62 shows some of the materials needed to print on a pretreated cyanotype fabric.

+ Cyanotype fabrics can be purchased precoated; see Additional Resources on page 91.
+ Sheet of glass or pushpins to secure objects
+ Transfer materials (images printed on a transparency, leaves, fabric, paper cut-outs)

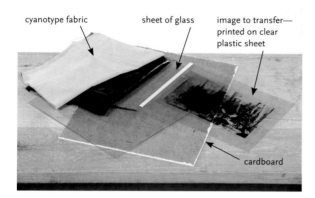

3.62 Materials needed to transfer design to a pretreated cyanotype fabric.

Application Method

+ Direct application by placing design or materials directly onto fabric

Workspace

+ Foam-core board or piece of cardboard
+ Pushpins or a sheet of glass to secure the fabric and materials during development
+ Any workspace is appropriate as long as there is a sunny window or access to direct sunlight where the images can lay undisturbed.

Instructions Using Cyanotype Fabric

1. Pin cyanotype fabric to a foam board or piece of cardboard.
2. Place items to transfer onto fabric. Transparency graphics work very well on cyanotype fabrics because it is dry during application. Photographs can easily be turned into high contrast images using a photo-editing program.

3. Secure objects to fabric using pushpins, rocks, or a sheet of glass (for transparency images).

3.63 Lay pretreated cyanotype fabric, a transparency image, and a sheet of glass on a piece of cardboard before placing in a sunny spot or UV light source.

4. Expose to sunlight or UV light. On sunny days exposure should only take 5 to 10 minutes; while on cooler, shadier days exposure could take as long as 30 minutes.
5. Remove from sunlight and rinse fabric in cool water until the water runs clear.
6. Lay flat out of sunlight until dry. Iron on high heat to set the color. During the ironing process the cyanotype fabric will change color slightly; as it cools it will return to its original color.

3.64 The image will darken once exposed to light. Once completely rinsed in cool water and dried, the image will remain.

Examples

Figures 3.65 through 3.67 demonstrate the results that can be achieved using Setacolor dyes or cyanotype fabric.

3.67 Leaves were used to create this print on a commercially treated cyanotype fabric.

3.65 Silk twill painted with purple and red Setacolor dye that was then diluted further with water before leaves were pressed into the surface and allowed to dry in the sun.

Additional Resources

Sourcing: Binders Art Store (www.bindersart.com), Dharma Trading Company (www.dharmatrading.com), Blueprints on Fabric (blueprintsonfabric.com)

Inspiration: *Blue Prints: The Natural World in Cyanotype Photographs* by Zeva Oelbaum (http://www.zevaphoto.com)

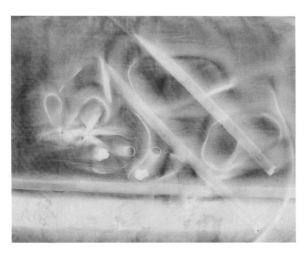

3.66 Cotton broadcloth was painted with a brown Setacolor, and objects such as zippers, zipper pulls, and ribbon were secured before it was placed in the sun to dry.

STUDENT PROJECTS

1. *Sample Book:* Create pages for a reference sample book. Select five techniques from this chapter and create at least three samples for each technique. Experiment with fabric, dye, and ink selection, but always ensure that the fiber content of the fabric is appropriate to the choice of printing medium. Each finished sample should be at least 4" × 4", so start with a larger piece of fabric and consider cropping parts of the print to achieve the most dramatic results. Present each sample on an 8 1/2" × 11" sheet of paper, include a brief description of the process, and answer the following:

   + What can be done to achieve better/different results?
   + How could this sample be used in a garment, accessory, or fine art?

2. *Printing:* Utilizing printing techniques is a quick and easy way to make repeat patterns. Select a printing technique and create a 1-yard piece of repeat-patterned fabric using two colored dyes. Before beginning, create a design (a simple graphic shape is best for beginners), plan how the repeat will be laid out, and determine what the scale will be.

   + How will adding alternate colors within the repeat effect the layout?

   The goal is to create a consistent repeat pattern on one piece of fabric. Make sure to make samples before beginning the final piece to reveal and troubleshoot any problems.

3. *Transfer:* Using transfer methods to create all-over, coordinating prints on fabric can be daunting and unpredictable; embrace mistakes! To begin, select two different transfer techniques and two pieces of light colored fabric, at least 1/2 yard. Using the two chosen techniques, create two different patterns on each fabric. Keep in mind that each piece of finished fabric should complement the other. For example, 1/2 yard of cotton fabric marbled in colors like green and yellow could be paired with a 1/2-yard piece of sun-printed silk. The sun printing should be a similar or complementary colorway and design. Because marbling creates very wavy unpredictable lines, perhaps using yarn of various thicknesses as a transfer onto the Setacolor dye would be appropriate. Always experiment and make samples before progressing to the final piece.

KEY TERMS

- block printing
- cyanotype and sun printing
- ebru
- fixed
- marbling
- monoprinting
- printing
- Prussian blue
- screen printing
- Setacolor
- squeegee
- transfer printing

ENDNOTES

1. Clarke, Simon. *Textile Design*. London: Laurence King Publishing, 2011.

2. "Sonia Romero." Accessed May 21, 2014. http://www.soniaromero.net

3. Maurer-Mathison, Diane. *The Ultimate Marbling Handbook*. New York: Watson-Guptill Publications, 1999.

4. Ware, Mike. *Cyanotype: History, Science and Art of Photographic Printing in Prussian Blue*. London: Science Museum and National Museum of Photography, Film and Television, 1999.

5. Ibid.

chapter 4

FIBER MANIPULATION

OBJECTIVES:

+ Using Fiber Etch to remove sections of fibers

+ Using heat to permanently disrupt a fabric's surface

+ Using specially designed tools to carve or stamp leather

+ Permanently reshaping a piece of leather

+ Creating felt by manipulating wool fibers

+ Using a needle to create felt

+ Combining wool roving and natural fabrics to create a lightweight fabric

+ Adding dimension to a felted piece

Fiber manipulation is the process of removing fibers to create sheerness or cut-outs within a piece of fabric. It can also be considered the creation of a piece of fabric by manipulating individual fibers, such as felt, or changing the surface texture of leather as in carving or molding. While most of the techniques discussed in this chapter are environmentally friendly, the process of removing fibers from fabric using chemicals can be somewhat hazardous. See the box on page 120 for advice on how to limit the environmental impact of fiber manipulation.

CHEMICAL REMOVAL

Removing fibers from fabric can be done with a product known as Fiber Etch. It is made of sodium bisulfate, water, glycerin, and printing paste. It works by removing the cellulose fibers from fabric creating a **devoré**, or *burnout,* effect on mixed fiber fabrics, and will remove sections of natural (cellulose) fibers on fabric, creating a cut-out effect.

The origins of devoré stem from cutwork first created by Italian nuns for ecclesiastical textiles and evolved from **drawn thread work**, or removing individual threads from a fabric. As the nuns developed the technique, they began removing large portions of fabric, resulting in cutwork. As the Roman Catholic Church expanded, it employed more people to produce the church vestments, and these employees in turn began to embroider their own linens and garments. The popularity spread quickly throughout Europe by the 14th century. Eventually, sodium bisulfate was introduced to the process of cutwork, making it quicker and easier. This chemical all but eliminated the need for the time-consuming act of cutting away small pieces of fabric. The results became known as **broderie chimique** in Europe because it was used to simulate machine embroidery[1] (see Cutwork Using Fiber Etch on page 102). In the 17th century, this technique became known as "poor man's lace" because it provided the look of lace without the cost. By the 1920s, the use of devoré on blended fabrics to create a burnout effect became mainstream and was widely used as a fabric treatment on a variety of textiles and products ranging from scarves to handbags to home décor.

Devoré, or *burnout*, is the removal of fibers from the surface of a fabric using a chemical called sodium bisulfate, sold commercially as Fiber Etch. This chemical is applied to the surface of the fabric and eats away the cellulose fibers in that fabric, leaving the synthetic and protein fibers untouched. Burnout creates sheerness in the area where it is applied, creating dramatic, lush garments or textiles (Figure 4.1). Often seen on velvet, this technique can be used with any blended fabric, as shown in Table 4.1.

Fiber Etch can be applied to the fabric using any of the print or transfer techniques mentioned in Chapter 3. Once the chemical is applied, it is allowed to dry thoroughly. The fabric is then ironed from the opposite side using only dry heat until the treated area turns a caramel color and begins to fall off. Once the fabric is rinsed and dried, it is ready for use.

4.1 Tadashi Shoji RTW Fall 2013 uses a devoré technique to create a sheer pattern on velvet.
Aquino/WWD; ©Condé Nast

Fabric Selection

It is important to choose a blended fabric to avoid leaving holes (unless that is the desired effect). Velvet works particularly well and is the traditional choice when it is constructed of a synthetic or protein base and a cellulose fiber pile. Any knit or woven fabric will work, as long as the lengthwise thread, or **weft**, is synthetic or protein and the horizontal thread, or **warp**, is cellulose (or vice versa). As always, do a burn test to be sure of the fiber content and test on the fabric before beginning a final project. See Table 4.1 for quick reference.

Table 4.1: Fiber Etch Fabric Selection Guide

Fibers That Will Dissolve	Fibers That Will NOT Dissolve
cotton	acrylic
linen	polyester
rayon	wool
hemp	silk

Materials

See Figure 4.2 for some of the materials needed for the devoré technique.

+ Blended fabric (see Table 4.1)
+ Dust mask
+ Fiber Etch (see Appendix B, Figure B.45)
+ Brushes for applying Fiber Etch
+ Protective gloves: rubber, vinyl, or latex depending on skin sensitivity
+ Pushpins or straight pins to secure fabric to work surface
+ Iron
+ Muslin or any undyed fabric

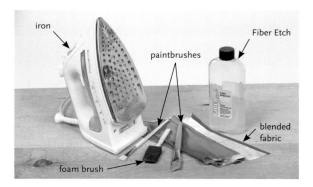

4.2 Materials required to complete a devoré sample using Fiber Etch.

Application Methods

+ Direct application
+ Stamping
+ Screen printing

Workspace

+ Fiber Etch can be used anywhere, but the fumes released when ironing can be toxic, so work in a well-ventilated area and wear a mask if necessary.
+ Fabric can be secured to a foam-core board or padded work table.

Safety: Always wear gloves when working with Fiber Etch, as the chemical can cause skin irritation and is flammable. When Fiber Etch is heated, it releases fumes that can be harmful. Always wear a dust mask and avoid all contact with eyes and surrounding surfaces.

Instructions

1. Secure fabric to work surface. The following example is of an acid-dyed devoré satin attached with pushpins to a foam-core board.
2. Apply Fiber Etch to fabric using any of the application methods listed above. This example shows the creation of a splatter pattern. The foam brush is saturated with Fiber Etch and flung over the surface of the fabric.

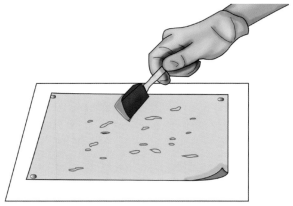

4.3 Using a foam brush saturated in Fiber Etch, create a splatter pattern on the fabric.

3. Blot off any excess Fiber Etch with a paper towel.

REMOVING EXCESS FIBER ETCH

Applying a thin layer of baking soda to unwanted areas of Fiber Etch will help eliminate any mistakes.

4. Allow the Fiber Etch to dry thoroughly. A hair dryer can be used to expedite the process.
5. Once the Fiber Etch has dried, sandwich it between two pieces of muslin. This helps to avoid cross contamination, as Fiber Etch can stick to the iron and ruin future projects.

4.4 Sandwich the fabric between two pieces of muslin with the back side of the fabric facing up.

6. Iron the back side of fabric in quick, light passes. Too much heat too fast can cause the fabric to burn and can also create holes.

7. The area where the Fiber Etch was applied will turn a caramel color and start to fall off. Be very careful to avoid burning the Fiber Etch or it will permanently stain the fabric.

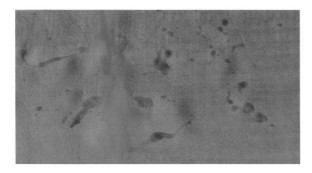

4.5 Once the Fiber Etch has been heated, it will turn a caramel color and start to flake off.

8. Rinse off any remaining Fiber Etch and allow fabric to dry.

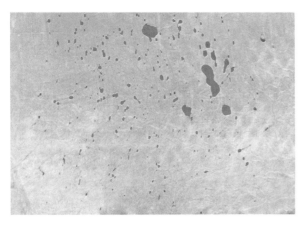

4.6 Dried and pressed example of Fiber Etch.

Examples

Figures 4.7 through 4.9 showcase three different examples of devoré.

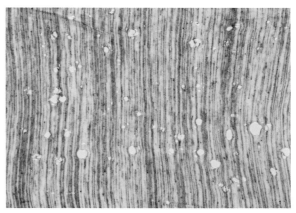

4.7 Fiber Ftch applied with a stamp on modal.

4.8 Fiber Etch applied with a screen onto a black silk/rayon blended velvet.

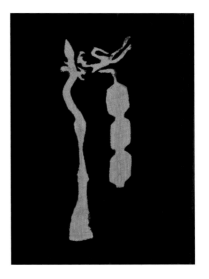

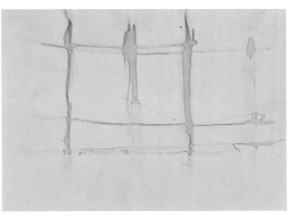

4.9 Fiber Etch applied using a synthetic paintbrush to a cotton/Lycra fabric dyed with an acid dye.

Dionne Swift is a textile designer who works in a variety of mediums. She studied embroidery at Goldsmiths, University of London, and earned her master's degree in textile at the University of Central England. Swift uses devoré on velvet as a way to explore "changing structural qualities in the landscape."[2] She dyes and hand paints the cloth, then overdyes and adds more handwork in order to create visual layers and depth. She believes that the techniques used are more important than the actual images: the results are beautiful, textured textiles (Figures 4.10a and b).

4.10a *Blue Valley View* was created by Dionne Swift by hand painting Fiber Etch onto devoré velvet.
Dionne Swift, textile artist

4.10b *Shadow Experiment* by Dionne Swift was created by layering a wool base under a discharge-printed linen and stitching the two pieces together with a synthetic thread. Devoré is then applied and eats away the cellulose fibers of the linen, revealing the wool beneath.
Dionne Swift, textile artist

Zuhair Murad RTW Fall 2013 showed textiles that could be created using Fiber Etch. Screen printing works best to get similar results: create a screen with a negative (reverse) dot pattern so the dots remain once the cellulose fibers are burned away (see Chapter 3, Screen Printing, page 72). Make sure the screen is made of a synthetic or protein fiber so that Fiber Etch does not eat away the screen (Figure 4.11).

4.11 Zuhair Murad RTW Fall 2013
© *firstVIEW*

Additional Resources

Sourcing: Dharma Trading Company (www.dharmatrading.com), Silkpaint (www.silkpaint.com)

Inspiration: Dionne Swift (www.dionneswift.co.uk), The Metropolitan Museum of Art (www.metmuseum.org)

Cutwork is traditionally created by stitching the outline of a design with a satin or buttonhole stitch and then carefully removing pieces of fabric with small embroidery scissors. This section will focus on the use of Fiber Etch to aid in cutwork designs on cellulose fabric, which eliminates the need for time-consuming cutting by chemically removing the desired fabric. All areas that will be removed must be reinforced with either the satin or buttonhole stitch using polyester thread to avoid any unwanted tearing.

There are many different styles of cutwork but they can all be identified by various stylistic trends. **Richelieu cutwork** consists of distinctive buttonhole bars crossed through the cut out areas (Figure 4.12). **Venetian cutwork** is characterized by a padded buttonhole stitch around open areas (Figure 4.13). **Madeira embroidery** is a white needlework technique composed of patterns of small holes or eyelets (Figure 4.14).

The use of Fiber Etch expedites the cutwork process, but only under certain conditions. It all depends on fabric choice—in some cases, hand cutting may be the only viable option. See Table 4.1 on page 97 for a quick guide.

4.12 Sass & Bibe used Richelieu cutwork in its RTW Fall 2013 collection.
Giannoni/WWD; © Condé Nast

4.13 Michael Van Der Ham created a modern Venetian cutwork garment for his RTW Fall 2013 collection.
Giannoni/WWD; © Condé Nast

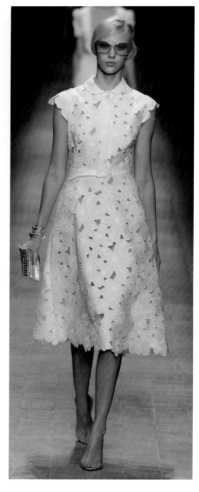

4.14 Valentino created summery frocks with Madeira embroidery in his RTW Spring 2013 Collection.
Giannoni/WWD; © Condé Nast

Materials

Figure 4.15 shows some of the materials needed to create cutwork using Fiber Etch.

+ Dust mask
+ Fiber Etch (see Appendix B, Figure B.45)
+ Foam brush
+ Items for transferring a design
+ Iron
+ Natural fiber fabric
+ Pins
+ Sewing machine
+ Scissors
+ Stabilizer
+ Synthetic thread
+ Muslin or any undyed fabric
+ Protective gloves: rubber, vinyl, or latex depending on skin sensitivity

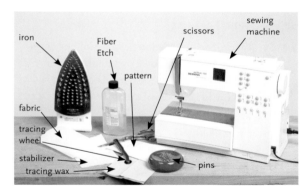

4.15 Materials needed to complete a cutwork sample using Fiber Etch.

Workspace

+ A sewing machine is useful with this technique but the buttonhole stitch, sometimes referred to as the blanket stitch, can be done by hand (see Chapter 6, Blanket Stitch, page 188).
+ A foam-core board and pushpins are necessary to secure the fabric during the Fiber Etch application.

Safety: Handle Fiber Etch carefully. It can cause skin irritation, it is flammable, and it should not be inhaled. Always wear protective gloves and a dust mask.

Instructions

1. Create a design (part A in Figure 4.16) and decide the width of the stitch (a minimum of 1/4 inch is necessary or some Fiber Etch may overflow into the design). Create a second line around the design to indicate the desired stitch width (part B in Figure 4.16).

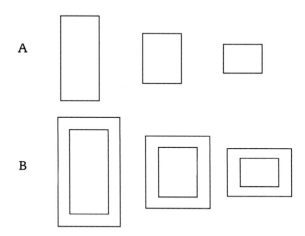

4.16 Cutwork design (A) with appropriate stitch width added and indicated (B).

2. Transfer design to fabric.
3. Stabilize fabric with a tear-away interfacing.
4. Pin fabric to stabilizer. Place pins far away from the design to avoid obstructing the machine during sewing.
5. Using a straight stitch, outline the design. Start by back stitching.
6. To go around a corner, leave the needle in the fabric and raise the presser foot. Rotate the fabric so that it aligns with the direction that is to be sewn.

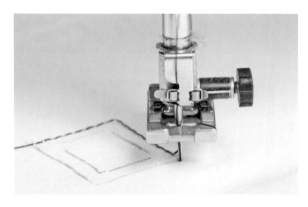

4.17 When turning a corner, leave needle in the fabric, raise presser foot, and rotate fabric until it is aligned in the desired direction.

7. Continue to stitch the outline of the design using a straight stitch until complete.

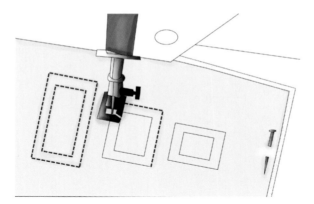

4.18 Using a straight stitch, sew along the lines of the design.

8. Set machine to zigzag stitch and adjust settings on sewing machine to accommodate the proper stitch width. Every machine is different, but the most important part is to make sure the stitch length is very short, as that will create the packed stitches.

9. Zigzag stitch within the two straight-stitched lines until the design is complete.

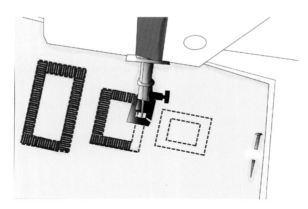

4.19 Fill in the design between the two straight-stitched lines with a tight buttonhole stitch.

10. Apply Fiber Etch with a foam brush to the areas that will be removed.

4.20 Apply Fiber Etch with a foam brush to the areas that will be removed.

11. Allow to dry.
12. Tear off interfacing.
13. Sandwich dried piece (back side up) between two pieces of scrap fabric or muslin and iron on a high heat. Do not use steam. See Figure 4.4 on page 98 for further clarification.
14. The areas with Fiber Etch will turn a caramel color and easily tear away.

4.21 The areas treated with Fiber Etch will turn a caramel color and easily tear away.

15. If necessary, more Fiber Etch can be added to remove any remaining fibers.

16. Rinse with water or use small embroidery scissors to remove any excess pieces of fabric.

17. If the fabric was rinsed, allow to dry. Press.

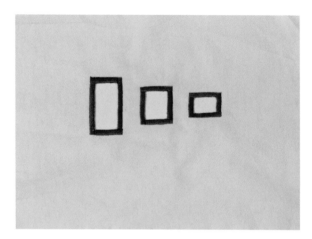

4.22 Final sample with areas removed using Fiber Etch.

Example

How to make lace: In order to make lace using Fiber Etch, layer a piece of synthetic tulle between the fabric and the interfacing and follow the previous instructions. After the Fiber Etch has been applied, dried, and ironed, take great caution when removing fabric pieces to avoid damaging the tulle (Figure 4.23).

4.23 Layering a piece of synthetic tulle under the sample creates a lace effect.

An extreme example of cutwork is Viktor & Rolf's RTW Spring 2012 collection in which huge sections of fabric were removed and then reinforced by attaching a tulle-like fabric, as just discussed (Figures 4.24a and b).

4.24a Viktor & Rolf RTW Spring 2012. *Giannoni/WWD; ©Condé Nast*

4.24b Viktor & Rolf RTW Spring 2012. *Giannoni/WWD; ©Condé Nast*

Additional Resources

Sourcing: Dharma Trading Company (www.dharmatrading.com), Silkpaint (www.silkpaint.com)

Inspiration: The Metropolitan Museum of Art (www.metmuseum.org), Style.com (www.style.com), *Women's Wear Daily* (www.wwd.com)

HEAT

Heat can be applied to natural, synthetic, and blended fabrics to create an array of amazing results, but it is unpredictable. If the heat is too high, the fabric will melt and create holes or completely burn away. Often used to create a distressed, or tattered, look on natural fabric (Figure 4.25), heat can also create unique, beautiful, bubbled, or twisted textures on synthetic fabrics.

4.25 Hein Koh created this piece by layering a few pieces of canvas and then using a chef's blowtorch to burn holes through each layer of canvas to create the "eye" shape. The swirl part of the eye was created by gluing butcher's twine in a spiral pattern between two pieces of canvas. It was lightly scorched to give it color. Finally, the two pieces are attached together using an acrylic matte medium and supplemented with pieces of burnt fabric where needed.
The All-Seeing Eye © Hein Koh 2011

Every fabric will react differently to heat depending on fiber content and finishes or dyes. Always test fabric first and keep in mind a few factors that can affect the results: the distance between the heat gun and the fabric, as well as how long the heat is concentrated in one area. Quick, even movement of the heat gun across the fabric produces the best results and, remember, as a general rule, synthetic fibers will melt and natural fibers will burn.

Materials and Tools

Figure 4.26 shows some of the materials required to manipulate fabric with heat.

+ Dust mask
+ Fabric
+ Granite slab or other heat-resistant surface
+ Heat gun

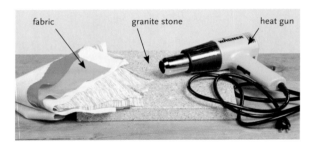

4.26 Materials needed to manipulate fabric with heat.

Workspace

+ Always work on a heat-resistant surface to avoid setting a fire.
+ Work near a water source in case of flames.

Safety: Working with a heat gun can be dangerous. It becomes very hot quickly and can easily cause fabric to catch on fire. Never touch the end of a heat gun.

Instructions

1. Find a space outside or a space with good ventilation and a nearby water source.
2. Loosely secure fabric to a nonflammable surface with masking tape or work in sections on a granite slab.
3. Hold heat gun about 6 to 8 inches away from fabric, and move gun evenly and quickly across the surface of the fabric.

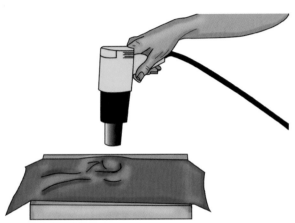

4.27 Hold heat gun 6 to 8 inches away from fabric and move quickly and evenly across the fabric.

4. Timing is not an exact science. Generally the heavier the fabric, the longer it takes to see results. Light fabrics can melt away in seconds. See approximate burn times in Table 4.2.

Table 4.2: Approximate Burn Times of Fabric

acrylic/tulle	1–2 seconds	poly interlock	3–4 seconds
acrylic ripstop	3–4 seconds	polyester tulle	1–2 seconds
cotton	5–6 seconds	polyester lining	4–5 seconds
polyester rayon	4–5 seconds	polyester organza	2–3 seconds
polyester chiffon	2–3 seconds	synthetic fur	3–4 seconds
polyester lace	1–2 seconds	silk jersey	2–3 seconds
polyester satin	3–4 seconds	wool jersey	3–4 seconds

Examples

Figures 4.28 through 4.32 illustrate the dramatic effects of heat on fabric.

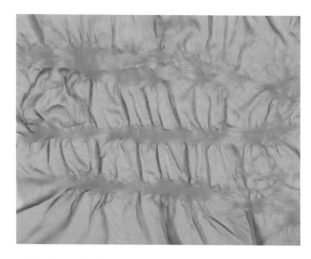

4.28 Polyester chiffon manipulated by passing the heat gun in straight lines equidistant from one another.

4.29 Polyester lining, when melted, creates a vein effect. Holding the heat gun over a particular area longer creates the darker areas.

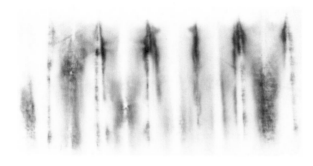

4.30 Accordion-folded muslin, scorched along only the edges of the folds.

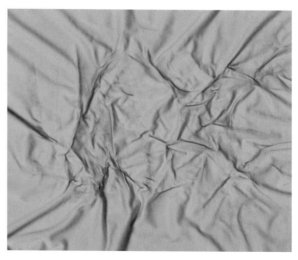

4.31 Silk Lycra creates intricate puckering when exposed to heat.

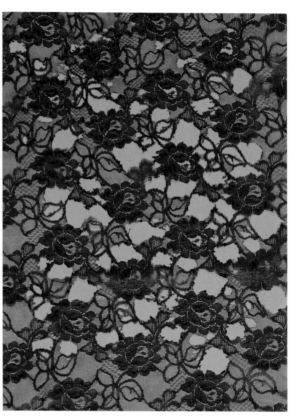

4.32 The delicate mesh areas of a polyester tulle melt away quickly when exposed to heat.

Sabi Westoby, a traditional quilter for more than 10 years, changed direction in 2008 and began making art quilts, textiles, and mixed media works.[3] Westoby combines paper, textiles, paint, stitching, and collage to create pieces inspired by both the natural and manmade worlds. She embraces the challenge of exploring unknown materials and new techniques, which led to a series of work in her "Monochrome Series" that used a heat gun to create unexpected effects and textures. Westoby chose to use Lutradur, a synthetic spun and bonded polyester, for its organic qualities and its ability to react to heat in unexpected ways. She experiments by holding the heat gun close to the fabric to speed up melting and further away to slow it down. Westoby says, "Lutradur and burning are among my favorite materials and techniques" (Figures 4.33a and b).[4]

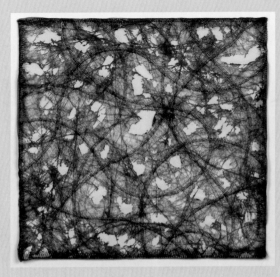

4.33a Sample created by Sabi Westoby by laying black Lutradur, synthetic spun polyester, over white cotton backing and a thin layer of polyester batting (sandwiched between the cotton backing and another piece of cotton). She added curved zigzag stitching through both pieces of fabric using a black cotton thread, important because a synthetic thread would melt along with the Lutradur. Westoby moved the heat gun along the fabric using long, slow strokes until the Lutradur melted away.
Photograph © Sabi Westoby

4.33b Sabi Westoby created this sample using black Lutradur. The goal was to make small holes for embellishments, so she concentrated the heat gun in certain areas until the desired shape and size was achieved. The burnt piece of Lutradur was then laid onto a white cotton fabric and Westoby machine stitched around each hole using cotton thread. French knots were then hand stitched into each hole. Intended to be an art piece, it was then mounted and framed.
Photograph © Sabi Westoby

Additional Resources

Sourcing: Most supplies can be found at local hardware and fabric stores.

Inspiration: Hein Koh (www.heinkoh.com), Sabi Westoby (www.sabiwestoby.com), Lisa Bledsoe (www.lisabledsoe.net)

LEATHER TOOLING

Leather tooling is the manipulation of the surface of leather with the use of knives, modeling spoons, or stamps to carve away material, creating a negative pattern or molding wet leather over a form to create a positive effect.

Creating marks on leather has been used as a form of communication since early civilizations began harvesting animal hides for shelter and clothing. Spanish Moors are considered the first to notably use intricately etched leather as decoration in their homes as early as the 8th century AD.[5] The Aztec culture in Central America is credited with creating many of the raised floral designs that increased the popularity of leather tooling through the Middle Ages and into the 1800 and 1900s, when leather tooling become popular among cowboys and ranchers. Not only did leather provide protection from the elements, it was also a large surface that could be used for self-expression and creativity.[6]

Only vegetable-tanned leather can be tooled, because it can absorb water, unlike most other commercially tanned leathers. For carving or stamping, select a leather that is at least as thick as the depth of the swivel knife or stamp, the thicker the leather the more definition that can be achieved. Molded leather requires very thin leather because it must have some stretch in order to fit around a mold.

Leather carving is the compression of parts of the leather's surface to create relief—embossed patterns created with stamps, knives, spoons, or other tooling mechanisms. Vegetable-tanned leather must be used when carving because it can easily absorb water. Damp leather is necessary when carving leather because the water softens the leather enough to be easily compressed with a stamp or knife. As it dries, the leather will harden into the compressed shape and become permanent.

LEATHER THAT CANNOT BE CARVED

Chrome- and oil-tanned leather, latigo, and suede cannot be carved.

Most commercial examples of carved or embossed leather are done in specialized tanneries where the leather is pressed with heavy metal sheets to permanently set the pattern into the surface of the leather (Figure 4.34). When mixed with other fabrics, the traditional Southwestern feeling of carved leather is easily transformed into cutting-edge, modern garments and accessories.

Materials and Tools

Figure 4.35 shows some of the tools and materials needed for leather carving and tooling.

+ Compass for etching (see Appendix B, Figure B.46)
+ Mallet
+ Modeling spoons (see Appendix B, Figure B.48)
+ Ruler
+ Stamps (see Appendix B, Figure B.47)
+ Swivel knife (see Appendix B, Figure B.49)
+ Vegetable-tanned leather
+ Water and sponge

Workspace

+ Granite slab or other very hard surface
+ Access to water

4.34 Just Cavalli RTW Fall 2013 collection. *Cristaldi/WWD; © Condé Nast*

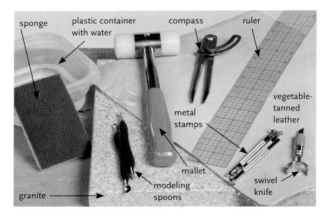

4.35 Materials required for carving leather.

Safety: Working with any sharp tools can be dangerous, so always use caution.

Instructions for Stamping

1. Stamps can be used randomly on a piece of leather or within a grid to create intricate geometric patterns using very few tools.

2. Determine grid size, which will directly correspond to the size of the stamp. Measure from tip to tip across the face of the tool. A general rule is that small tools will fit on a 1/4-inch grid, medium on a 3/8-inch grid, and large on a 1/2-inch grid.

3. Use a ruler to adjust compass so that it is the same width as the desired grid size.

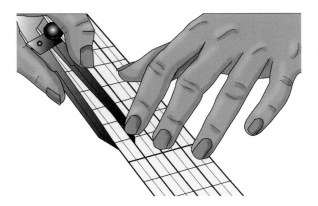

4.36 Adjust a compass so that it is the same width as the desired grid size.

4. Create grid, using a compass to indent the leather and a clear plastic ruler to guide the compass.

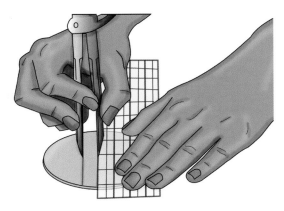

4.37 Using the edge of a ruler as a guide, lightly press the compass into the surface, leaving a shallow indentation.

5. Place leather on a granite slab and dampen leather with a sponge. If the leather is too saturated, the stamp will not work; and if the leather is too dry, the stamp will disappear as the leather dries. Experimentation is key to finding the right balance, but keep in mind that leather color changes significantly from wet to dry.

4.38 Dampen the leather using a sponge—the color of vegetable-tanned leather changes significantly from dry to wet: be sure to experiment.

6. Position the stamp on the grid so that the center of the tool is directly on the "+" created by the grid and pound firmly with a rubber mallet.

4.39 Position the stamp on the center of the "+" created by the grid.

7. Continue placing the stamp in the same position along the grid until the desired pattern emerges.

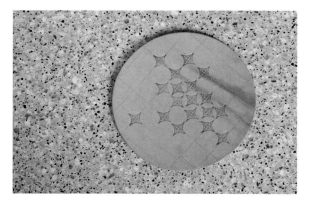

4.40 Continue placing the stamp along the grid until the desired pattern emerges.

8. Once the leather has dried, leather dye can be applied (see Chapter 1, Leather Dye, page 14).

Instructions for Carving

1. Create a design on paper and transfer to the surface of vegetable-tanned leather using a stylus, tip of the compass, or the edge of a modeling spoon. Carefully indent a shallow line: this will act as a guide.

4.41 Transfer design onto the surface of leather using the tip of a compass.

2. Dampen leather using a sponge. It can take some practice determining the ideal amount of water. See Instructions for Stamping on page 113 for visual direction.

3. Carve out the lines with the swivel knife. Always hold the blade at a 45-degree angle to the leather. Twist the blade as it moves along the line to create a cut in the leather.

4.42 Using a swivel knife, carve into the surface of the leather. Always hold the knife at a 45-degree angle to the leather.

4. Using a small modeling spoon, place the edge on the line and drag the tool along the line, creating a beveled edge.

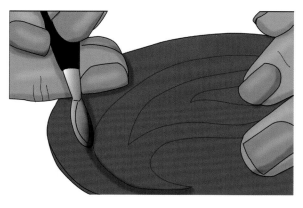

4.43 Place the edge of a modeling spoon into the cut created by the swivel knife and press back the leather.

5. For thicker lines, a wider tool can be used, but it is best to start with a small one to make a precise indent and then work up to a larger spoon.

6. To add depth, continue running the beveling tool in the indentation. Each additional pass will create a deeper gouge.

4.44 Additional passes with a modeling spoon create deeper grooves.

7. Continue to dampen leather as necessary. If the tool begins to skip across the surface, it is a good indication that the leather is too dry.
8. Once the desired edges have been achieved, more detail can be added using the swivel knife for lines or stamps for simple shapes. Always dampen leather before each additional process.

4.45 A swivel knife can be used to add further detail.

9. A small modeling spoon can be used to add more dimension to the additional fine line.
10. Once the piece has dried, leather dye can be applied (see Chapter 1, Leather Dye, page 14).

Examples

Figures 4.46 and 4.47 show examples of carved leather.

4.46 Different sized stamps can be used to create various results and the leather can be dyed once dried.

4.47 Dyeing carved leather highlights the details.

Mark Evans, born in North Wales in 1975, works with large hides and a variety of knives and scalpels to create large-scale leather etchings. Evans doesn't use traditional carving tools such as the swivel knife, but the technique is the same and the results astounding. He carves away less than 1/10 of a millimeter at a time to reveal the suede of the leather. Varying depths create different tones of color used for shading. Evans calls his work "microsculpting" and can spend months on just one piece. Precision is the key to his work, because once a line has been carved out or indented it cannot be undone (Figure 4.48).

4.48 Artist Mark Evans, in the process of creating a detailed etching of a lion onto leather.
Mark Evans, www .markevansart.com

Additional Resources

Sourcing: Tandy Leather Factory (www.tandyleatherfactory.com), Zack White Leather (www.zackwhite.com)

Inspiration: *Leather: The New Frontier in Art* by J. Robert Buck

Leather molding is creating a three-dimensional design by carefully stretching wet, vegetable-tanned leather over a waterproof form, securing it, and allowing it dry thoroughly. Once the leather has dried and hardened, it will retain the shape of the waterproof mold. Some stabilization might be needed, depending on the depth of the design, to help the leather maintain its shape. Beeswax, glue, or even fiberglass for larger projects, are all suitable options for reinforcement.

Leather molding is a popular and effective technique for adding dimension and drama to a leather garment but is more prominent in the accessory market because of its ability to transform simple designs into highly functional pieces (Figure 4.49).

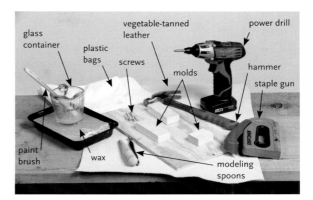

4.50 Materials needed to mold leather.

+ Modeling tools (see Appendix B, Figure B.48)
+ Paintbrush for applying wax
+ Sandpaper
+ Screwdriver
+ Staple gun and staples
+ Thin vegetable-tanned leather (1–2 mm)
+ Two pieces of plywood for creating mold—though molds can be made from almost anything, so experiment.
+ Wax and Pyrex dish for melting wax (any commercial wax will work)

Workspace

+ Work on a sturdy surface that can handle the pressure of pressing the leather.
+ Cover any surfaces with plastic.
+ Have access to a sink or water source.

Safety: Working with power tools can be dangerous, always use caution when handling and wear protective eyewear.

4.49 The "Victory Case" by Will Ficner is designed to be functional and beautiful. Not only can it hold lots of items, it also has a closure to keep everything protected and in its place. *wilboro.com*

Materials and Tools

Figure 4.50 shows some of the materials and tools necessary for molding leather.

+ Jigsaw, if creating a mold from plywood
+ Hammer

Instructions

1. Dampen leather by soaking it in water for a minimum of 24 hours. Leather should be slightly stretchy before beginning.

2. To create a mold using plywood, trace the block shapes onto the surface and add another 1/8 inch around the edges (a larger area may be needed if the leather is thicker). This allows for the leather to fit between the block and the cut-out.

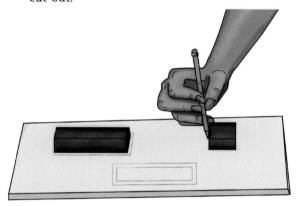

4.51 To create a pattern on plywood, mark the desired shapes and then add a minimum of 1/8 inch around each edge to allow for the leather to fit within the mold.

3. Set mold onto an object that will allow it to be suspended. The bottom of a stool works well. Sawhorses can be used for larger projects.

4. To create the mold, first drill holes at each corner of the rectangle, then insert the jigsaw blade into the hole and saw along the outside lines.

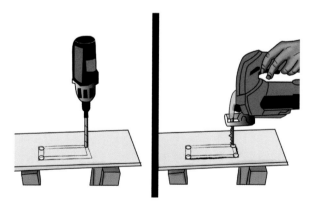

4.52 Create the mold by drilling holes into each corner of the rectangle, insert jigsaw blade into hole, and saw along outside lines of pattern.

5. Once the shapes are cut out, use sandpaper to smooth any rough edges.

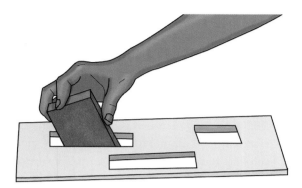

4.53 Sand away any rough edges of the plywood.

6. Lay the leather onto the mold, leather side down. The suede side should be facing up.

7. Staple the leather to the edge of mold to hold it in place during stretching.

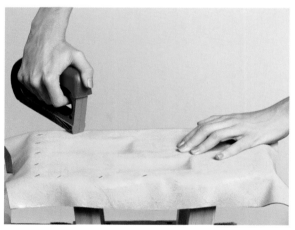

4.54 Lay the leather over the mold suede side up and staple into place along the edges.

8. Using the molding tools and the blocks, press the leather until it begins to take shape. Continue to wet the leather as necessary. This can take a very long time, depending on the depth and detail of the design. This example took about an hour to press to the appropriate depth.

4.55 Work the leather using the modeling tools until the desired shape emerges. This can take over an hour.

9. Place the blocks into the indented areas and place another piece of plywood on top of the blocks and screw the pieces of plywood together. At this point tearing may occur on the leather if it is not stretched sufficiently.

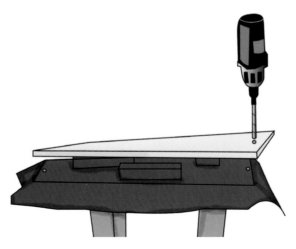

4.56 Insert block molds into stretched leather and lay another piece of plywood onto leather. Screw in each corner to press the blocks further into the leather.

10. Allow to dry overnight.
11. Melt wax in a Pyrex cup. Use caution when handling the hot wax.
12. Once dried, use a paintbrush to apply melted wax into rectangular indents. Add thin layers, allowing each layer to dry between coats.

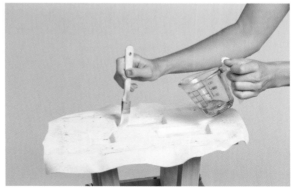

4.57 Once the leather has dried, melted wax can be applied with a paintbrush into the molded areas to maintain the leather's shape.

13. Once dried, the leather can be dyed (see Chapter 1, Leather Dye, page 14).

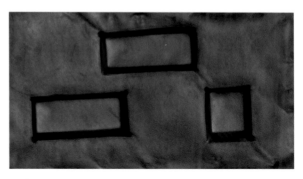

4.58 Once dried, the piece can be dyed with leather dye.

Example

Figure 4.59 demonstrates an application for molded leather.

Additional Resources

Sourcing: Tandy Leather Factory (www.tandyleatherfactory.com), Zack White Leather (www.zackwhite.com)

Inspiration: Dmitry Byalik (www.dmitrybyaliknyc.com), Susanne Williams (www.willinilli.com)

4.59 Kimberly Irwin created this handbag using very thin, damp, vegetable-tanned leather stretched across a sheet of plywood with squares cut out. The leather was slowly pressed into these squares creating the pyramid shapes. To maintain the shape while the leather dried, clay pyramids were inserted into each section and secured. Once the leather dried, a thin layer of fiberglass was added to maintain the shape and protect the pyramids from collapse. *Handbag by Kimbelry Irwin, Photo credit: Colby Blount*

ENVIRONMENTAL IMPACT: FIBER MANIPULATION

Fiber Etch, the product used to remove cellulose fibers from fabric, is made using sodium bisulfate, a strong acid. This acid can cause serious skin and eye irritation, so always wear gloves and protective eyewear when handling. If the Fiber Etch does come in contact with your eyes, immediately rinse for at least 15 minutes. Never dispose of leftover Fiber Etch outside, because the acid will eat away any natural fibers it encounters, including plants and wood. Dilute Fiber Etch with plenty of water before disposing of it down a sink drain. If Fiber Etch is ingested, do not induce vomiting; instead seek medical attention or contact the Poison Control Center at 800-222-1222. Do not store in metal containers; Fiber Etch can react with metal and release fumes and toxins into the air.

Using heat to manipulate fabrics releases some fumes and toxins, particularly when burning or melting synthetic fabrics. Always work in a well-ventilated area and wear a dust mask. When using a heat gun or open flame, there is always a fire danger; work outside near a hose or fire extinguisher. Fabric is flammable, and a small spark can quickly turn into a big fire. Take precautions to avoid damaging your home or environment.

Manipulating leather poses very few environmental concerns. Both carving and molding are done on vegetable-tanned leather, the most environmentally friendly of the tanning processes. The tools used to manipulate leather, if high quality, can last a lifetime, and molds can be used several times before they start to warp or decay.

Felting is created using heat, water, pressure, and agitation of wool. Even though wool is a renewable resource, environmental concerns arise when considering how the wool is processed. Always chose a reputable wool distributer and do some research to find out what they are doing to protect their livestock. Dyeing wool has the biggest ecological footprint, and the process can vary greatly from company to company. Acid dyes are usually used and pose very little environmental threat if disposed of properly. With a little research, it is easy to find companies that use only natural ingredients to dye the wool used for roving.

The actual process of binding the wool fibers, creating the felt, is not mechanized (for the purposes of this text) and requires human energy rather than electricity. Simple, safe, dish detergent and water are used to agitate the fibers and can be discarded down a sink drain.

FELTING

Felt is a nonwoven cloth that has been pressed together and has no internal structure such as threads or an adhesive to maintain its stability. Instead of being woven or knitted, like the fabrics previously discussed, it relies on wools ability to mat and tangle to create a stable fabric.

Felt is one of the oldest known textiles because it is the least reliant on technology: moisture, heat, friction, and wool fibers are the only materials required to create it.[7] Felt's natural warmth and durability made it ideal for the nomadic people of Central Asia, where the process was perfected and used for clothing, horse blankets, and tents because its light weight made it portable. It was also used in shoes and hats because of its ability to mold and maintain shape.

Felt was common in cultures where sheep and wool were prominent because natural fibers like wool have microscopic scales that lay in one direction as a way to repel moisture and dirt form the sheep's skin. Using heat, moisture, and friction, the fibers—applied in layers perpendicular to the layer below—begin to bond. Once fully bonded, the piece can be cut without fear of fraying. There are some other fibers that felt but none as well as wool does. Alpaca, angora, llama, and cashmere are readily available and can felt well, either with a needle or a wet-felting technique. Longer fibers such as bison, yak, and camel take longer to felt but result in a softer, more pliable fabric.

Felt can be used in everything from fashion (Figure 4.60) to home goods (Figure 4.61). Felt's durability makes it ideal for almost any application, and its ability to blend with other natural fabrics makes it versatile and light, so felt does not necessarily have to be heavy.

4.60 Alexander McQueen used twisted wool roving to create the neckline and wispy wool fibers for the dress in his RTW Fall 2000 collection.
© Daily Mail/Rex/Alamy

4.61 Dana Barnes created giant crocheted and felted squares for her NYC loft.
© Bruce Buck 2010

Wet felt can be created by layering precarded and predyed wool, or **roving**, so that each layer runs perpendicular to the one below to ensure that the fibers entangle. The wool can be laid out in any design, and the thickness depends on the number of layers of wool used. Wool will quickly turn from puffy to limp and flat when water is applied, so consider this factor when purchasing roving. You will often need more than you think.

Once the roving has been laid in the desired pattern, it is then exposed to heat, water, pressure, and an agitator (like dish soap), causing the fibers to mat together. The fibers will shrink and harden into a strong fabric, which can be manipulated to create intricate ball gowns or a simple shift dress. Combinations of colors create a depth that can only be achieved with the layering process of felting.

Materials

Figure 4.62 shows some of the materials needed for wet felting.

+ Bubble wrap, shelf liner, or bamboo blind
+ Dowel rod
+ Fabric strips of nylon stockings
+ Lukewarm, soapy water in a spray bottle
+ Wool roving

4.62 Materials needed for wet felting.

Workspace

+ Plastic to cover work area
+ Access to warm water
+ Old towels to absorb excess water

Instructions

1. Begin by separating fibers. Hold the roving with two hands and pull small bundles of wool away from the roving. Hands should be placed as far apart as the desired length of the fibers: otherwise the roving cannot be pulled apart.

VIDEO

Go to Chapter 4 Video Tutorial Part 1: Preparing Wool for Felting

STUDIO:

SEPARATING WOOL FIBERS FROM ROVING

Never cut wool roving, as the sharp edge will make it difficult to felt the fibers together.

4.63 Separate wool roving by pulling off small segments—do not cut roving.

2. Lay out small pieces of wool, starting at the corner and work in one direction. Overlap the wool slightly.

4.64 Beginning in one corner, lay out pieces of roving, overlapping them slightly.

3. Continue to lay out rows of wool always overlapping it with the previous row.

4.65 Continue to lay out roving, slightly overlapping each row.

4. Check to make sure there are no gaps in the wool placement before adding a second layer.
5. Lay out the second layer of wool perpendicular to the first layer.

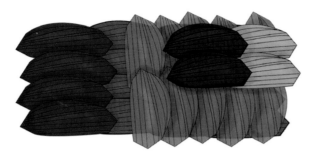

4.66 Apply the second layer of roving at a 90-degree angle to the layer below.

6. Continue to add layers of wool perpendicular to the row below until the desired thickness is achieved.
7. Wet the felt with a spray bottle filled with lukewarm soapy water or a sponge. If the water is too hot at this time, the wool will not felt evenly. Start in the center of the project and work toward the edges, pressing the wool to make sure it is thoroughly saturated.

4.67 Thoroughly wet roving using a spray bottle filled with warm soapy water.

8. Sandwich the fabric between two sheets of bubble wrap (bubble side should be touching the wool), shelf liner, or bamboo mats (if using a bamboo mat, place a piece of tulle between the felt and mat to avoid tangling into the mat). This will aid in agitating the wool fibers, causing them to tangle faster.

VIDEO

Go to Chapter 4 Video Tutorial Part 2: Wetting and Rolling Felt

STUDIO:

4.68 Place wet felt between two pieces of bubble wrap—the bubble side should be against the wool to assist in agitation.

9. Place the dowel rod at one end and roll the felt and bubble wrap.

4.69 Roll the bundle around a dowel rod.

10. Tie the wrapped roll together with nylon stocking or strips of fabric.

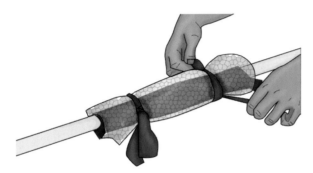

4.70 Bind the bundle with nylon stocking or strips of fabric.

11. Lay down a towel and roll the bundle back and forth starting at the wrist and rolling until it reaches the elbow. This can also be done on the floor by rolling the bundle back and forth using your feet.
12. Roll back and forth about 50 times; the amount will differ with every project depending on the thickness.
13. Unroll the bundle and turn it 90 degrees: straighten out the felt and remove any wrinkles.

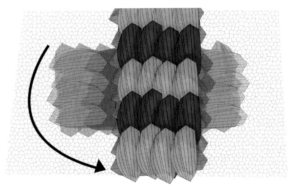

4.71 After a minimum of 50 rolls, unwrap the bundle, and turn the felt piece 90 degrees from its original position.

14. Reroll the bundle and repeat Steps 11 through 13. Always make sure to turn the felt 90 degrees each time to ensure even felting.
15. Test the felt using the pinch test. Pinch a small amount of wool roving. If it easily pulls away from the surface, the felting is not yet complete. If it is difficult to pull small amounts of fibers from the surface, then the felting process is complete.
16. Allow to dry flat.

4.72 Completed and dried sample.

Examples

Figures 4.73 and 4.74 demonstrate two approaches to wet felting.

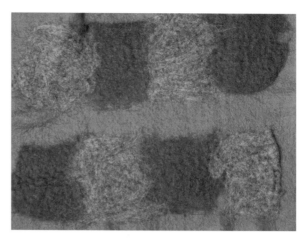

4.74 Patterns can be created using wet felting when working on a felt background.

Additional Resources

Sourcing: New England Felting Supply (www.feltingsupply.com), Hobby Lobby (www.hobbylobby.com)

Inspiration: Horst Couture (www.horstcouture.com), Irit Dulman (www.iritdulman.blogspot.com)

4.73 Wool yarns can be included in the wet felting process.

Needle felting, also known as *dry felting*, is the act of creating felt using only wool and a barbed needle that is moved through the surface of the wool into a foam board until the fibers begin to bond and tangle. There is no need for soap and water in this process, so it can be used to sculpt three-dimensional pieces and to create beautiful edge designs and open patterns (Figure 4.75).

4.75 Jill Stuart RTW Fall 2013 collection.
Chinsee/WWD; ©Condé Nast

Commercial felting is created on a machine similar to a traditional sewing machine called an **embellisher**. But unlike a home sewing machine, this machine has no thread or bobbin. The needle simply moves up and down through the roving until the fibers become tangled. Some home machines can even be converted to felting machines with the proper attachments.

Needle felting can also be combined with wet felting when separate pieces of felt need to be bound together. The needle is punctured through the layers to bond the two pieces together, which is a way of making seams (see Dimensional Felting, page 132).

Materials

Figure 4.76 shows some of the necessary materials for needle felting.

+ Felting needles: single needles and multineedle options are available (see Appendix B, Figure B.43)
+ Foam pad designed for felting (see Appendix B, Figure B.44)
+ Wool fabric
+ Wool roving
+ Wool yarns

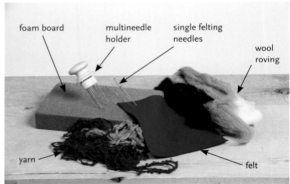

4.76 Materials needed for needle felting.

Workspace

+ Any workspace is appropriate—just be sure that the foam pad is large enough and thick enough to accommodate the project size and depth of needles.

Safety: Felting needles are very sharp, so be very careful when handling to avoid cutting yourself.

Instructions

1. Layer felt piece, yarn, and roving onto a foam board.

2. Using a single needle or a multineedle holder, push through the felt into the pad and repeat. Try to start in the center and work to the edge until the wool is secured.

4.77 Press the needle through the layers, allowing the barbed needle to tangle the wool fibers. A multineedle holder can make the felting process go faster.

3. Occasionally pull the felt off of the foam board. Notice that the fiber punctures through the felt piece and tangles on the back side.

4.78 Occasionally pull the felt from the board. Notice the felt fibers have migrated to the back and have begun to tangle.

4. Once completed, the wool roving should be secured to the felt piece.

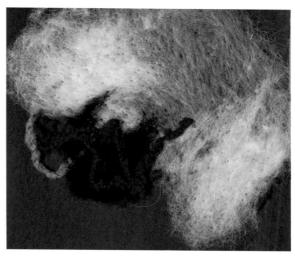

4.79 Completed sample of needle-felted piece.

Examples

Figures 4. 80 through 4.82 show a variety of needle felting results.

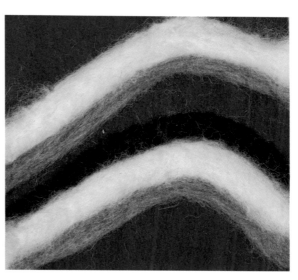

4.80 Roving applied with a needle-felting technique can produce neat wool lines of varying heights.

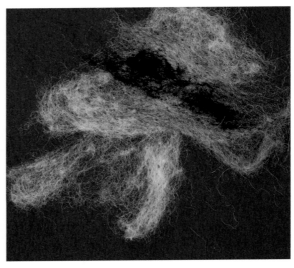

4.81 Other items, such as rope, can be introduced when needle felting—avoid puncturing sturdier objects with the needle or it will break.

4.82 Light wispy wool roving can be applied using a needle-felting technique.

Additional Resources

Sourcing: Dharma Trading Company (www.dharmatrading.com), New England Felting Supply (www.feltingsupply.com), Hobby Lobby (www.hobbylobby.com)

Inspiration: *The Complete Photo Guide to Felting* by Ruth Lane

Felting with natural fibers is also known as **nuno felting** and was named by Polly Stirling and Sachiko Kotaka in 1994. They were looking for a way to make a lighter-weight felt for the warmer climates of Australia. They combined loosely woven fabric and felted in a layer of wool.[8] The fibers of wool move through the weave of the fabric to the back of the fabric, where it becomes entangled, often causing shrinkage in the fabric, creating inconsistent puckers. This technique can be applied to either side of the fabric to create delicate puckering or to add body to a lightweight fabric (Figure 4.83).

4.83 Conny Groenewegen RTW Fall 2013 collection felted white roving to a silk organza blouse for added body: the natural puckering of the felt was embraced in this look.
Giannoni/WWD; ©Condé Nast

Materials

Figure 4.84 shows some of the materials necessary for felting with natural fibers.

+ Dowel rod
+ Liquid dish soap
+ Natural fabric
+ Pantyhose
+ Spray bottle
+ Wool roving

4.84 Materials needed to felt with natural fabrics.

Workspace

+ Plastic to cover work area
+ Access to warm water
+ Old towels to absorb excess water

Instructions

1. Cover work surface with plastic.
2. Lay out a natural-fiber fabric on work surface and dampen with warm soapy water.
3. Separate fibers from roving (see Wet Felting: Step 1 on page 122).
4. Lay out design on one side of fabric, overlapping the wool roving slightly.

4.85 Lay out wool roving in the desired pattern, being sure to overlap the roving slightly.

5. Wet fibers with warm soapy water using a spray bottle or sponge. See Figure 4.67 on page 123 for further clarification.

6. Press on fibers to make sure that all air bubbles have been removed.

7. Flip fabric over and apply wool in the same areas as the front side but at a 90-degree angle. During the felting process, the wool fibers will migrate through the natural fabric and tangle with one another.

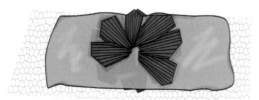

4.86 Flip fabric over and apply wool roving to the back side, perpendicular to the wool on the opposite side. During the felting process the wool fibers will migrate through the fabric and tangle with one another.

8. Spray with warm soapy water.

9. Sandwich between two pieces of bubble wrap and wrap around a dowel rod. (See Figures 4.68 and 4.69 on pages 123–124 for more detailed instructions.)

10. Secure with nylon stockings or fabric strips. (See Figure 4.70 on page 124.)

11. Roll back and forth at least 50 times.

12. Open up bundle and turn the fabric 90 degrees and reroll.

13. Continue to roll the bundle back and forth in increments of 50, rotating fabric until the wool is securely fastened to the fabric and the desired results have been achieved. The piece should pass the pinch test.

14. Rinse fabric to remove excess soap and allow to dry flat. Puckering will occur as the wool shrinks and tangles.

4.87 Completed sample—notice that as the wool fibers felt together, shrinkage occurs, which creates puckering.

Examples

Figures 4.88 through 4.90 show three examples of felting with natural fibers.

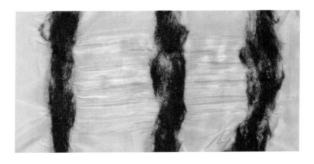

4.88 Applying roving in parallel lines to the front and back of a natural fabric will create a shirring effect.

4.89 Wool roving can be applied to one side of silk gauze and allowed to migrate to the back of the fabric, muting the color and creating delicate puckering.

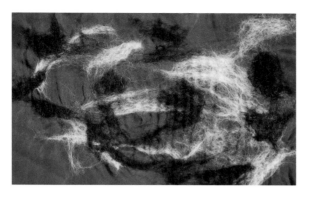

4.90 Silk habotai acid-dyed and felted with wispy pieces of wool roving.

Additional Resources

Sourcing: Dharma Trading Company (www.dharmatrading.com), New England Felting Supply (www.feltingsupply.com), Hobby Lobby (www.hobbylobby.com)

Inspiration: *The Complete Photo Guide to Felting* by Ruth Lane, Ecouterre (www.ecouterre.com)

COLLECTION SPOTLIGHT: BOTTEGA VENETA FALL/WINTER 2013

Bottega Veneta's Fall 2013 collection is the perfect example of the striking beauty of the nuno method—but instead of using the puckered side of the fabric, the wool side is displayed, creating a bold painterly effect on flannel. The addition of small embellishments adds even more depth to the fabric creating a truly unique look.

4.91a Bottega Veneta RTW Fall 2013
Giannoni/WWD; ©Condé Nast

4.91b Detail of the fabric seen in Figure 4.91a, designed by Tomas Maier of Bottega Veneta, created with embroidery, silk, and wool with a flannel base.
Giannoni/WWD; ©Condé Nast

Dimensional felting, also called *inclusion felting*, is the practice of adding a third dimension to the surface of the felted fabric. Most small objects can be included into the surface of the felt using the needle-felting technique and perhaps some additional roving to thoroughly secure the object.

The inclusion technique can cause unexpected shrinking as the felt wraps and molds around the object, so it is important to do practice samples to estimate the amount of shrinkage that will occur. This technique creates high-relief texture and can even add glimpses of color or shine to the surface of the fabric, depending on material choice. Felted balls are some of the best ways to create dimension because they easily attach to the surface and are lightweight and durable (Figure 4.92).

4.92 Conny Groenewegen uses felted balls to add texture to a sleek wool blazer in her RTW Fall 2013 Collection. *Giannoni/WWD; ©Condé Nast*

Materials for Felted Balls

Figure 4.93 shows the materials needed to create felted balls.

+ Felting needles (see Appendix B, Figure B.43)
+ Foam board (see Appendix B, Figure B.44)
+ Wool roving

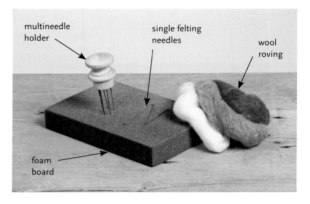

4.93 Materials needed for creating felted balls.

Materials for Inclusion Felting

Figure 4.94 shows some of the materials needed for inclusion felting.

+ Dowel rod
+ Liquid dish soap
+ Natural fabric
+ Spray bottle
+ Wool roving
+ Pantyhose

4.94 Materials needed to felt wool roving with the inclusion of felted balls.

Workspace

+ Plastic to cover work area
+ Access to warm water
+ Old towels to absorb excess water

Safety: Felting needles are sharp, so never look away from the needle when felting.

Instructions for Felted Balls

1. Begin by separating a small piece of roving (see Figure 4.63 on page 122) and placing it onto a foam felting board.
2. Roll one end into a small ball and puncture with a felting needle a few times until the fibers are tangled.

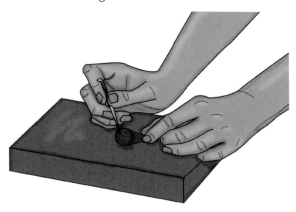

4.95 Roll a piece of roving into a small ball and puncture with a felting needle to tangle fibers.

3. Roll some more roving over the ball and puncture again until sturdy.
4. If more roving is needed, add another piece to the tail of the ball and puncture a few times with a felting needle to tangle fibers.

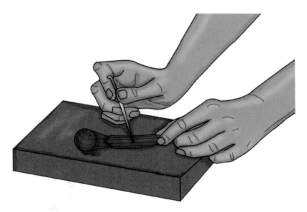

4.96 To create a larger ball, lay another piece of wool roving onto the tail of the ball and puncture with the felting needle to tangle fibers and connect the strips of roving.

5. Continue this process until a felted ball of the desired size and density is created.

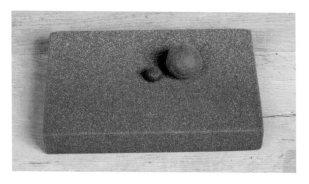

4.97 Any size or density felted ball can be created using this process.

Instructions for Inclusion Felting

1. Lay out wool roving on a piece of bubble wrap, bubble side up, and be sure to overlap wool fibers when laying out the design. Apply felted balls to roving in the desired pattern.

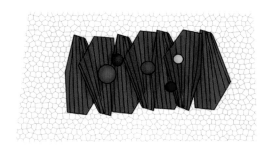

4.98 Lay roving onto bubble wrap (bubble side up), being sure to overlap fibers slightly and add felted balls in the desired pattern.

2. Lay more wool roving over felted balls at a 90-degree angle to the first layer of roving.

4.99 Lay another layer of wool roving over the balls at a 90-degree angle to the first layer of roving.

3. Squirt with warm soapy water, starting at the center and working to the edges. (See Figure 4.67 on page 123.)

4. Press the wool during wetting to remove any air bubbles.

5. Apply another piece of bubble wrap, bubble side down, and wrap around a dowel rod. This can be difficult with the included pieces, but try to keep the bundle as tight as possible. (See Figures 4.68 and 4.69 on pages 123–124.)

6. Secure the bundle with nylon strips and roll back and forth. (See Figure 4.70 on page 124.)

7. After 50 rolls, unwrap the felt, turn it 90 degrees, and reroll.

8. Continue this process until the fabric becomes dense and passes the pinch test. No wool should be easily disrupted from the surface.

9. Allow to dry.

10. Next, use a foam board and a felting needle to define the edges of the included pieces.

4.101 Completed piece demonstrating the technique's ability to create a three-dimensional surface.

Examples

Figures 4.102 through 4.104 show various dimensional felted pieces.

4.100 Use a foam board and a felting needle to define the edges of the included pieces.

11. Once completed, the included pieces will be raised from the surface to create a three-dimensional texture.

4.102 Objects like belt buckles and toggles can be included in felt pieces. This is most easily created with the use of a felting needle and a foam board.

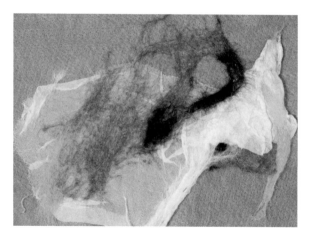

4.103 Any fabric can be included in a piece of felt as long as the wool roving that sandwiches it has been thoroughly tangled with the back side of the fabric—again a felting needle and board work best because of the control that can be achieved.

4.104 Felted balls can easily be attached to a natural fabric by repeatedly piercing them with a felting needle, causing the fibers to tangle with the fabric below.

Additional Resources

Sourcing: Dharma Trading Company (www.dharmatrading.com), New England Felting Supply (www.feltingsupply.com), Hobby Lobby (www.hobbylobby.com)

Inspiration: *The Complete Photo Guide to Felting* by Ruth Lane

1. *Felting:* Each felting technique creates vastly different results but uses many of the same materials. Select three felting techniques and create a collection of samples. Design each piece so they coordinate with each other; consider the thickness, texture, color, and fiber layout. Record results and discuss at least two specific applications for the felt collection in the context of fine art, fiber art, textile, interior, or fashion design.

2. *Fiber Etch Sample Book:* The success of Fiber Etch is directly related to the fabric selection. Choose at least 10 different cellulose-fiber or blended-fiber fabrics: when in doubt do a burn test. Each piece of fabric should be at least 4" × 4". Apply Fiber Etch using a variety of application methods—stamping, painting, or screen printing to name a few—and follow the instructions in this chapter. Present each sample on a 8 1/2" × 11" sheet of paper and include a brief description of the process, what fabric was used, how the Fiber Etch reacted to each fabric, what could be done to achieve better/different results, and how the sample could be used in a garment, accessory, interior, or fine art.

3. *Heat:* Heat is a nontraditional method for adding surface texture or color to fabric. While the results can be stunning on individual pieces of fabric, they are even more compelling when layered upon one another. Choose at least five 1-yard pieces of fabric and layer them. Consider what could happen with each fabric before determining the order that they will be secured together using pins or stitching. Using a heat gun, melt or burn your way through the layers. Try different approaches in different areas of the fabric. For instance hold the heat gun near to or far from the fabric, lightly move the heat across the fabric's surface, or burn through multiple layers of fabric at a time. Record your results and consider practical applications for the final piece.

KEY TERMS

- broderie chimique
- cutwork
- devoré
- dimensional felting
- drawn thread work
- embellisher
- felt
- leather carving
- leather molding
- leather tooling
- Madeira embroidery
- needle felting
- nuno felting
- Richelieu cutwork
- roving
- Venetian cutwork
- warp
- weft
- wet felt

ENDNOTES

1. Llado i Riba, Maria Teresa, and Eva Pascual i Miro. *The Art and Craft of Leather: Leatherworking Tools and Techniques Explained in Detail*. New York: Barron's, 2006.

2. "Dionne Swift: Textile Artist." Accessed June 2, 2012. http://www.dionneswift.co.uk.

3. "Sabi Westoby: Artist Statement." Accessed May 7, 2014. http://www.sabiwestoby.com/artists-statement .html.

4. Sabi Westoby, email message to author, May 8, 2014.

5. Maddox, William A., Dr. *Historical Carvings in Leather*. San Antonio, TX: The Naylor Company, 1940.

6. Ibid.

7. Mullins, Willow. *Felt*. New York: Berg, 2009.

8. Lane, Ruth. *The Complete Photo Guide to Felting*. Minneapolis: Creative Publishing International, Inc., 2012.

chapter 5

FABRIC MANIPULATION

OBJECTIVES:

+ Applying ribbon, trim, or braids to fabric

+ Combining shapes of fabric to create a design

+ Using a sewing machine to quilt fabrics

+ Creating a three-dimensional design on fabric using batting

+ Using cording to create a pattern on fabric

+ Creating basic shirring patterns by hand

+ Using elastic to shirr fabric

+ Creating pleats

+ Creating tucks

+ Using tucks to create intricate patterns on fabric

+ Using stitches to bind small bundles of pleats together

+ Sewing small stitches and gathering to create a pattern on fabric

Fabric manipulation is the act of manipulating the surface of fabric to create a three-dimensional pattern through additional sewing, stuffing, or folding. While the act of manipulating fabric has very little environmental impact, there are a few things to consider in order to limit your footprint; see the box on page 150 for further discussion.

APPLIQUÉ

Appliqué is the process of attaching another fabric, or patch, called **patchwork**, or ribbon or trim, called **passementerie**, to the surface of another fabric.

Appliqués have been used in various ways in many different cultures—all of which achieved distinct effects. The chosen patterns depended on the purpose of the garments and the natural resources available. During the Victorian era, the technique of passementerie was widely used when silk ribbons became popular; the motifs were often dominated by floral, paisley, and scroll patterns.[1] The results are timeless, and this technique is still seen on the runway today (Figure 5.1).

Patchwork was used prior to the mass production of textiles during the industrial revolution when fabric was scarce.[2] Small pieces of silk or velvet were patchworked together to create larger, more functional pieces of fabric. English patchwork was particularly well-known because of the complex geometric patterns created using tiny hexagon shapes (Figure 5.2).

5.1 Valentino created a beautiful and modern example in his Spring Couture 2013 collection by appliquéing tubes, similar to a spaghetti straps, onto a sheer organza base.
Giannoni/WWD; ©Condé Nast

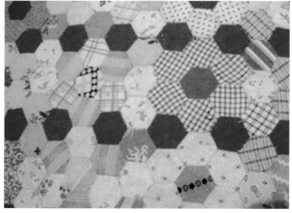

5.2 Complex geometric patterns can be achieved by sewing tiny hexagon pieces of fabric together, referred to as English patchwork. *Courtesy of Polly Medley*

Passementerie is the addition of ribbons, braids, or trim to the surface of fabric to resemble a woven or embroidered pattern. Passementerie can be applied in any style of ornamentation, but are often seen as loops, scrolls, or paisley motifs (Figure 5.3).

5.3 Rue Du Mail designed a beautiful and modern shirt for its RTW Fall 2013 collection using ribbons of varying sizes applied in controlled waves.
Giannoni/WWD; © Condé Nast

Nearly any trim can be used for passementerie, but the best way to know is to do a test: wrap the ribbon in the desired shape and determine if the look is appropriate. Does it remain flat? Is that the intent or is a dimensional look the goal? The ribbon does not need to be tacked down everywhere, so three-dimensional loops can easily be created.

Materials

Figure 5.4 shows some of the materials needed for passementerie.

+ Fabric to which to attach ribbon
+ Ribbon, braids, or trim
+ Scissors
+ Stabilizer
+ Thread

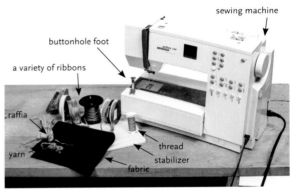

5.4 Materials for passamenterie.

Workspace

+ A sewing machine with a standard presser foot is used to attach the ribbon to the fabric using a straight stitch.

5.5 A standard presser foot.

Instructions

1. Pin a tear-away stabilizer to the back of the fabric to which the ribbon will be attached.

2. Lay ribbon onto fabric to determine the layout.

3. Determine the stitch length and thread color. A contrasting color will stand out against the ribbon, while a matching color will hide mistakes and become invisible.

4. To begin, lay the ribbon upside down on the fabric and stitch straight 1/4 inch from the edge. Fold the ribbon over the stitches so that the right side is facing up. This will finish the edge of the ribbon.

5.6 Lay ribbon upside down on the fabric and stitch across the top. Fold ribbon over stitching and lay flat to finish the edge.

5. Adjust the needle of the sewing machine so that it is aligned with one side of the ribbon.

5.7 Adjust the needle so that it is aligned with one edge of the ribbon.

6. Stitch down one side of the ribbon, stopping 1/4 inch to 1/2 inch from the edge. Fold the end under the ribbon and stitch through both layers to finish off the end of the ribbon.

5.8 To finish the bottom edge of the ribbon, fold ribbon under and stitch flat.

7. Move back to the top of the ribbon and adjust the needle to align with the opposite side of the ribbon.

8. Stitch down the other side of the ribbon, stopping slightly before the end and folding the edge under as in Figure 5.8.

9. Continue adding strips of ribbon, stitching on both sides of the ribbon until the design is complete.

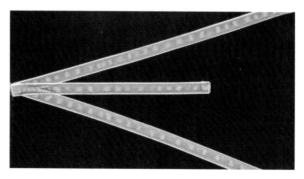

5.9 Ribbons can be applied in straight lines.

Examples

Figures 5.10 and 5.11 show different passementerie options.

5.11 Almost any flat ribbon can be used for passamenterie. From left to right: flat gold ribbon, yarn, flat braid, raffia, gold scrolled ribbon, leather lacing, glittered ribbon.

Additional Resources

Sourcing: Any local craft or fabric store will have the appropriate materials.

Inspiration: Houles Paris (www.houles.com), Samuel and Sons Passementerie (www.samuelandsons.com)

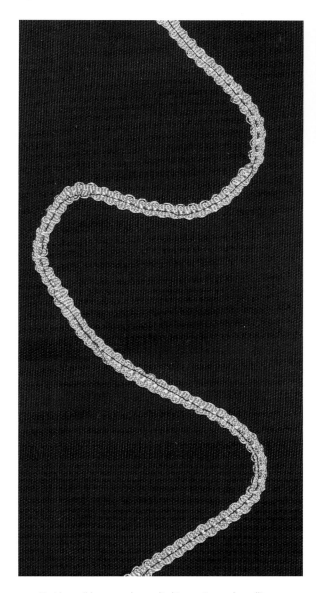

5.10 Braids or ribbons can be applied in curving and scrolling patterns.

Traditionally patchwork is the creation of fabric by sewing together smaller, often mismatched pieces to create a large piece of fabric, as seen in one of Roberto Capucci's iconic masterpieces in Figure 5.12. However, a modern interpretation of patchwork can include the application of fabric pieces or patches to an existing garment. Patchwork is not limited to fabric but can be created using any number of unconventional objects (Figure 5.13).

Before sewing any two fabrics together, always make sure they can be sewn together. Some lighter weight fabrics may require stabilization in order to support the stress on the seam (see Appendix A, Stabilizers, page 253). Always create a sample and test the strength of the seam by tugging on the fabric.

5.12 Roberto Capucci patchworks and pleats strips of colorful taffeta to create this beautiful evening gown.
© *Massimo Listri/Corbis*

5.13 Maison Martin Margiela demonstrates the use of unconventional materials in its Fall 2012 collection with the use of flattened baseball gloves to create a patchworked vest.
Giannoni/WWD; ©*Condé Nast*

Materials

Figure 5.14 shows some of the materials needed to create patchwork.

+ Fabric
+ HeatnBond (see Appendix B, Figure B.54)
+ Scissors
+ Stabilizer
+ Thread. Contrasting thread will cause the shape to stand out, while complementary color thread will create the illusion of the stitching being part of the shape.

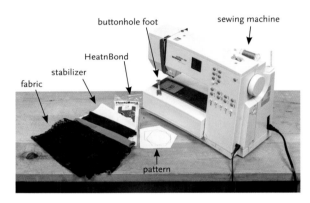

5.14 Materials needed to patchwork fabric.

Workspace

+ Use a sewing machine with a standard presser foot or buttonhole foot. (See Figure 5.5 on page 141.)

Instructions

1. Create design, separate the pieces, and cut out the pattern pieces.
2. Lay out design on fabric. For tightly woven fabric, HeatnBond can be attached to keep the shape in place while sewing. Iron HeatnBond to the back of the shape and cut out (teal fabric is backed with HeatnBond).

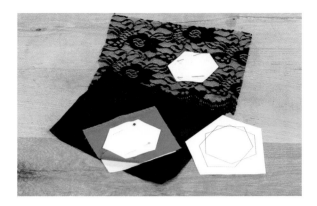

5.15 Lay out pattern pieces and iron HeatnBond to any tightly woven fabric.

3. Cut shapes out of fabric.
4. Beginning with the shapes at the back of the design, remove HeatnBond backing if necessary and iron into place on fabric.
5. Stabilize fabric with a tear-away stabilizer and pin to the back side of fabric.
6. Adjust sewing machine to a zigzag setting. Use a very tight zigzag stitch to secure the shape onto the fabric. The stitch length should be below 1, while the width can be as wide as the design calls for—this example is stitched using a width of 4.
7. Begin at one corner of the design and stitch around. Make sure that the edges of the patch are completely covered with thread. The edge of the fabric should be in the center of the presser foot.

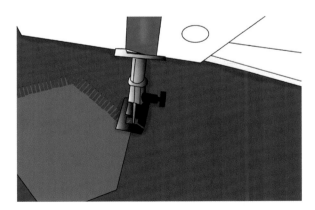

5.16 Beginning at one corner of the design stitch onto background fabric using a very tight zigzag stitch.

8. At corners, leave the needle in the fabric, raise the presser foot, and pivot the fabric.

9. For fabrics that cannot be secured with HeatnBond such as lace or sheers, cut out shape and use a straight stitch to secure the fabric into place.

10. Use a zigzag stitch to secure the lace. Align the edge of the fabric with the center of the presser foot to be sure that all edges are secured. The stitch width can be different for each patch, but make sure it is not too similar or it will look like a mistake.

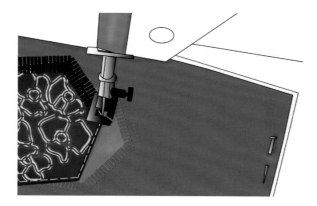

5.17 Sheer or open weave fabrics should first be attached to background fabric using a straight stitch before securing with a tight zigzag stitch.

11. Once complete, remove interfacing.

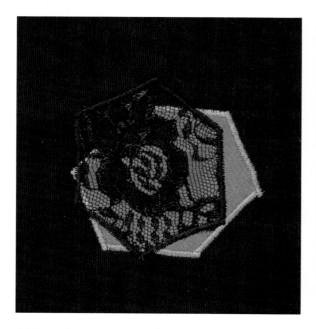

5.18 A complete patchwork example.

Examples

Figures 5.19 and 5.20 show appliqué examples.

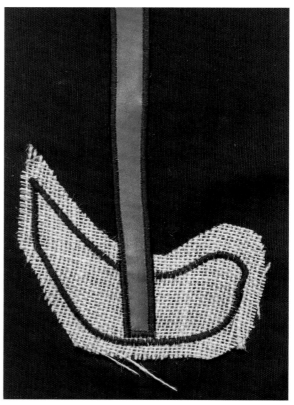

5.19 Placing the zigzag stitch inside of a shape allows the burlap to fray naturally.

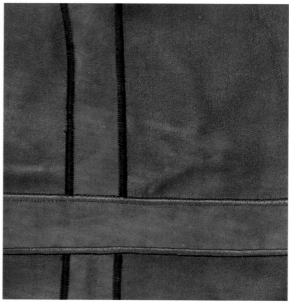

5.20 Suede patchworked onto leather using contrasting color threads.

Loewe created art deco patterns on sheepskin and leather jackets for its RTW Fall 2013 collection with the use of traditional patchwork designs, modernized with a vibrant color scheme. The choice of leather creates an unexpected toughness to an otherwise traditional graphic and technique. (Figures 5.21a and b). To create a similar look, a pattern must first be created, cut apart, and given seam allowance. The design is sewn back together and created into a garment. To achieve the narrow lines without having to sew tiny strips of fabric together, use an appliqué approach. For example, in Figure 5.21b, the pink areas would be cut larger and the neighboring color applied and sewn to the pink. This larger piece could then be patchworked into the garment relatively easily.

5.21a Loewe RTW Fall 2013. To create a similar effect, a pattern must first be created, cut apart, and seam allowance added to each piece. Fabric or leather is cut using the shapes with seam allowance as a pattern. Each piece of fabric is sewn together until the final design emerges.
Giannoni/WWD; ©Condé Nast

5.21b Loewe RTW Fall 2013.
Giannoni/WWD; ©Condé Nast

Additional Resources

Sourcing: Any local craft or fabric store will have the appropriate materials.

Inspiration: Roberto Capucci (www.fondazionerobertocapucci.com), FIDM Museum (www.fidmmuseum.org), The Metropolitan Museum of Art (www.metmuseum.org)

QUILTING

Quilting is stitching that fastens three layers of fabric together: a top, a fiber filling called **batting**, and a lining. Stitched designs are indented into the surface to hold the layers together and create a decorative effect. Quilting is a versatile technique and could be used for a variety of purposes in fashion (Figure 5.22) and in home decorating (Figure 5.23).

Hand quilting has ancient origins, when it was first used as protection for animals against abrasive armor. The extra batting also helped to keep soldiers warm during long journeys. Its use began in Asia, and the skill spread along the trade route to parts of Europe.[3] In medieval times, it was used in decorative wall hangings and bed covers, but by the 17th century it was used in fashion to create dresses and petticoats. By the 19th century, quilting became popular in rural areas, giving rise to the domestic quilting tradition.[4]

Another form of quilting, called **cording,** which is the placement of cotton cords or yarn between two pieces of fabric that are then sewn into place, has a rich history in India, Persia, and Turkey. Cording reached the height of its popularity during the 13th and 14th century in Italy, France, and England where its highly decorative nature led to its use in bedspreads and wall hangings. Cording was often paired with **trapunto,** a technique used to create dramatic reliefs on fabric by raising details or segments of a design within a larger pattern using batting; in the 17th and 18th centuries, it was used to decorate linen caps, jackets, and petticoats.

Common quilting practices today include trapunto and cording but most often in conjunction with some sort of **machine quilting,** the use of a sewing machine to assist in the creation of straight, even, and consistent stitch lines across the fabric. Often, machine quilting only uses a thin layer of batting between two layers of fabric in order to keep the fabric from becoming too stiff and heavy.

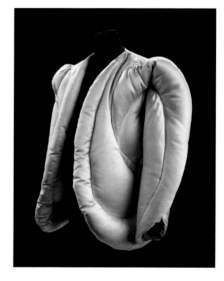

5.22 Charles James quilted satin jacket filled with down from 1937. It was created much in the same way as a down comforter—some areas were stuffed fully, while others were left unstuffed to allow for the natural movement of the body.
Charles James © V&A Images

5.23 These chairs were created by product designer Tokujin Yoshioka from a kind of quilted fabric used to protect machinery in transit.
Tokujin Yoshioka, photo courtesy of www.moroso.it

Machine quilting is done with the aid of a sewing machine. It makes the process much faster and easier than hand stitching and is particularly useful in creating straight-line designs (Figure 5.24).

5.24 Fleamadonna RTW Fall 2013.
Koski/WWD; ©Condé Nast

Three layers are used when machine quilting: the top fabric, batting (thickness depending on application), and lining. Quilting can be done with almost any fabric—just make sure that the weight of the three layers is consistent, because if the lining is too thin, it can tear easily.

Materials

Figure 5.25 shows some of the materials needed to machine quilt.

+ Base fabric
+ Items for transferring design
+ Sheet batting (see Appendix B, Figure B.56)
+ Top fabric
+ Thread
+ Pins

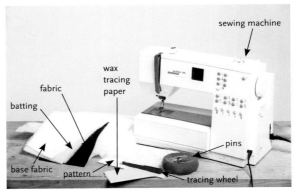

5.25 Materials needed for quilting fabric.

Workspace

+ A sewing machine with a standard presser foot is necessary to quilt quickly and consistently. Quilting can be done by hand following the same instructions below.

ENVIRONMENTAL IMPACT: FABRIC MANIPULATION

Fabric manipulation itself has very little environmental impact, aside from the energy used to run a sewing machine and the manufacturing of thread. The creation of any textile has significant environmental impacts, ranging from the farming of plants, like cotton, to the toxic chemicals used to dye fabric. The production of all fabrics emits greenhouse gases.

One significant issue with the topics addressed in this chapter is the amount of fabric used. Most techniques can consume double or triple the amount of fabric necessary to simply shape a piece of fabric around a body or to drape across a window. That is why it is so important to create smaller samples to determine exactly how much fabric will be needed to achieve the desired effects before beginning any project. One thing we can do as designers is try to be mindful of how we consume our medium— fabric. There is no harm in taking apart old garments or accessories and using the scraps to work out details before moving to a larger scale. Not only will it help to save money, it will also keep lots of fabric out of landfills.

Instructions

1. Create and transfer design to fabric. See Appendix A, Transfer Methods, page 253.

2. Pin together fabric with transferred design, sheet batting, and base fabric.

3. Begin stitching lines in one direction, being careful to miss the box at the center. Always back stitch at the start and end of each stitch line.

5.26 Transfer design onto fabric and layer over a sheet of batting and a base fabric.

5.27 Begin stitching the lines of the design, piercing the top fabric, batting, and base fabric.

4. Stitch the other direction of lines, back stitch at both ends. At this point the dimension created by the batting should be obvious.

5. Continue to stitch the design until it is complete.

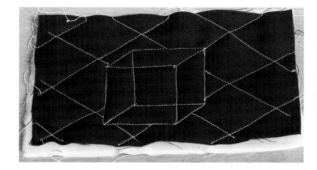

5.28 Upon completing all of the stitching, a raised pattern will emerge.

Examples

Figures 5.29 through 5.31 demonstrate quilting variations.

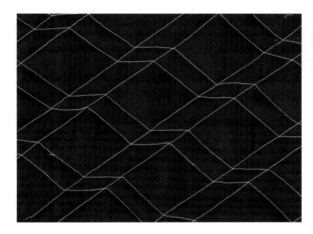

5.29 Geometric patterns paired with thin batting creates a modern look.

5.30 Curving patterns and thick batting create dramatic results.

5.31 Quilting patterns can be used as a border.

Additional Resources

Sourcing: Most local craft and fabric stores have the appropriate materials for machine quilting.

Inspiration: Maya Schonenberger (www.mayaschonenberger.com), Arlé Sklar-Weinstein (www.arlesklar.com), Stacy West (www.stacywest.com)

Trapunto, also known as *Italian quilting*, is traditionally created by stitching the outline of a shape or pattern through two layers of fabric—the top fabric and the lining. Tiny slits are cut into the back, where the batting is stuffed, to pad and raise the shapes.

Trapunto can be used in combination with other quilting techniques to create dramatic effects. It is versatile and can create subtle effects with lightweight batting or thick, padded shapes, as Elsa Schiaparelli demonstrates in her iconic Skeleton Dress from 1938, seen in Figure 5.32. This technique is executed easily with a sewing machine and can be manipulated to create limitless designs and patterns. Trapunto tends to appear most dramatic on solid color fabrics but can be used to add dimension to a portion of a print.

Materials

Figure 5.33 shows some of the materials needed to create a trapunto sample.

+ Awl or chopstick
+ Base fabric
+ Batting (see Appendix B, Figure B.55)
+ Items for transferring design onto fabric
+ Thread

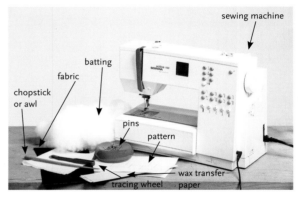

5.33 Materials needed for trapunto.

Workspace

+ A sewing machine with a zipper foot (Figure 5.34) is necessary for creating a trapunto design.

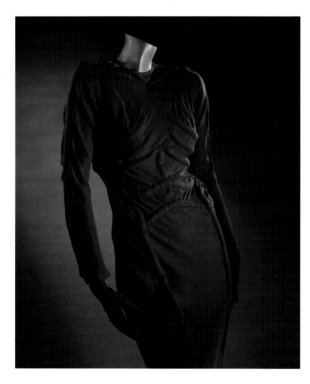

5.32 The Skeleton Dress was created in 1938 by adding trapunto to a skin-tight silk crepe dress to create a three-dimensional skeletal pattern.
Schiaparelli, Elsa ©V&A Images

5.34 Zipper foot.

Instructions

1. Create design and determine the order the shapes will be stitched. Overlapping shapes adds further dimension to the piece.
2. Lay the top fabric over a base fabric. Any fabric can be used for trapunto, but try to use similar weaves; so do not mix a plain weave fabric with a knit.
3. Transfer design to fabric using any of the methods mentioned in Appendix A, Transfer Methods, page 253.
4. Using the zipper foot, stitch around the first shape. Leave a small area open for adding batting; back stitch.

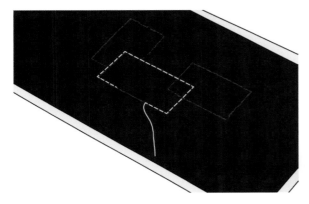

5.35 Stitch around the first shape, leaving a small area open for inserting batting.

5. Use an awl or chopstick to push the batting between the two layers of fabric, filling in the stitched shape.

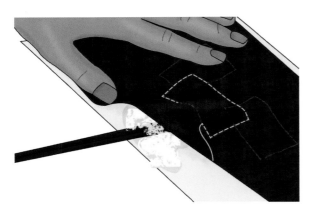

5.36 Use an awl or chopstick to push batting between the two layers of fabric into the stitched shape.

6. Close the shape, making sure to back stitch at both ends.

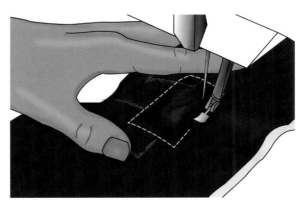

5.37 Once the batting is inserted, stitch the shape closed using a zipper foot.

7. Continue to create shapes, leaving small areas open to insert batting.
8. Add further dimension by stitching over already stuffed areas.
9. Once the piece is complete, a raised, padded shape will emerge.

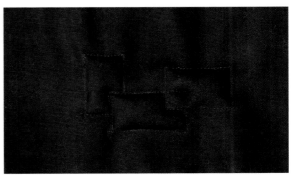

5.38 Once complete, a raised pattern emerges.

Examples

Figures 5.39 through 5.41 show trapunto variations.

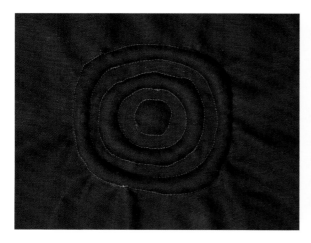

5.39 Circular shapes can be created using trapunto. Always start in the center.

5.41 Organic shapes are easily achieved using trapunto.

Additional Resources

Sourcing: Most local craft and fabric stores have the appropriate materials for trapunto.

Inspiration: Elsa Schiaparelli (www.schiaparelli.com), FIDM Museum (www.fidmmuseum.org), The Metropolitan Museum of Art (www.metmuseum.org)

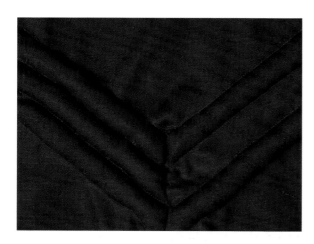

5.40 Trapunto tubes create graphic texture.

Cording is a narrow-stitched channel filled with yarn or cord to create ridges. Like traditional quilting, a cord (batting) is placed between the two layers of fabric and stitched into place. A cord can be anything, from a shoelace to rubber tubing. Just be sure that the cord meets the functionality of the project. It would be impractical, not to mention uncomfortable, to upholster a chair with thick, stiff cording. Always consider the final objective before selecting what to use for cording.

There are a couple of problems that arise when using cording, the first being that it does not offer the insulation that a sheet of batting can provide. It also creates a firmer, heavier, less flexible fabric, so it is used almost solely as a decorative feature. It is usually applied in parallel rows and creates rounded ridges directly related to the size of the cording used. Large, firm cording can be used to create dramatic looks (Figure 5.42), while thin, even rows add discrete details (Figure 5.43).

5.42 Comme des Garçons used large, firm cording in its RTW Fall 2013 collection.
Giannoni/WWD; ©Condé Nast

5.43 David Koma used thin cording to accent leather garments in his RTW Fall 2013 collection.
Giannoni/WWD; ©Condé Nast

Materials

Figure 5.44 shows some of the materials needed to create corded fabric.

+ Base fabric
+ Cording (see Appendix B, Figure B.53)
+ Pins
+ Thread
+ Top fabric

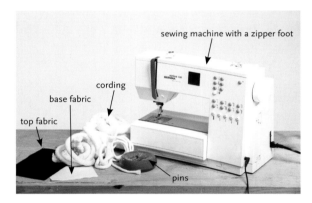

5.44 Materials needed for cording fabric.

Workspace

+ A sewing machine with a zipper foot is required to cord; see Figure 5.34 on page 152.

Instructions

1. Layer two pieces of fabric—a top and a base fabric. These should be similar in weight and weave.
2. Determine the cording's size and path; straight and curvy lines are easily achieved.
3. Using a zipper foot, stitch a line—this will serve to hold one side of the cording in place. Back stitch.
4. Insert cording between the two pieces of fabric; be sure to press it tightly against the stitched line.

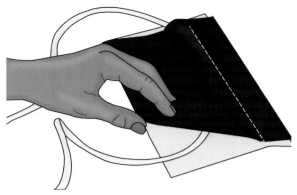

5.45 Insert cording between the two pieces of fabric and press it against the stitched line.

5. Using a zipper foot, stitch along the other side of the cording. Keep the zipper foot as close as possible to the cording. If there is too much space, it will shift inside the tunnel of fabric.

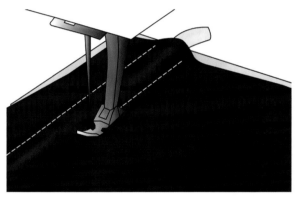

5.46 Using a zipper foot, stitch the other side of the cording. Stitch as closely to the cording as possible to ensure the cord does not shift.

6. Continue repeating Steps 3 through 5 until the design is complete.

Examples

Figures 5.47 and 5.48 demonstrate the variety of designs that can be achieved using cording.

5.47 Any sized cording can be used, each creating different effects.

5.48 Curving lines can be easily achieved with cording.

Additional Resources

Sourcing: Most local craft and fabric stores have the appropriate materials for cording.

Inspiration: FIDM Museum (www.fidmmuseum.org), The Metropolitan Museum of Art (www.metmuseum.org)

SHIRRING

Shirring is creating fabric that is contracted into a smaller size when gathered along multiple parallel rows of straight stitching sometimes filled with cording (Figure 5.49). Shirring is usually executed using thread if done by hand—**basic shirring**—or with a band of elastic with the aid of a sewing machine—**elastic shirring**.

Shirring was first developed to gather large pieces of fabric to fit snuggly against the body. It is especially useful around necklines and cuffs because it stretches over the body and then fits snuggly against it with sliding or pulling. Not much is known about the history of shirring other than it was likely derived from smocking and became very fashionable in the late 1800s.[5]

5.49 Miu Miu RTW Spring 2014 used vertical shirring to create volume and texture on this cocktail dress.
Giannoni/WWD; ©Condé Nast

Basic shirring is constructed by stitching threads across the surface of the fabric in parallel lines. The threads at one end of the fabric are secured and then the fabric is slowly scrunched up the threads until the desired amount of puckering has occurred. The remaining thread is cut and secured so that the shirring will remain intact. For further stability, a **stay**—piece of fabric used to stabilize an area—may be required.

Using basic principles, a variety of options for shirring emerge. Stitch length is the biggest variable, as smaller stitches create tiny, delicate puckering, while long stitch lengths create large folds on the fabric.

Materials

Figure 5.50 shows some of the materials needed for shirring.

+ Disappearing ink pen
+ Fabric
+ Thread

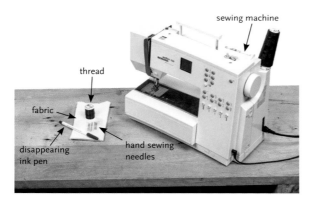

5.50 Materials needed to shirr fabric.

Workspace

+ A sewing machine with a standard foot, or needle and thread.

Instructions

1. Decide how large the desired piece should be after shirring. For slight fullness cut a piece about one and a half times the finished size. For medium fullness start with a piece two times the desired size, and for generous fullness start with three times the amount of fabric. Samples should always be created before beginning a final piece.

2. Determine the length of the final piece and add seam allowance to all edges if necessary.

3. Plan a pattern of parallel lines and mark on the back side of the fabric using a disappearing ink pen.

4. Stitch along the line with hand-sewn stitches, machine-sewn straight stitches, or a zigzig stitch (4 width, 2.5 length) over a string or cord. DO NOT BACK STITCH.

PREPARING THE CORD OR STRING

When using cord or string, be sure to cut it a few extra inches longer at each end. Ensure that the zigzag stitch is large enough to fit over the cord without puncturing it. If the cord gets snagged in a stitch it will not shirr properly.

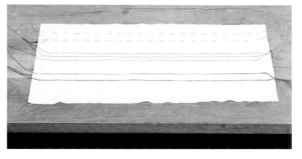

5.51 Shirring can be created with a variety of stitches. Top: hand stitched; center: long machine-sewn stitches; bottom: cord secured with a zigzag stitch (2.5 length, 4 width).

5. At one end of the fabric, knot the loose threads together. When using a sewing machine, tie the bobbin and needle threads together. If stitching by hand, tie multiple rows of thread together.

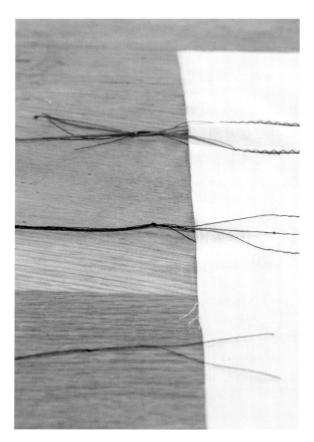

5.52 Secure threads on one side of the fabric by knotting the needle thread and bobbin thread or knotting together rows of hand stitches.

6. Hold onto the threads or cord on one end of the fabric. Using the other hand, draw the fabric toward the secured threads. Work inch by inch.

5.53 Hold the unknotted threads in one hand and move fabric down the threads until the desired fullness has been achieved.

7. Secure stitches by tying the bobbin thread and needle thread together (Figure 5.52). Using a small machine stitch, stitch along the edge of the fabric to secure the threads.

8. Set the shirring by arranging the gathers to the desired appearance and steam with an iron.

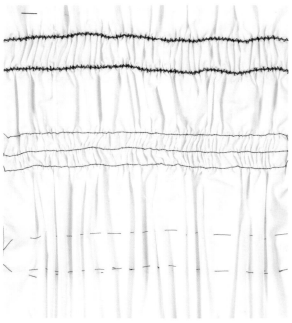

5.54 Different stitching creates different shirred effects.

9. If more stability is desired, a stay can be attached to the back of the shirring by hand stitching a piece of fabric along the first and last rows of shirring. The stay does not overlap with unshirred fabric.

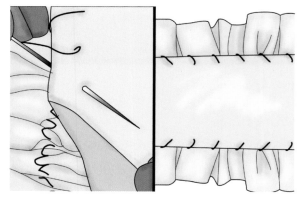

5.55 Left: Hand sew the edge of the stay to the top row of shirring, but do not overlap the stay with unshirred fabric. Right: Stich along the bottom as well to secure the stay completely.

Examples

Figures 5.56 through 5.59 demonstrate a variety of shirring options.

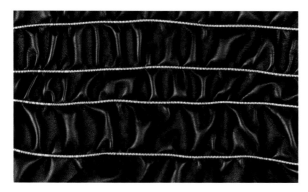

5.56 Leather shirred with cording and a zigzag stitch.

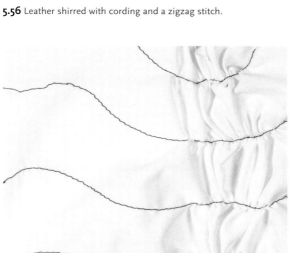

5.57 Stitch rows of parallel wavy lines, knot threads at one edge of the piece, and move fabric along threads until the desired effect is achieved.

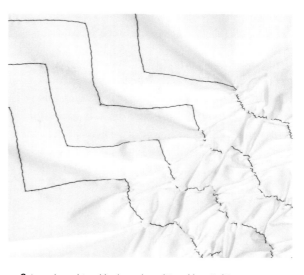

5.58 A random shirred look can be achieved by stitching a step pattern onto fabric.

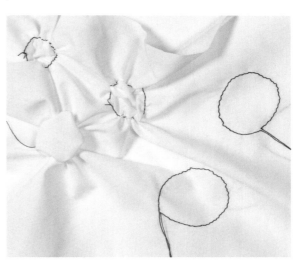

5.59 To create puckers and dips in the fabric, stitch circles and leave long threads. Knot one thread and pull the other to create until the desired shape emerges.

Additional Resources

Sourcing: Most local craft and fabric stores have the appropriate materials for basic shirring.

Inspiration: FIDM Museum (www.fidmmuseum.org), The Metropolitan Museum of Art (www.metmuseum.org)

Using elastic bands is a quick and easy way to make shirred fabric. Elastic is inserted into channels of fabric and secured at one end. The elastic is pulled tight until the desired puckering is achieved. Finally, the elastic is secured at the other end of the channel (Figure 5.60).

5.60 Bruno Pieters used elastic-band shirring in its Spring 2004 collection to create form-fitting shirts with gaping holes held close to the body with elastic bands.
Photography Alex Salinas, www.alexsalinas.com

Elastic shirring works very well along edges and opening of garments because it keeps the fabric from stretching and gaping. It is considered an easier alternative to basic shirring because the results are more consistent and it doesn't, usually, require additional stabilization. The elastic does the work inside the fabric channel with little intervention from the designer.

Materials

Figure 5.61 shows some of the materials needed to shirr using elastic.

- ✦ Elastic in any width
- ✦ Fabric to be shirred—almost any will work, but bulky fabrics tend to become too full once shirred.
- ✦ Thread

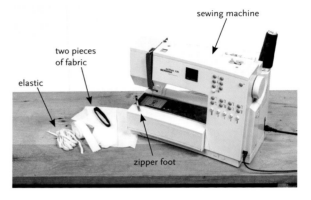

5.61 Materials needed to shirr with elastic.

Workspace

- ✦ A sewing machine with a zipper foot (see Figure 5.34 on page 152) is needed.

Instructions

1. Determine the size of the final piece. Cut two pieces of fabric one to three times the length of the desired final piece (see Basic Shirring Step 1 on page 159 for more in-depth explanation).
2. Determine the length of the desired final piece and add seam allowance around all edges. Cut two pieces.
3. Draw parallel lines on the fabric the width of the elastic.
4. Lay the two pieces of fabric on top of each other.
5. Using the zipper foot, sew along one side of where the elastic will be placed and then back stitch to knot the threads.
6. Insert the elastic between the two pieces of fabric and press it against the stitched line.
7. Hold the elastic tightly against the stitched line and use the zipper foot to stitch a second line parallel to the first against the edge of the elastic, and then back stitch.

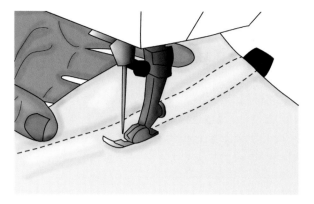

5.62 Use a zipper foot to stitch a line against the side of the elastic. This line should be as close as possible to the elastic without sewing through it.

8. Once all of the elastic is inserted, sew a stay stitch along one edge to secure the elastic.

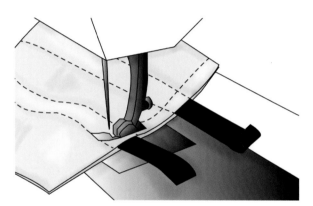

5.63 Elastic is stitched to the fabric along one edge of the piece to secure it before the fabric can be gathered.

9. Hold the elastic in one hand and slowly move the fabric toward the secured edge.

5.64 Pull the elastic and slide the fabric along it until the desired effect is achieved.

10. Once the desired width and fullness ae achieved, sew a stay stitch along the side where the elastic was pulled to secure the piece.

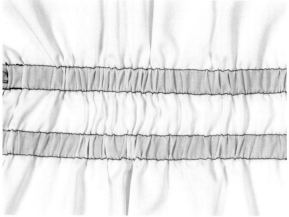

5.65 Stitch the fabric and elastic together on the side of the piece where the elastic was pulled in order to secure it into place.

Example

Figure 5.66 shows shirring using a variety of elastic widths.

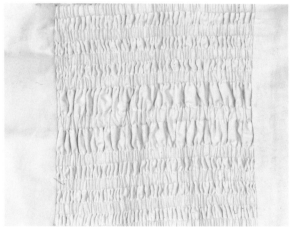

5.66 Various sized elastic can be used and inserted into a garment.

Additional Resources

Sourcing: Most local craft and fabric stores have the appropriate materials for elastic shirring.

Inspiration: FIDM Museum (www.fidmmuseum.org), The Metropolitan Museum of Art (www.metmuseum.org)

PLEATING AND TUCKS

Tucks and pleats are very similar in structure—folds of fabric are pulled from the surface and secured using stitches. **Tucks** are stitched from one end of the fabric to the other, while **pleats** are stitched at one end to create fullness at the other.

Pleats and tucks have been used in fashion since the days of the Grecians, when large pieces of square fabric were manipulated to create form-fitting garments by folding fabric upon itself. In the early 1900s, Mariano Fortuny was a pioneer in the process of pleating and created delicately pleated garments (see Designer Profile on page 168). After the Second World War, Italy was beginning to organize its fashion industry and urged its citizens to revitalize the textile industry. Roberto Capucci, a young Italian designer emerged with his stunning ball gowns constructed from yards of pleated fabric to create astonishingly beautiful garments that helped Italy to become a leader in the fashion world. As the pleating process mechanized and synthetic fabrics were widely used (synthetic fabrics can, in most cases, maintain pleats permanently), pleating became used extensively in interior design and fashion because the cost was reduced significantly. Today pleats and tucks can be seen in garments and home décor and found at almost every price point.

The variety of tucks and pleats is limited only by the imagination, and with some basic understanding, a huge number of options open up to a designer. **Standard pleating** is the most basic option and only requires the consistent folding of fabrics to create fullness. **Standard tucks** are more controlled folds of fabric that are stitched along the entire fold and add more stability than a pleat. **Pattern tucks**, often referred to as *pintucks*, are simply tiny folds of raised fabric secured with stitching along the entire fold. Because patterned tucks use much less fabric and are easier to control, the results are often more delicate and much more intricate than traditional pleats and tucks.

Standard pleats are folds of fabric that are either leveled off or manipulated to project from the surface of the fabric. They can be created in a very strategic order, as Madame Gres is so well known for (Figure 5.67), or left unpressed to create fullness (Figure 5.68). This section will explore basic techniques that can be used in many creative ways.

5.68 Marco De Vincenzo RTW Fall 2013 collection.
Giannoni/WWD; ©Condé Nast

+ Metal straightedge
+ Paper
+ Pencil
+ Pins
+ Scissors

5.67 Created by Madam Gres in 1944 from one large piece of white silk jersey.
Photo Courtesy Museum Associates/LACMA

Materials

Figure 5.69 shows some of the materials required for standard pleating.

+ Disappearing ink pen
+ Fabric
+ Iron

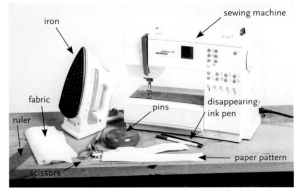

5.69 Materials needed to pleat fabric.

Workspace

+ A sewing machine is needed to tack pleats into place.
+ An iron is needed to set pleating.

Instructions

1. Determine the depth of the pleat.

2. Using strips of paper, create a pattern. The final pattern will be the length of the final fabric.

3. For 1/2-inch deep pleats, mark a strip of paper every 1/2 inch. For 1-inch pleats, mark the paper every 1 inch, and so on.

4. Fold the paper in the manner of the desired pleat. For knife pleats, pinch the paper until two parallel marked lines match up and fold over. Always fold each pleat in the same direction. For a box pleat, pinch the paper as with a knife pleat, but fold each pleat in an opposite direction. This will cause the creases of two folds to butt up against one another.

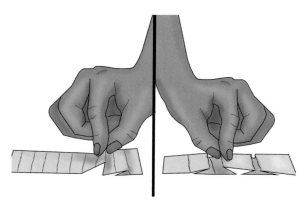

5.70 Left: Knife pleats are always folded in the same direction. Right: Box pleats are folded in opposite directions.

5. Continue adding strips of paper until the desired length is achieved.

6. Define fold lines on the pattern by cutting a small notch into the edge of the paper.

7. Cut fabric to the length of the desired final piece (include the hem or seam allowance). If necessary, sew pieces of fabric together to create the proper length of fabric; try to create seams inside of folds.

8. Finish hem if necessary.

9. Using the notches created on the paper pattern, mark the fabric with a disappearing ink pen or notch with small scissors at the top and bottom to indicate where each fold will occur.

10. Begin folding fabric in the same manner as the paper pattern. A metal straightedge can be used to help keep the pleats straight before pressing.

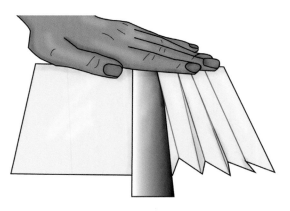

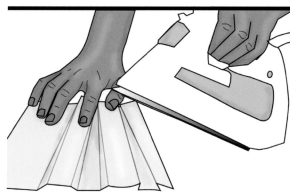

5.71 Top: A metal straightedge can be used to keep the pleats straight. Bottom: Box pleats consist of two folds, each folded in opposite directions.

11. Continue until the entire length of fabric is pleated.

12. Secure the pleats along the edges using a basting stitch (very long stitch that is easily removed). If the pleats are meant to hang free baste the top side only. For contained pleats, baste both ends of the fabric.

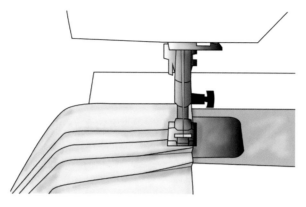

5.72 Pleats are secured using a basting stitch across the top of the pleats.

Examples

Figures 5.73 through 5.75 show pleating variations.

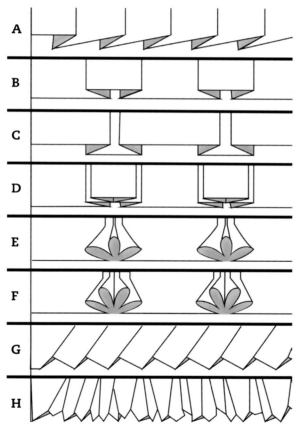

5.73 Pleating variations. A: knife pleats, B: box pleats, C: inverted box pleats, D: double box pleats, E: three-fold pinch pleats, F: four-fold pinch pleats, G: accordion pleats, H: broomstick pleats, created by wrapping wet fabric around a dowel rod and all allowed to dry resulting in an irregular pleat pattern.

5.74 Pressed knife pleats with lowered release points. Left: basted at top and bottom. Right: pleats not basted at the bottom to provide fullness.

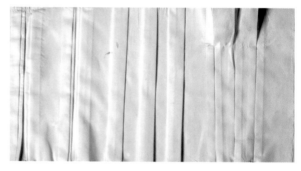

5.75 Box pleat variations. Left: double inverted box pleats. Center: evenly spaced single box pleats. Right: projecting box pleat secured with a topstitch one third of the way down the pleat.

Additional Resources

Sourcing: Most local craft and fabric stores have the appropriate materials for standard pleating.

Inspiration: Roberto Capucci (www.fondazionerobertocapucci.com), FIDM Museum (www.fidmmuseum.org), The Metropolitan Museum of Art (www.metmuseum.org), Issey Miyake (www.isseymiyake.com)

Mariano Fortuny was a Spanish-born designer who practiced in Italy. His first encounter with textiles came by way of his parents' extensive collection of historical fabrics, which he continued to collect throughout his life. Fortuny was strongly influenced by the past and often looked to Ancient Greece, the Italian Renaissance, South America, and even Chinese brush painting for inspiration. But his interest in the fine pleating of the ancient Grecian garments led to his most iconic garment, the Delphos Dress, seen in Figures 5.76a and b. Fortuny created the dress with the use of a machine he invented to heat-stamp the fabric into permanent pleats after struggling with the fragility of pleats and their ability to shift and come undone. In 1910, he was granted a patent and was free to use the heat-stamping technique with no competition. This was the main catapult of his business and one of the major reasons Fortuny is still a name recognized in fashion today.[6]

5.76a The Delphos Dress is Fortuny's signature gown, popular among avant-garde women in the 1920s and 30s. The dress is simply a finely pleated column of fabric that was available in a variety of lengths. Most likely created with hand-gathered pleats and heat set after a number of dye baths to create the peach color, though the exact process is unknown.
Image copyright © The Metropolitan Museum of Art. Image source: Art Resource, NY / ©Artres

5.76b Detail of the Delphos Dress.
Image copyright © The Metropolitan Museum of Art. Image source: Art Resource, NY / ©Artres

Standard tucks are folds of fabric that are sewn at an equal or slanted distance from the folded edge through two layers of fabric. The options with tucking are limitless because they are easy to control and create a more structured, precise look than can be achieved with pleating. One thing to consider when working with tucks is that the tuck will sit on top of the fabric, making it difficult to sew into seams. Therefore, it is advisable to always create a sample in the final fabric to get an idea of what sort of issues can arise.

Materials

Figure 5.77 shows some of the materials needed to tuck fabric.

+ Disappearing ink pen
+ Fabric
+ Paper
+ Pencil
+ Pins
+ Ruler
+ Scissors
+ Thread

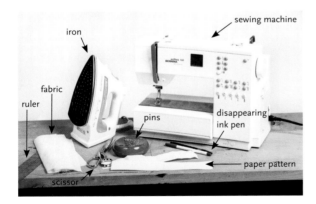

5.77 Materials needed to tuck fabric.

Workspace

+ Sewing machine with standard foot

Instructions

1. Determine the width of the tuck (the space between the fold and the stitch) and the visible space between each tuck.
2. Using strips of paper, a ruler, and a pencil, mark the measurements for the tuck and the visible space between each tuck. Remember that the tucks fold onto themselves, so there should be two lines per tuck.
3. Crease each line on the paper and pinch until the two lines meet. Cut a notch into the paper or mark with a pencil the lines that create each tuck.

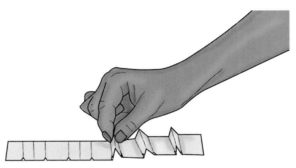

5.78 Pinch the paper until two lines match up to create a tuck.

4. Attach pieces of paper as necessary to achieve the desired length of fabric.
5. Cut fabric according to the length of the opened pattern. Include any seam allowance or hem needed on finished piece.
6. Hem if necessary.
7. Mark fabric according to pattern using a disappearing ink pen or with small notches (cuts into the fabric). Straight lines can be drawn to indicate folds and assist in stitching.

8. Begin pinching fabric at the center of the notches and pull up. Once the notches touch, crease with a finger and then iron. The creased line, created by the notches touching, will become the stitch line.

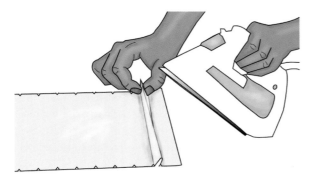

5.79 Begin pinching the fabric to create each tuck. Two notches should align with each tuck.

9. Pin each tuck at the top and bottom to secure as the remaining tucks are created.

10. Using a sewing machine and a straight stitch, sew along the creased line to secure the tuck in place. Fabric will be folded, so be careful not to stitch through more than the two layers of fabric to make each tuck.

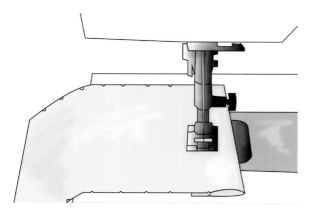

5.80 Sew along each creased line to secure the tuck.

11. Press with an iron if desired, or allow the tuck to stand upright. If connecting into a seam, iron the areas around the seam allowance and baste into place.

Examples

Figures 5.81 through 5.83 show a variety of tucking options.

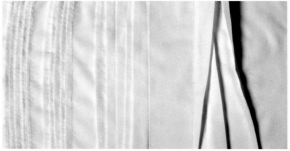

5.81 Left to right: pin tucks, evenly spaced tucks, graduated tucks, tapered tucks.

5.82 To create crisp, stiff tucks, back the fabric with a stabilizer.

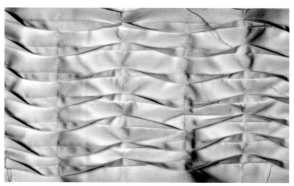

5.83 Rows of tucks are folded in alternating directions and secured using a top stitch.

Viktor & Rolf's winter 2011 collection included many examples of standard tucks used to create high drama. In Figure 5.84a, standard tucks on organza create a sheer shell around the model; this look can be achieved with small, consistent tucking of strips of fabric. Once the strips are complete, one end of the strip is inserted into a seam on the garment. In Figure 5.84b, Viktor & Rolf created a structured wool coat using standard tucks. To create the shoulder piece (circle with tucks), each piece needs to be created separately and attached to the garment. For this look, one of the circle slices is longer and fuller, allowing it to wrap around the bicep and attach to the circle on the back of the coat. When examined closely, it is clear that there is another layer of fabric at the elbow to aid in the construction of the sleeve.

5.84a Viktor & Rolf RTW Fall 2011. *Giannoni/WWD; ©Condé Nast*

5.84b Viktor & Rolf RTW Fall 2011. *Giannoni/WWD; ©Condé Nast*

Additional Resources

Sourcing: Most local craft and fabric stores have the appropriate materials for tucking.

Inspiration: FIDM Museum (www.fidmmuseum.org), The Metropolitan Museum of Art (www.metmuseum.org)

Pattern tucking is the use of hand-stitched pin tucks with curving, angular, or straight lines to create tiny ridges along the fabric's surface. It is versatile and can follow almost any line: lines that converge, cross, and start and stop anywhere on the fabric (Figure 5.85).

5.85 Mint design RTW Fall 2013 collection. *Giannoni/WWD; ©Condé Nast*

Often fabrics with stretch or that are cut on the bias work best when it comes to pattern tucking. A slight stretch to the fabric will provide some forgiveness and make curving patterns easier to achieve.

Materials

Figure 5.86 shows some of the materials needed to create pattern tucks.

+ Disappearing ink pen
+ Fabric
+ Needle
+ Scissors
+ Thread

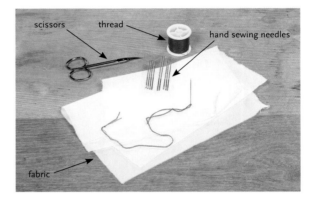

5.86 Materials needed to pattern tuck.

Workspace

+ Any workspace is appropriate to pattern tuck.

Instructions

1. Determine the size of the fabric needed. Always do a sample, because fabric size will depend on how many pin tucks, the size of the tucks, and the shape of the tucks.
2. Transfer design onto fabric using a disappearing ink pen (always test on fabric to make sure it disappears completely).
3. Thread needle with color appropriate to the design. Outcomes are generally more favorable when the thread matches the fabric, but for demonstrative purposes the color will contrast significantly in the following examples.

4. Knot thread and pull up through the back of the fabric at the distance from the line that will equal the height of the tuck.

WORKING WITH LARGE TUCKS

Higher or larger tucks are often harder to control and lead to more puckering, which, in some cases, can be desirable. But if a smooth line is the goal, consider working on the bias or using a fabric with a slight stretch.

5. Pinch the fabric at the drawn line and pass the needle through the fabric to the other side so that it is an equal distance from the line as the initial thread.

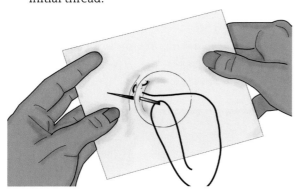

5.87 Pinch the fabric together along the drawn line and stitch through both layers of fabric every 1/4".

6. Continue to pass the thread through both layers of fabric every 1/4 inch, depending on the fabric and the desired result. Larger stitches will lead to more puckering.
7. Make sure the thread is pulled tightly during stitching but not tight enough to create excess puckering.

8. Once the shape is complete, pass thread to the back, and secure with a knot.

5.88 Stitch until the pattern is complete. Make sure that thread is tight but not tight enough to cause puckering, and tie off thread on the back of the fabric.

9. Almost any shape is attainable with this technique. Knit and bias-cut fabrics work exceptionally well for complicated patterns.

Examples

Figures 5.89 through 5.91 show pattern tucks.

5.89 Curving shapes are easily achieved using pattern tucking.

5.90 Thread can be passed over the fold before passing though both layers of fabric.

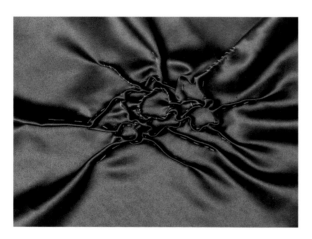

5.91 A silk satin is manipulated using patterned tucks.

Additional Resources

Sourcing: Most local craft and fabric stores have the appropriate materials for pattern tucking.

Inspiration: FIDM Museum (www.fidmmuseum.org), The Metropolitan Museum of Art (www.metmuseum.org)

SMOCKING

Smocking secures finely pleated or folded fabric. **English smocking** is similar to shirring but goes one step further by securing selected pleats together with a decorative stitch. **Direct smocking** is a hand-stitching technique that gathers fabric into small shapes as the threads are pulled tight on the back of the fabric. The stitches are sometimes visible to help organize the folds in direct smocking, too.

Smocking was prominent in the 18th and 19th centuries because of its ability to stretch. Prior to the advent of elastic, this was the only way to secure large amounts of fabric while still allowing for movement of the body. Originally, it was designed for laborers to provide fitted and flexible work wear. But with the industrial revolution, laborers were no longer able to wear the bulky fabric because it could get caught in machinery.[7] At this time, smocking became a decorative statement rather than a functional one and was seen on women's clothing mostly in the bodice, sleeve, or neckline (Figure 5.93).

5.93 A day dress created in the 1870s demonstrates work wear influencing fashion. Smocking was originally used in rural areas and worn by laborers, but as the urbanites idealized the simplicity of rural life, smocking became a popular decorative technique.
© 2008 FIDM. All rights reserved

English smocking is a two-step procedure that first structures the fabric into narrow pleats using a straight stich (similar to shirring). The pleats are then bound and organized using an embroidery stitch (see Chapter 6 for detailed instructions of various embroidery stitches). English smocking is often seen in children's wear, but its applications in women's wear results in a sophisticated sweetness (Figure 5.94). It can also be used in housewares, particularly curtains and linens, and in handbags as well (Figure 5.95). Most fabrics are suitable for smocking, but a general rule is the thicker the fabric, the more dramatic the peaks and valleys become.

5.95 Bulgari smocks leather in its Spring 2013 handbag collection. *Giannoni/WWD; ©Condé Nast*

5.94 Miu Miu's Spring 2012 collection uses English smocking to draw the full fabric close to the body. *Giannoni/WWD; ©Condé Nast*

Materials

Figure 5.96 shows some of the materials needed to complete an English smocking sample.

+ Disappearing ink pen
+ Embroidery floss
+ Fabric
+ Needles
+ Scissors
+ Thread

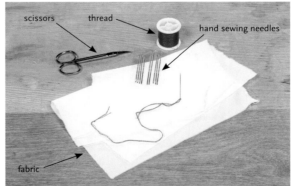

5.96 Materials needed to create an English smocking sample.

Workspace

+ Any workspace is appropriate to create smocking.

Instructions

1. Estimate the amount of fabric that will be needed—about three times the desired length. Always do a sample to be sure.
2. Create parallel lines along fabric and mark with small dots using a disappearing ink pen. The dots indicate stitch placement.
3. Hand stitch the fabric along the dots bringing needle and thread up through one dot and down through the next.

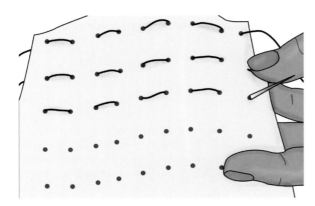

5.97 Hand stitch the fabric, bringing the needle up through one dot and down the next.

4. Once each line is stitched, knot the threads together on one end of the fabric.
5. Holding one end of the threads, slowly gather the fabric along the thread. See Shirring earlier in this chapter for more information.

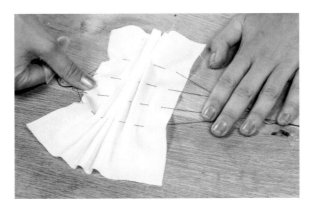

5.98 Knot one end of the threads together and slowly move the fabric down the threads until neat pleats are formed.

6. After the fabric has been shirred and the threads are secured at both ends, carefully arrange pleats so that they are even. Steam to set.
7. Thread an embroidery needle and knot the end of the thread.
8. Pull the needle and thread through two or more pleats at the same depth as the shirring line, then loop the needle and thread around the pleats and back through the same two pleats, very close to the original thread.

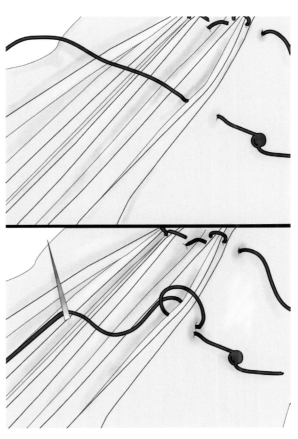

5.99 Top: Draw the needle and thread through a predetermined number of pleats. This example binds two pleats together. Bottom: Loop the needle and thread over the group of pleats and draw back through the same bundle of pleats.

9. Draw the needle through the next two pleats and continue to bind until the row is complete.
10. On the next row DO NOT bind the same group of pleats. Alternate which pleats are bound to create a honeycomb pattern.

5.100 Each row should alternate which pleats are bound together to create a honeycomb pattern.

Examples

Figure 5.101 shows smocking stitch patterns and Figure 5.102 shows the same stitches on fabric.

Additional Resources

Sourcing: Most local craft and fabric stores have the appropriate materials for English smocking.

Inspiration: FIDM Museum (www.fidmmuseum.org), The Metropolitan Museum of Art (www.metmuseum.org)

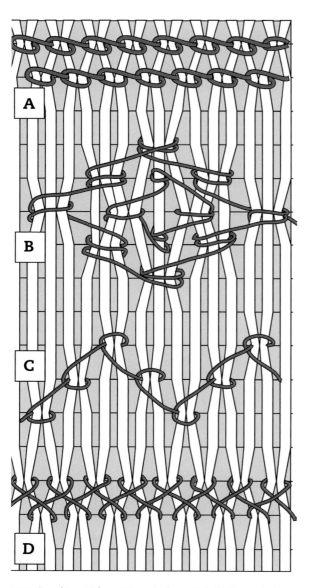

5.101 Smocking stitch variations. A: chain stitch, B: diamond stitch, C: feather stitch, D: cable stitch.

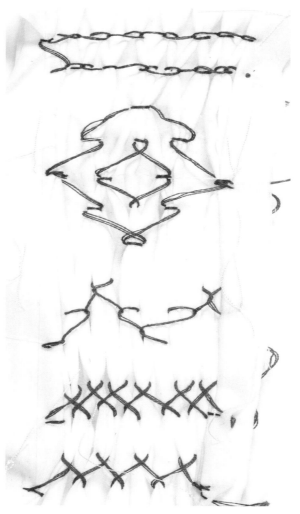

5.102 English smocking stitches on fabric.

Direct smocking is a grid-based pattern of dots that are connected with a thread in an organized and precise manner. When the thread is pulled tight, a pattern emerges. Direct smocking does not stretch naturally unless an elastic cord is used in place of a traditional thread. Direct smocking can be applied at any area of a garment but is best suited in areas that are meant to fit closely to the body (Figures 5.103a and b).

5.103b Detail from Bottega Venetta's RTW Spring 2007 collection. *Miranda/WWD; ©Condé Nast*

5.103a Bottega Veneta used direct smocking in its RTW Spring 2007 collection to draw in excess fabric and to create a monochromatic detail using the diamond smocking procedure. *Miranda/WWD; ©Condé Nast*

Materials

Figure 5.104 shows some of the materials needed for direct smocking.

+ Disappearing ink pen
+ Fabric
+ Needles
+ Scissors
+ Thread

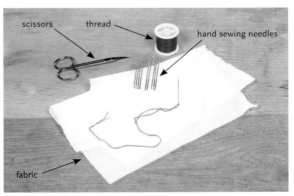

5.104 Materials needed for direct smocking.

Workspace

+ Any workspace is appropriate to create direct smocking.

Instructions

1. Select a grid pattern from Figure 5.105.

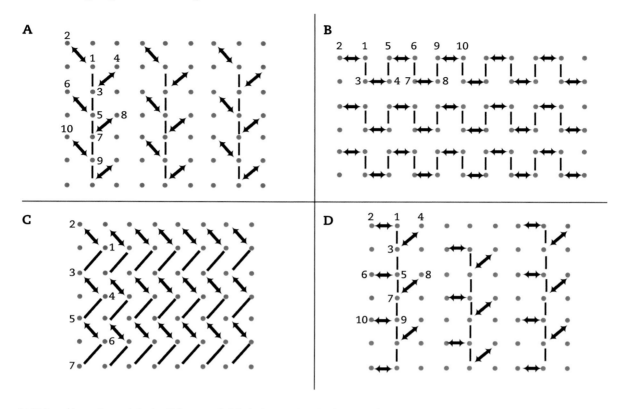

5.105 Smocking patterns. A: lattice, B: lozenge, C: tight lattice variation, D: alternating lattice variation.

2. Determine how much fabric is needed for the final piece—one and a half to three times the size of the final piece, depending on the size of the design. Complete a sample.

3. Mark the dotted pattern on the back side of the fabric using a disappearing ink pen. The following example is of a lattice pattern.

4. Follow the stitching path shown on the pattern beginning at point #1. Knot thread and draw through #1.

5. Move to point #2 and catch a small amount of fabric. Draw the needle and thread back to point #1 and grab another small amount of fabric. Always point the needle's tip in the direction you will be pulling the thread when making stitches.

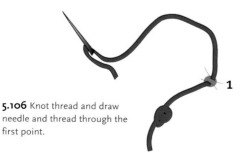

5.106 Knot thread and draw needle and thread through the first point.

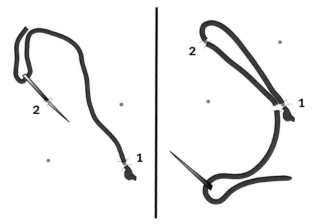

5.107 Draw the needle and thread from point #1 to point #2, grabbing a small amount of fabric with the needle then go back to point #1 and grab another bit of fabric.

6. Draw points #1 and #2 together and secure with a small stitch. This step is indicated by the arrow on the grid according to Figure 5.105.

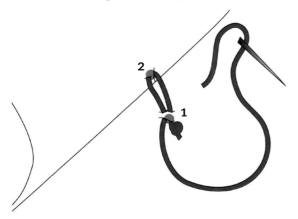

5.108 Draw points #1 and #2 together and secure with a small stitch.

7. Draw the needle and thread to point #3 and catch a piece of fabric. Do not pull the thread tight. Move to point #4, catching another small amount of fabric and back to point #3.

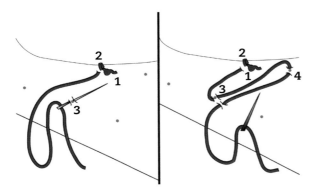

5.109 Draw the needle and thread to point #3, grabbing a small amount of fabric, then to point #4, catching another small amount of fabric, and then back to point #3.

8. Draw points #3 and #4 together with the thread and secure with a small stitch.

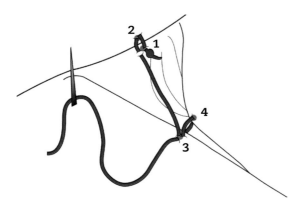

5.110 Draw points #3 and #4 together and secure with a small stitch.

9. Continue until the pattern is complete. From the front side a braidlike pattern will emerge, called the lattice pattern (see Figures 5.113 and 5.114).

Instructions for Flower Pattern

1. Create grid pattern on the front side of fabric using a disappearing ink pen.
2. Draw the needle and thread across the fabric surface, catching a small amount of fabric at each dot.

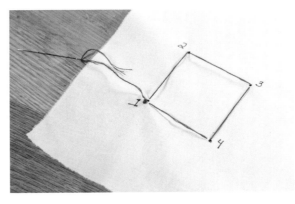

5.111 Draw the needle and thread across the surface of the fabric, catching a small amount of fabric at each point.

3. Once a square shape is created, draw the threads together.

5.112 Once a square shape is created, draw the threads together.

Examples

Figure 5.113 and 5.114 show direct smocking variations.

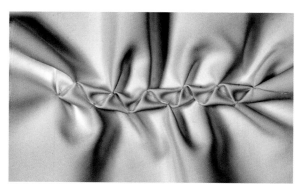

5.114 Lozenge-patterned smocking.

Additional Resources

Sourcing: Most local craft and fabric stores have the appropriate materials for direct smocking.

Inspiration: FIDM Museum (www.fidmmuseum.org), The Metropolitan Museum of Art (www.metmuseum.org), Francesca Chiorando (www.fchiorando.blogspot.com)

5.113 Lattice-patterned smocking.

STUDENT PROJECTS

1. *Sample Book:* Create pages for a reference sample book. Select six techniques from this chapter and create small samples. The finished size should be 4" × 4", so it is important to start with a larger piece of fabric because fabric manipulations have a tendency to consume a lot of material. Experiment with fabric selection and thread choice to create interesting effects. Present each sample on an 8 1/2" × 11" sheet of paper and include a brief description of the process, and address:

   ✦ What can be done to achieve better/different results?

   ✦ What kinds of fabric worked best/worst?

   ✦ How could this sample be used in a garment, accessory, or fine art?

2. *Combining techniques:* Create two samples of fabric: the finished piece should be at least 12" × 12". For each sample, select two techniques from this chapter and combine them. For example, sample 1 could be fabric that is pattern tucked and then pleated; sample 2 could be fabric that has been smocked and then quilted using cording. Think outside the box and remember that this is all about experimentation.

   Some combinations will be harder to create than others, so record your results and be prepared to discuss how each sample could be improved, also consider practical applications for the sample. Would the combined techniques function well on garments or upholstery or would it be best suited for a fine art piece?

3. *Being Vionnet:* Madeleine Vionnet is well known for intricate pin tucking on bias garments. Choose any inspiration and create a collection of three pin-tucked patterns that represent your inspiration. For example, perhaps the inspiration is Salvador Dali. Research his art and look at the way he uses lines and shapes to place the viewers into a surreal environment. Think about how you can evoke the same emotions using very simple lines and shapes. Sketch out some ideas and choose three to make into samples. Create a few small samples to experiment with fabric and thread before moving on to the final pieces. Each finished sample should be at least 4" × 4" and should compliment each other in color and design. Record your results and think about possible applications within your field of study.

KEY TERMS

- appliqué
- basic shirring
- batting
- bias cut
- cording
- direct smocking
- elastic shirring
- English smocking
- fabric manipulation
- machine quilting
- passementerie
- patchwork
- pattern tucks
- pleats
- quilting
- shirring
- smocking
- standard pleating
- standard tucks
- stay
- trapunto
- tucks

ENDNOTES

1. Conlon, Jane. *Fine Embellishment Techniques.* Newtown, CT: The Taunton Press, 2001.

2. Crabtree, Caroline, and Christine Shaw. *Quilting, Patchwork & Applique.* London: Thames & Hudson, 2007.

3. Ibid.

4. Ibid.

5. *Merriam-Webster's Dictionary.* Online edition. Springfield, MA: Merriam-Webster, 2003. Also available at www.merriam-webster.com.

6. Deschodt, Anne-Marie, and Doretta Davanzo Poli. *Fortuny.* New York: Harry N. Abrams, Inc. Publishers, 2000.

7. Conlon, Jane. *Fine Embellishment Techniques.* Newtown, CT: The Taunton Press, 2001.

chapter 6

EMBROIDERY

OBJECTIVES:

+ Creating basic embroidery stitches

+ Using metal threads to create embroidered designs

+ Creating raised and padded embroidery

+ Removing threads within a fabric and binding the edges with embroidery stitches

+ Using a sewing machine to create weblike stitching patterns

+ Using a bobbin and sewing machine to stitch thick threads to fabric

Embroidery is needlework or trim sewn onto and through fabric using embroidery thread, yarn, ribbons, metallic threads, straw (Figure 6.1), grass, or any other long thin strand that can fit through a **needle eye**—the loop at the top of the needle that the thread passes through.

Unlike other techniques in this text, embroidery has a relatively small environmental impact because the materials are often used in small amounts. Consult the box on page 216 for further discussion.

EMBROIDERY STITCHES

Early needles and threads were used to sew together animal hides to make simple clothing and shelter, but eventually sewing evolved into a decorative craft. Embroidery developed throughout Siberia and the Middle East as early as the Bronze Age (4500–100 BC) and in China during the Zhou Dynasty (1100–256 BC).[1] It spread into Europe by the 12th century where it was found on religious banners and streamers bearing coats of arms. Embroidery was used to communicate messages such as love, faith, and hope to an illiterate populace. Women often used embroidery to express themselves in male-dominated societies. By the 16th century embroidery patterns were being published and sold worldwide and were often drawn by well-known artists. In 1834, Josue Heilmann of Mulhouse invented the embroidery machine and changed the art from a craft industry to a commercial one.[2]

Embroidery has been a major part of fashion and textiles, and while the basic stitches have remained unchanged, the materials have evolved and the patterns have become increasing complicated. When multiple stitches are combined with beading, a lush blanket of threads and beads can become a timeless piece of art.

6.1 Custo Barcelona Spring 2012 created these tribal-inspired heels using nontraditional straw to create diamond patterns using the satin stitch. Even more dimension was added with the long, full straw stitches at the top and the tightly woven stitches wrapping from the toe to the sole of the shoe.
Courtesy Custo Barcelona

Materials

Figure 6.2 shows some materials that could be used for embroidery.

+ Embroidery hoop
+ Needle. There are countless options on the market but there are two basic choices: The **embroidery needle**, also known as a *crewel needle*, is medium length but has a long eye, so it can easily accept embroidery floss. The second is a **tapestry**, or *chenille*, **needle**. This needle is blunt and shorter than an embroidery needle and has a larger eye, for use with wool threads and ribbons.
+ Fabric to embroider onto
+ Small embroidery scissors
+ Stabilizer
+ Thread, yarn, or ribbon to embroider

Instructions

For every stitch:

1. Mark where the stitches will be on the fabric with a disappearing ink pen to keep them evenly spaced.
2. Knot the thread at one end, and draw the other end through the eye of an appropriately sized needle for the fabric and thread.

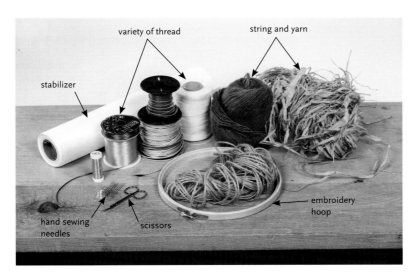

6.2 Selection of materials for embroidering.

A **blanket stitch** is often used as a finishing stitch along the edge of blankets, but it can also be used to combine pieces of fabric to create a larger piece or be used decoratively on any part of the fabric. Tightly packed blanket stitches are often referred to as **buttonhole stitches**. Blanket stitches are always worked from left to right.

VIDEO
*Go to Chapter 6
Video Tutorial:
Embroidery*

Instructions

1. Bring needle up through point #1, down at point #2, and up at point #3 with the thread looped under the needle. Pull the thread equally and tightly for each stitch.

2. Continue moving to the right until the desired length is achieved. Secure final loop with a small stitch along the lower line of the stitch at point #4.

6.3b Continue moving the needle to the right until the desired length is achieved, and secure final loop with a small stitch at #4.

Examples

Figure 6.4 shows blanket stitch samples using a variety of "threads" and stitch sizes.

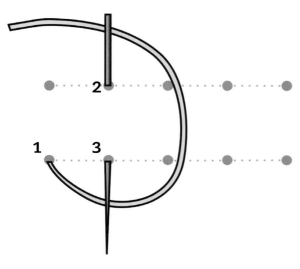

6.3a Bring the needle up at #1, down at #2, and up at #3 while keeping the thread looped under the needle.

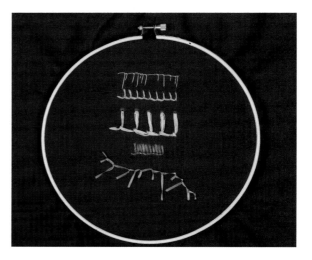

6.4 Blanket stitches, top to bottom: metallic thread, flat yarn, raffia, fuzzy yarn, and ribbon.

A **chain stitch** can create straight or curvy lines and is a series of looped stitches that resemble a chain once complete. A chain stitch is always worked from top to bottom.

Instructions

1. Bring needle up through point #1 and insert the needle back into the fabric very close to the original point (point #2). Bring needle up through point #3, only a short distance from point #1 while looping the thread beneath the needle.

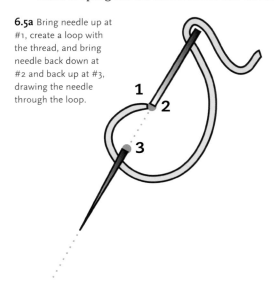

6.5a Bring needle up at #1, create a loop with the thread, and bring needle back down at #2 and back up at #3, drawing the needle through the loop.

2. Insert needle very close to point #3, inside the loop created from the stitch above, loop thread below the needle (as before), and bring needle out at point #4.

6.5b Insert needle very close to #3, inside the loop created from the earlier stitch. Loop the thread below the needle and out at point #4.

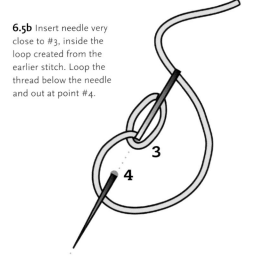

3. Repeat until the desired length is achieved, making sure to keep the stitches a consistent length.

4. To finish the stitch, secure the last loop with a tiny stitch.

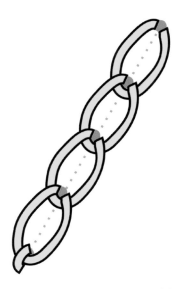

6.5c Continue to create small looped stitches until the desired length is achieved; keep all of the stitches a consistent length and end the row by securing the last loop with a small stitch.

Examples

Figure 6.6 shows chain stitch examples using a variety of threads and stitch sizes.

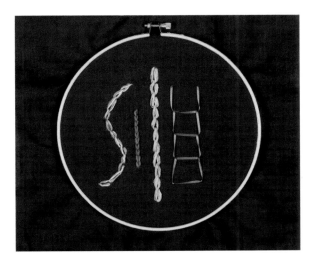

6.6 Chain stitch, left to right: multicolored yarn, fuzzy yarn, raffia, and ribbon.

Couching is an embroidery technique in which yarns or thick threads are laid onto the surface of a fabric and attached with small consistent stitches always worked from left to right.

Instructions

1. Lay thick thread or yarn onto the surface of the fabric. Bring thread up at point #1, very close to the laid thread, and down at point #2. Repeat at regular intervals until the laid thread is secured.

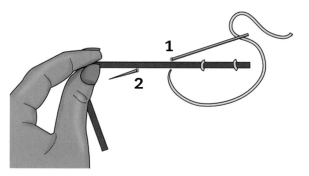

6.7 Lay thick thread or yarn onto fabric and secure with small, consistent stitches.

2. To turn a corner, lay the thread in the direction required and make small horizontal stitches over the turning point.

Example

Figure 6.8 shows couching examples using a variety of threads and stitch sizes.

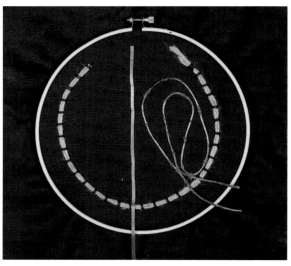

6.8 Couching, left to right: raffia secured with embroidery floss, leather strip secured with fishing line, metallic cord secured with consecutive stitches with a fuzzy yarn.

Cross stitches are X-shaped stitches that can be created singularly or worked in rows.

Instructions for Single Cross Stitch

1. Bring needle up at point #1, down at point #2, up at point #3, and down at point #4.

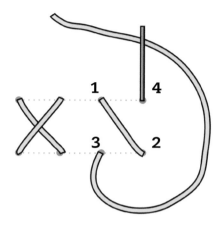

6.9 For a single stitch, bring needle up at #1, down at #2, up at #3, and down at #4 to create an X.

Instructions for Lines of Cross Stitches

1. Bring needle up at point #1, down at point #2, and up at point #3. Continue until the desired length is achieved.

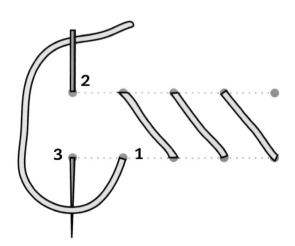

6.10a For a line of stitches, bring needle up at #1, down at #2, and up at #3 until the desired length is achieved.

2. At the end of the line of diagonal stitches, reverse the direction of the stitches taking the needle down through point #4 and up at point #5. Repeat until the row is complete.

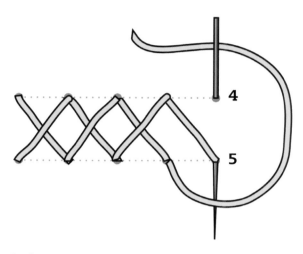

6.10b At the end of the row of diagonal stitches, reverse directions to create a row of X-shaped stitches.

Example

Figure 6.11 shows cross stitch samples using a variety of threads and stitch sizes.

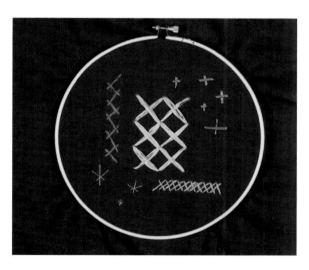

6.11 Cross stitches, center: raffia; clockwise from top: blue ribbon stitched to resemble a T, flat pink yarn shows a compact version of the cross stitch, metallic thread creates starbursts, and green fuzzy yarn shows a staggered cross stitch.

The **French knot** is used to create raised, knotted points on the surface of the fabric. It is often used to add emphasis to an area.

Instructions

1. Bring the needle up at point #1. Hold the thread tight and wrap it tightly around the needle two or three times.

3. For larger knots use thicker thread or yarn. Do not wind the thread around the needle more than three times.

Example

Figure 6.13 shows French knot examples using a variety of threads and stitch sizes.

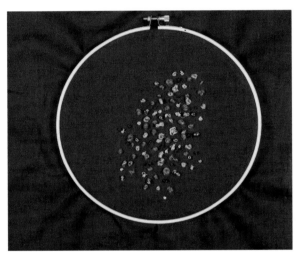

6.13 French knots using a variety of threads and yarns.

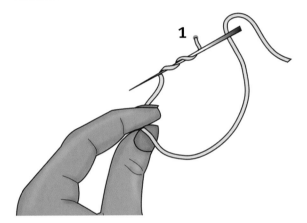

6.12a Bring the needle up at #1 and wrap the thread around the needle two or three times.

2. While still holding the thread tight, insert the needle close to point #1 and pull the needle to the back of the fabric making sure that the twists lie neatly on the fabric.

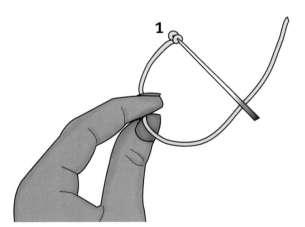

6.12b While holding the thread tight, insert the needle close to #1 and pull the needle to the back.

A **satin stitch** is a solid stitch often used to fill in large areas. It can be made at an angle or straight across and consists of side-by-side stitches.

Instructions for Straight Satin Stitch

1. Bring needle up at point #1, down at point #2, and up at point #3. Repeat until the area is filled with tightly packed stitches.

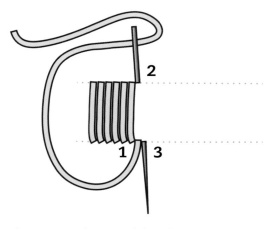

6.14 To create a straight satin stitch, bring the needle up at #1, down at #2, up at #3, repeating until the area is tightly packed with stitches.

Instructions for Slanted Satin Stitch

1. Choose the direction of the slant. Begin at the center of the shape, bring needle up through point #1, down at point #2, and up at point #3. Work parallel stitches from the center out to the right. Return to the center and work out to the left.

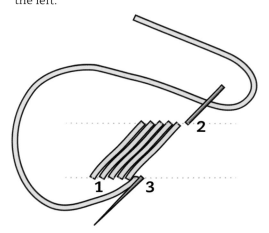

6.15 For a slanted satin stitch, begin at the center of the design and work to the right. Bring the needle up at #1, down at #2, and up at point #3.

Example

Figure 6.16 shows satin stitch examples using a variety of threads and stitch sizes.

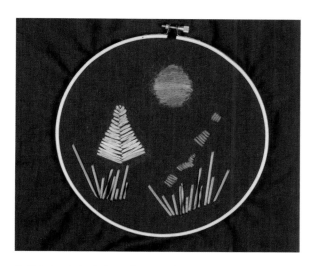

6.16 Satin stitch, clockwise from top: fuzzy yarn is used to create a circle; green fuzzy yarn shows a random placement of satin stitches; blue ribbon shows various length satin stitches; raffia demonstrates a slanted satin stitch.

Leather embroidery refers to any of the above stitches created on a piece of leather. Because needles cannot penetrate the leather cleanly, holes need to be made before stitching begins.

Materials

Figure 6.17 shows some of the materials needed to embroider on leather.

+ Awl or leather punch
+ Thick cork piece or cutting board
+ Thread, yarn, or ribbon to embroider
+ Mallet
+ Needle

Instructions

1. Before beginning any stitches, create holes in the leather at a size that will allow for the thread to easily pass. Use an awl and a piece of cork to create small holes or a specially designed leather punch for larger holes.

2. Determine the placement of holes as appropriate to the desired stitch and create the stitch following any of the previous instructions.

Example

Figure 6.18 shows examples of embroidery on leather using a variety of threads and stitch sizes.

6.17 Materials needed to puncture leather for embroidery.

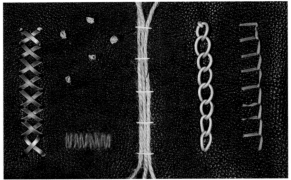

6.18 Left to right: Cross stitch using leather strips, French knots made of raffia, satin stitch using a fuzzy green yarn, jute couched with embroidery floss, chain stitch created with leather cord, and a blanket stitch using blue ribbon.

Albert Lesage founded the house of Maison Lesage in 1924 after acquiring Michonet Embroidery Company. Lesage was well known for its jewel-studded embroidery, and in over 50 years in business, he created nearly 25,000 samples. In the 1930s, Albert Lesage worked with Elsa Schiaparelli to create embroidered pieces used in garments and accessories (Figure 6.19) that reflected Schiaparelli's surrealist style. After Albert's sudden death, his son François took over in 1949. The 1950s brought Dior's new look: daintier, muted garments without extravagant embroidery. Although Dior chose to work with Lesage's competitor, Rebe, some designers like Balmain and Givenchy stuck with Lesage, which essentially kept the company in business. The 1960s arrived and nontraditional materials like shells, leather, wood, and feathers were embroidered onto the surface of fabric to create very dramatic relief work. In the 1980s, **trompe l'oeil**—embroidery that simulates other techniques like quilting, passementerie, and bobbin work—became very popular, and, once again, Lesage met the demands of the industry and created simulated three-dimensional embroidery.[3]

6.19 Lesage created silk crepe gloves embroidered with metalic and silk threads and then embellished with pearls for Elsa Schiaparelli's Fall 1939 collection. *Gloves, Fall 1939 (silk crepe, metallic & silk thread embroidery with pearls), Schiaparelli, Elsa (1890–1973) / Philadelphia Museum of Art, Pennsylvania, PA, USA/Gift of Mme Elsa Schiaparelli, 1969/ The Bridgeman Art Library*

Maison Martin Margiela's Fall/Winter 2013 collection used chunky yarns and big bold stitches to create a painterly effect on sheers. In Figure 6.20a, the effect is created using layers of thick yarns embroidered in a random fashion. The yarn remains above the fabric for long strokes and is secured sporadically with a tiny stitch to the back. What makes the look so interesting is the layering of the yarns to create a delicate piece of armor. Because the fabric is lightweight and the volume of yarns creates added weight, a stay or stabilizer is required to ensure that the structure of the garment will not be compromised. Large yarn and thick thread were used in the garment shown in Figure 6.20b—but in a more controlled way. Mostly created using a varying sized chain stitch, satin stitch, and blanket stitch, the design looks random, but actually requires careful planning. In some areas, more than one thread is embroidered at the same time. This helps to create color variation within each stitch.

6.20a Maison Martin Margiela RTW Fall 2013 collection. *Giannoni/WWD; ©Condé Nast*

6.20b Maison Martin Margiela RTW Fall 2013 collection. *Giannoni/WWD; ©Condé Nast*

EMBROIDERY TECHNIQUES

The development of embroidery techniques within cultures was specifically related to the materials available, the skill of the workforce, and the message presented. Only a few embroidery techniques will be highlighted in this section, including metal-thread embroidery, stumpwork, and drawn work. Each technique is distinctive, yet they can be combined with one another for dramatic results.

Metal-thread embroidery is perhaps the most dramatic of the three but it is also very expensive and was once only accessible to the very wealthy. It was mostly reserved for ecclesiastical garments, military uniforms, and textiles of the nobility. It was popular in Spain, Germany, and Hungary during the 15th century because of its intrinsic value and also because of the dimension and drama it added to otherwise ordinary fabric. [4]

Stumpwork, raised or padded embroidery, began in the 1400s and was often combined with metal-thread embroidery to give a lavish appearance to ecclesiastical garments. It became very popular in England in the late 17th century and was created with beads and pearls to make scrolling flower and plant designs on clothing, handbags, bookbinding, and pincushions.[5]

Drawn work is the manipulation of threads within a fabric. The earliest forms of drawn work embroidery came from countries all around the Mediterranean Sea and were traditionally created on natural or white linen because of its well-defined warp and weft. Threads were strategically removed and the loose edges bound using a white thread. In the 16th century, the British combined lace-making techniques with drawn work creating complex patterns filled with weaving threads.

Every embroidery technique will require a lot of practice to achieve the desired results but a little planning can go a long way. Before committing to any technique on a final piece, make sure to do some samples.

Metal-thread embroidery is created with gold or silver hollow metal threads called **purls** or with flat metal strips called **battus**.

WHY COUCH METAL THREADS?

Metal thread is usually applied to the surface of the fabric using a couching stitch to avoid damaging the fabric.

The impact of metal-thread embroidery depends on how the light reflects upon its surface, so it is important to use a variety of threads in different reliefs. Low-relief metal-thread embroidery is call **guipure**. A high-relief metal thread pattern is called **rapport** and is usually created on a separate piece of fabric and then applied to the final piece, where it can be combined with guipure for an even more dramatic look (Figure 6.21).[6]

Materials

Figure 6.22 shows materials that could be used for metal-thread embroidery.

6.21 A work by Lesage for Elsa Schiaparelli's Winter 1936 collection uses a variety of metal threads and gold paillettes to create a very dramatic looking black wool evening jacket.
Dinner Jacket, Winter 1936–37 (wool, gold, and metal thread embroidery with gold paillettes), Schiaparelli, Elsa (1890–1973)/Philadelphia Museum of Art, Pennsylvania, PA, USA/Gift of Mme Elsa Schiaparelli, 1969/The Bridgeman Art Library

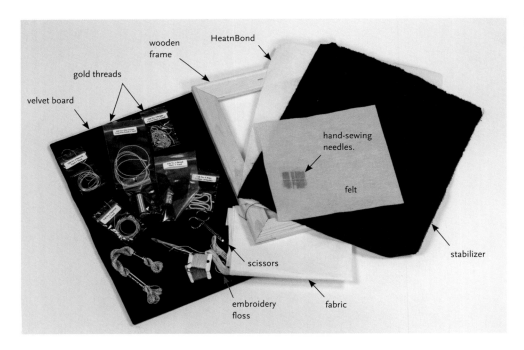

6.22 Materials needed for gold-work embroidery.

- #10 or #11 needles
- Double-sided fusible interfacing (HeatnBond)
- Fabric—heavier weight fabric works best because metal threads can become heavy.
- Gold threads—No. 4 check purl, No. 6 wire bullion, fine Grecian twist, No. 6 smooth purl, No. 4 jaceron (see Appendix B, Figure B.42)
- Plunging needle (thick needle with eye large enough for gold thread to pass through)
- Scissors used only for gold work
- Silk threads—gold colored or metallic
- Stabilizer
- Tweezers
- Yellow felt for raised areas
- Velvet board for materials

Instructions

1. Create design. Determine which areas will be raised (with yellow felt), and decide which gold threads will be used.

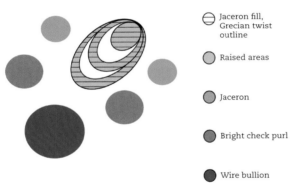

- Jaceron fill, Grecian twist outline
- Raised areas
- Jaceron
- Bright check purl
- Wire bullion

6.23 Design and pattern for metal-thread embroidery sample.

2. Transfer design onto fabric using a thin pencil line or any of the options mentioned in Appendix A, Transfer Methods, page 253. This example uses tailor's tracing paper because of the dark fabric.

3. Stabilize fabric with tear-away stabilizer appropriate to the weight of the fabric (see Appendix A, Stabilizers, page 253). This example uses black canvas, so the stabilizer is similar to a sheet of paper.

4. Attach fabric and stabilizer to a stretcher (see Appendix A, Stretching Fabric, page 254).

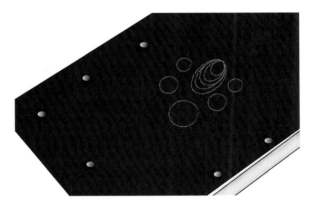

6.24 Transfer design onto fabric. Attach fabric and stabilizer onto a stretcher using pushpins.

5. Transfer design to felt pieces and attach HeatnBond to the back side. Cut out felt pieces.

6. Iron HeatnBond-backed felt pieces onto the stretched fabric. Depending on the height of the stretcher, towels may be used to hold the stretched fabric stable while ironing.

7. Stitch felt to fabric to secure it further using one thread from an embroidery floss.

6.25 Stitch felt to fabric using a lightweight thread.

8. Begin and end the gold threads to be couched using the **plunging method**. This technique uses a large needle to plunge the gold thread to the back side of the fabric and then securing with a knot or tape.

6.26 Begin and end thick threads by puncturing a hole with a large needle and drawing the thread to the back and securing with a knot or tape.

9. Couch the plunged gold thread around the edges of the felt. A Grecian twist thread is ideal because it is the same height as the felt, thus completely covering the felt edges.

10. Fill in the felted areas using a couching stitch.

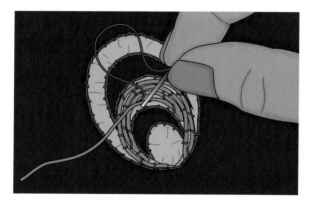

6.27 Fill in the felted areas with a couching stitch.

11. Small circles are created by plunging a gold thread to the back side with a thick needle and then securing with a couching stitch. Slowly wrap the gold thread in a spiral and secure using a couching stitch.

6.28 Create circular shapes by first plunging the gold thread to the back and securing with a couching stitch. Then slowly wrap the gold thread around the plunged thread while couching until the desired size is achieved.

12. Circular shapes can be achieved with any gold thread, each creating a unique and dramatic look. Feel free to experiment.

Example

Figure 6.29 shows a variety of gold threads couched to create a lush and dramatic design.

6.29 A variety of gold threads couched onto fabric, inspired by crop circles.

Tia Cibani Fall/Winter 2013 created a stunning sweater using metal-thread embroidery. This guipure embroidery look is created using the couching stitch to attach the threads in a figure-eight pattern directly onto the fabric, but another option is the rapport method. Since there are three distinct bands, each could be created separately and then attached to the garment's surface. With either method, a stay, or stabilizer will be necessary to avoid unwanted stretching of the fabric. However, the stabilizer will also cause the fabric to lose any of its natural elasticity in the area of the embroidery (Figure 6.30).

6.30 Tia Cibani RTW Fall 2013. *Aquino/WWD; © Condé Nast*

Additional Resources

Sourcing: Berlin Embroidery Designs (www.berlinembroidery.com), Sarah Homfray (www.sarahhomfray.com)

Inspiration: *Beginner's Guide to Goldwork* by Ruth Chamberlin, Mary Corbet's Needle 'n Thread (www.needlenthread.com), Royal School of Needlework (www.royal-needlework.org.uk)

Stumpwork is the name given to any raised or padded embroidery; pieces are usually prestitched and applied to the fabric over padding. Stumpwork can be applied to almost any tightly woven fabric but stabilization might still be necessary because the detailed work can become heavy.

When stumpwork is combined with other embroidery techniques, the results can be mesmerizing. It gives the designer the ability to tell a tactile story and add a fourth dimension to the work (Figure 6.31).

6.31 "Umbrella Man" created by Rose Gray was completed in steps. First, for the clothing, small pieces of cloth were hand woven and then small stitches were added to create different textures. Next, those pieces were stitched onto the background fabric over batting. Lastly, the umbrella was given dimension with a skeleton of copper wires.
© Waterrose Designs

Materials

Figure 6.32 shows the material needed for stumpwork.

+ Awl or chopstick
+ Batting for stuffing designs (see Appendix B, Figure B.55)
+ Embroidery hoops
+ Embroidery floss—these flosses usually come with six threads to every one floss. Often these need to be split into smaller clusters of thread for easier stitching (Figure 6.33).
+ Fabric
+ Felt
+ HeatnBond (see Appendix B, Figure B.54)
+ Needles
+ Tear-away stabilizer

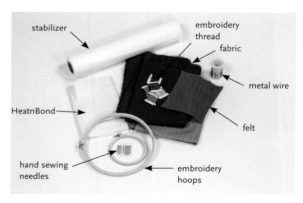

6.32 Materials needed for stumpwork.

6.33 Split embroidery floss into small groups of threads.

Instructions

1. Create pattern and determine which parts of the design will be embroidered onto the **ground fabric**, or background; which parts will be padded with felt to raise the design; and which will be created separately, padded, and attached to ground fabric. Wire can also be used to raise stitching and add further dimension.

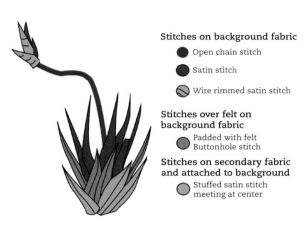

Stitches on background fabric
- ● Open chain stitch
- ● Satin stitch
- ◉ Wire rimmed satin stitch

Stitches over felt on background fabric
- ● Padded with felt Buttonhole stitch

Stitches on secondary fabric and attached to background
- ● Stuffed satin stitch meeting at center

6.34 A pattern for a stumpwork design.

2. Determine which stitches will be used. Blanket or satin stitches are often used to tightly bind the raw edges and keep them from fraying.

3. Separate design. There should be one pattern for the background (indicating where any felt padding will be applied) and one pattern for the pieces that will be attached separately.

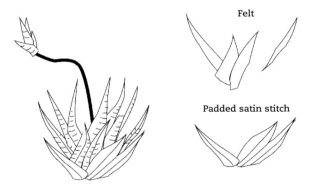

Felt

Padded satin stitch

6.35 Break pattern into pieces for easier cutting and transferring.

4. Select fabrics and threads. Almost any fabric will work but it should be strong enough to hold the weight of the embroidery.

5. Transfer design onto fabric. Indicate placement of raised felt areas and the parts of the design that will be applied and stuffed with batting. Stabilize fabric.

6. Transfer stuffed areas to a separate piece of fabric and stabilize with a tear-away interfacing.

7. Place stabilized fabric in embroidery hoops.

8. Attach HeatnBond to felt pieces using an iron and cut-out shapes.

9. Peel off the back of the HeatnBond and iron the felt pieces to the background fabric. Using a single thread from a six-thread embroidery floss (see Figure 6.33), stitch to secure. Only one thread is used so that it is easily hidden with filling stitches.

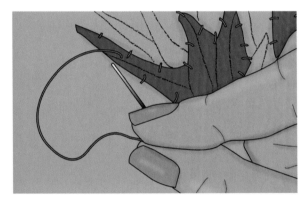

6.36 Once the felt pieces are ironed to the background fabric, secure the pieces further with small stitches using one embroidery thread (see splitting threads, Figure 6.33).

10. Cover felt pieces—this example uses a tight blanket stitch (buttonhole stitch).

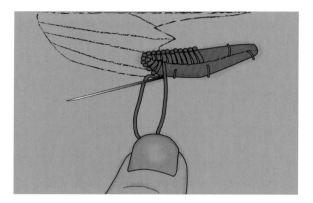

6.37 Cover felted pieces using embroidery floss and a tight blanket stitch (buttonhole stitch).

11. Next, attach wire pieces. Begin by plunging both ends of the wire through the fabric and securing it with a piece of tape to the back side of the fabric. Couch the wire into place using two or three threads from the embroidery thread.

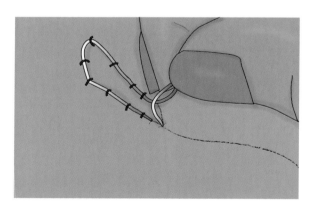

6.38 Begin and end the wire by plunging it to the back of the fabric and secure with a couching stitch.

12. Fill in wire area by passing three threads over and around the wire, alternating going under and over to create a zipper pattern. Note: Do not puncture the fabric during this step.

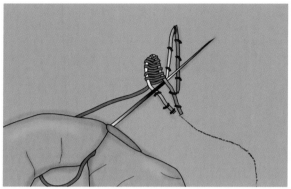

6.39 Fill in the wire pieces by passing three threads over and under the wire, alternating at each side creating a zipper pattern. Pack threads tightly using the tip of the needle.

13. Begin to fill in the background with the desired stitches as determined from the pattern in Figure 6.34 until only the area that needs to be stuffed remains.

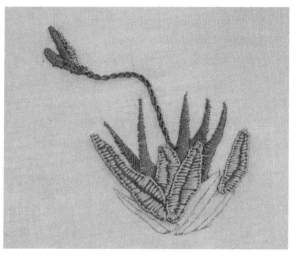

6.40 Fill in the background until only the area to be stuffed remains.

14. Working on a second embroidery hoop, begin to fill in the embroidery on the piece that will be raised using three threads from the embroidery floss.

15. Using sharp embroidery scissors, carefully cut the embroidered piece from fabric, being careful not to snip any threads while still cutting very close to the stitching.

6.41 The raised area is stitched on a separate embroidery hoop and carefully cut out.

16. Begin stitching around the edges, leaving one small section open to stuff batting.

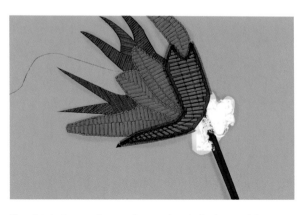

6.42 Stitch the area that is to be raised to the background; leave a small area open to insert batting using an awl or chopstick.

17. Continue stitching until the piece is thoroughly secured to the background and all remaining stitches are complete.

Example

Figure 6.43 shows a complete stumpwork piece.

6.43 Completed stumpwork sample.

Additional Resources

Sourcing: Materials to complete stumpwork are available at most local craft stores.
Jane Nicholas Stumpwork Embroidery (www.janenicholas.com), Needlelace.com and Leisure Needle (www.needlelace.com)

Inspiration: *Stumpwork: Historical and Contemporary Raised Embroidery* by Muriel Best, The Floss Box (www.theflossbox.blogspot.com), Annette Bolton (www.annettebolton.co.uk).

Drawn work, also known as *open work*, it is the manipulation of threads within a fabric. Horizontal or vertical threads are removed, and the remaining edges are bound with embroidery stitches.

Drawn work can be done on any plain weave fabric, but the fabric structure is very important to the final result. Tightly woven fabrics will hold their shape well, even after threads have been removed (Figure 6.44), while loosely woven fabrics tend to pull and shift with drawn work. Experimentation is always critical with this technique.

Materials

Figure 6.45 shows materials needed for drawn work.

+ Embroidery hoops
+ Embroidery threads
+ Fabric—defined weave fabrics work the best, like linen or burlap
+ Needles
+ Scissors

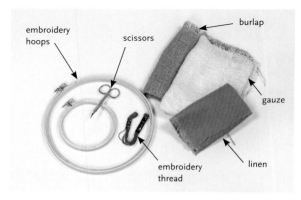

6.45 Materials needed for drawn work.

Instructions for Pulling Threads

1. Select a fabric that has a defined weave, and using a small needle, grab one thread and slowly pull it from the length of the fabric.

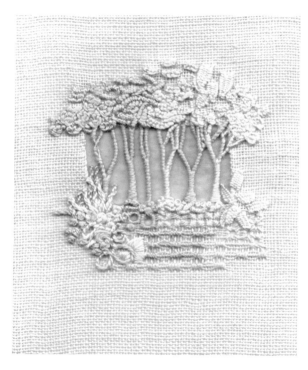

6.44 Jennifer Rochester created *Sunset Through the Trees* on linen and used silk threads to bind the threads of the fabric together. The piece was then mounted onto a dyed background to add more depth and interest.

© *Jennifer Rochester (textile artist)*

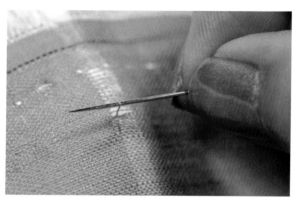

6.46 Use a needle to separate one thread from the weave and slowly pull from the fabric.

Spoke stitch—work from left to right on the wrong side of the fabric.

1. Secure thread to the left of the area that will be stitched. Pass needle and thread from right to left behind a predetermined number of threads and pull into a bundle.

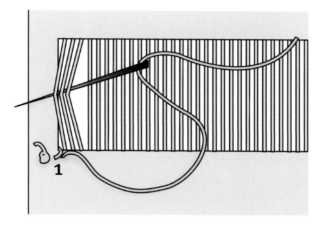

6.47a Working on the back side of the fabric, pass the needle from right to left behind a group of threads.

2. Wrap needle and thread around the bundle. Once to the right of the bundle, move the needle through the fabric at point #2. Continue moving to the right until the line is complete.

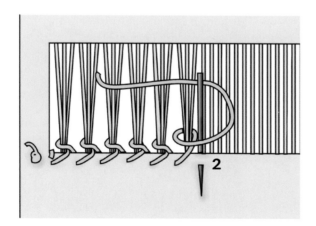

6.47b Wrap the needle around and to the right of the bundle and pass the needle through the fabric at #2.

Knotted border stitch—begin by creating a spoke stitch along both sides of the border. Thread is worked on the right side of the fabric from right to left.

1. Secure the thread on the right. Create a loop in front of the desired bundle of threads and draw thread behind the bundle and out through the loop.

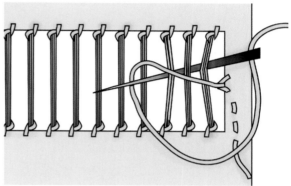

6.48a Create a loop in front of the desired bundle of threads and draw the needle behind the bundle and through the loop.

2. Pull the thread tight and continue working to the left.

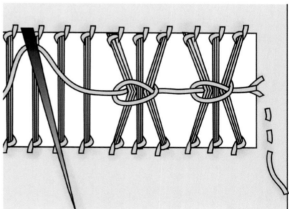

6.48b Pull the thread tightly and continue working to the left.

Overcast bar stitch—this stitch may or may not be combined with the spoke stitch, depending on the desired look. In this stitch, the number of threads must be equal to the number required for each bundle. The bar stitch is worked right to left.

1. This stitch does not begin with a knot. Instead, hold the thread along the threads that are going to be overcast. Pass the needle and thread behind a bundle of threads from right to left.

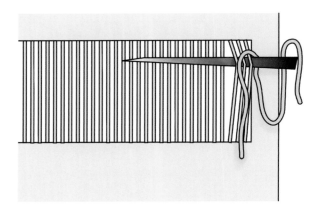

6.49a Hold the thread along the threads of the bundle that is to be overcast. Wrap the needle and thread behind the bundle from right to left.

2. Wrap the thread around the bundle until it is completely covered. After the first few passes the thread can be pulled tightly. Use the needle tip to keep the stitches packed.

3. Draw the needle and thread back up through the coils of the bundle, pull tight, and trim thread.

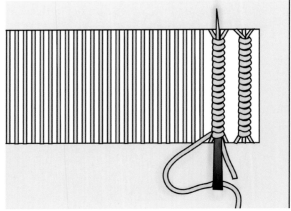

6.49b Once the bar is complete, draw the needle and thread up through the coils of the bundle and pull tight. Trim thread.

Additional Resources

Sourcing: Drawn work supplies can be purchased at most local craft and fabric stores. Embroiderysupplies.com (www.embroiderysupplies.com)

Inspiration: *Beginers Guide to Drawn Thread Embroidery* by Patricia Bage, Willow Fabrics (www.willowfabrics.com), Italian Needlework (www.italian-needlework.blogspot.com), Kate Davies (www.katedaviesdesigns.com)

MACHINE EMBROIDERY

A sewing machine can be used to create embroidery with very accurate stitch lengths for a uniform look with techniques like **bobbin work**—when the bobbin thread is used to create a pattern. Sporadic and sketchy effects can be achieved with methods like **free-motion embroidery**, in which a machine is used to achieve web-like stitching or to draw with thread directly onto fabric (Figure 6.50). The machine allows for quicker completion of the project but lacks the hand quality associated with traditional embroidery.

Machine embroidery doesn't have the rich history that hand embroidery does and wasn't developed until specialized sewing machine parts became available on the mass market. But as the cost of sewing machines went down, home sewing became more popular and people began decorating their fabric for art's sake rather than necessity or communication. Both of the techniques in this section require careful planning and an artful eye. Each is essentially drawn onto the fabric, so machine control is paramount. Make sure to practice, start off easy, and get a feel for how quickly or slowly to move the fabric under the needle, and then progress to more intricate designs. The possibilities are as endless as with pencil and paper.

6.50 Ditte Sørensen combined dyed fabric with free-motion embroidery to create a beautiful scene on fabric. © Ditte Sørensen

Free-motion embroidery is a free moving, painterly embroidery technique that allows for thread to be drawn directly onto fabric. It is created using a sewing machine with a special free-motion foot attached that can be purchased for most commercial and home machines. It provides clearance between the presser foot and the fabric so that it can be moved freely under the needle. The stitch length can vary and can be controlled with the speed of the machine and movement of the fabric under the needle. Every time the needle pierces the fabric, the thread will be secured, so short or long stitches can be created without manipulating the sewing machine functions.

Any design can be stitched using this method, although sketchier, open patterns or text tend to work best. Think of it as moving a paintbrush across a surface of a canvas, but instead the tools are the needle and thread.

Materials

Figure 6.51 shows some of the materials needed for free-motion embroidery on fabric.

+ Fabric
+ Tear-away stabilizer
+ Thread—high-quality embroidery thread

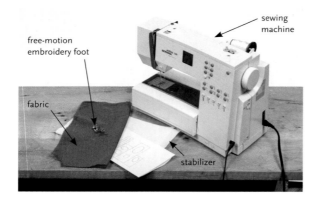

6.51 Materials for free-motion embroidery.

Workspace

+ A sewing machine with a free-motion embroidery foot (Figure 6.52) is required.

6.52 A free-motion embroidery foot.

Instructions

1. Set up sewing machine with free-motion foot and lower the feed dog. On most home sewing machines there is a button on the side similar to the one shown in Figure 6.54. Consult the sewing machine's handbook for further information. On industrial machines, masking tape can be placed over the feed dog to smooth out the surface.

6.53 Lower the feed dog: usually done with a button found on the side of the machine.

2. Thread machine with high quality embroidery thread.

3. Select and transfer design to fabric. Designs that have continuous connected lines work best, as well as those that allow for some interruption during the sewing process.

4. Stabilize fabric using a tear-away stabilizer.

5. Place fabric between the presser foot and the feed dogs. There should be clearance for the fabric to move, even when the presser foot is in the down position.

6. Begin stitching the design, moving fabric under the needle. The faster the fabric is moved, the longer the stitches will be. Slow movements create small stitches.

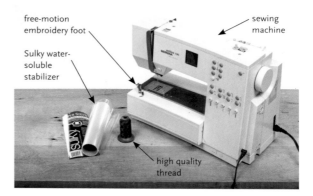

6.55 Materials needed to create lace using a free-motion embroidery technique.

Workspace

+ A sewing machine with a free-motion embroidery foot is required (see Figure 6.52, page 210).

Instructions

1. Layer four pieces of water-soluble stabilizer, pin together, and draw the general shape of the final piece using a permanent marker.

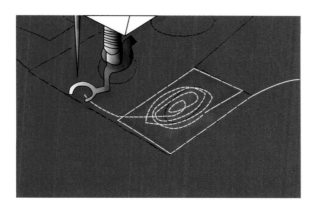

6.54 Move the fabric under the needle while stitching. Quick movements will create long stitches, while slow movements will create short stitches.

7. Continue moving the fabric under the needle until the design is complete.

8. Tie off loose threads on the back of the piece and tear away stabilizer.

9. Additional colors can be added to the piece, but it is always best to complete one color before moving onto the second.

Materials

Figure 6.55 shows the materials needed to create lace using free-motion embroidery.

+ Water-soluble stabilizer/Sulky (see Appendix B, Figure B.60)

+ Permanent marker

+ Thread—any thread will work, but these projects look best when high quality embroidery thread is used.

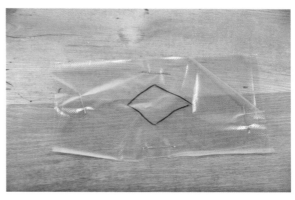

6.56 Pin together four or five layers of water-soluble Sulky and draw the desired shape onto the Sulky using a permanent marker.

2. Prepare sewing machine by adding free-motion foot and lowering the feed dog (see Figure 6.53). Thread machine with matching bobbin and top threads.

3. Stitch threads in tiny, overlapping circles until the design is filled in. Pieces of fabric, yarn, or ribbon can also be stitched into the design. Be sure that there are lots of threads that connect, or once the stabilizer is washed away, the design will simply unravel.

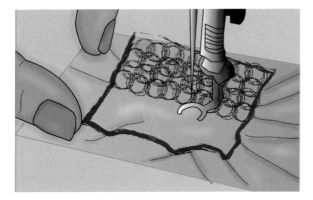

6.57 Stitch small, overlapping circles onto Sulky.

4. Continue stitching, changing color thread if necessary, until a thick tangled bed of threads emerges.

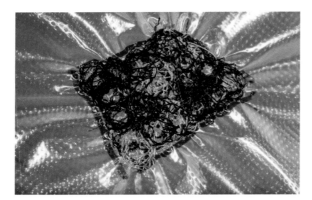

6.58 Continue sewing threads onto Sulky until a tangled bed of threads is created.

5. Soak in water until the stabilizer rinses away. Some small areas might need some extra help; an old toothbrush works great, just do not press too hard or the threads can be damaged.

6. Lay flat and allow to air dry.

Examples

Figures 6.59 and 6.60 show examples of free-motion embroidery.

6.59 An example of free-motion embroidery on fabric.

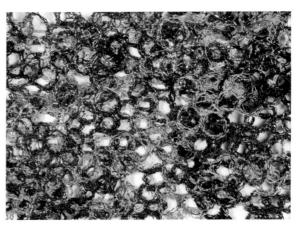

6.60 Lace created using free-motion embroidery on Sulky.

Additional Resources

Sourcing: Most local craft and fabric stores will have the supplies needed for free-motion embroidery. Sewing machine manufacturers will have information as to where to purchase a free-motion embroidery foot.
Nancy's Notions (www.nancysnotions.com), Sewing Parts (www.sewingpartsonline.com)

Inspiration: Fr. Frank Sabatté (www.sabatte-arts.com), Lizz Aston (www.lizzaston.com)

Augustin Teboul's Fall/Winter 2013 collection was shown at Berlin's Mercedes-Benz fashion week and included garments with spider-webbed details and intricate lace stitching. Free-motion embroidery is ideal for creating looks very similar to Teboul's. For larger areas that wrap around the body as in Figure 6.61, it is best to create the pattern on a sheer fabric and insert the panel into the garment. Free-motion can be very delicate, and repeated use could cause the thread to break. Small areas that are not on a moving part of the body can be created on a dissolvable stabilizer and inserted into the garment as a lace piece.

6.61 Augustin Teboul RTW Fall 2013. © *firstVIEW*

Bobbin work is used when a thread is too thick to fit through the eye of the needle, so instead it is wound around the bobbin. The fabric is then stitched with the back side facing up (front side facing the bobbin) to create a decorative pattern. The bobbin thread is essentially "couched" into place by the upper thread. Designs can be transferred to the back of the fabric for guidance—the sewer will not know what the bobbin thread looks like until the design is complete.

COMBINING FREE-MOTION AND BOBBIN WORK TECHNIQUES

A free-motion technique can also yield great results, but practice is pivotal to success. Begin your practice with a straight, consistent stitch to make sure the tension is correct and the stitch lengths are appropriate (8 to 10 stitches per inch is a good place to start).[7]

Bobbin work is great for bands and borders and to create highly textured effects. With this technique, the bobbin thread itself takes center stage, so it is best to pair it with a clear stitching thread or one that matches the background color of the fabric (Figure 6.62).

6.62 threeASFOUR RTW Fall 2010.
Chinsee/WWD; © Condé Nast

Materials

Figure 6.63 shows the materials needed for bobbin work.

+ Bobbin thread (thick thread or flat ribbon)
+ Fabric
+ Thread (usually the same color as the fabric so the stitches blend)

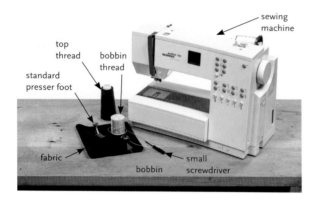

6.63 Materials needed for bobbin work.

Workspace

+ A sewing machine, bobbin, and a standard presser foot.

Instructions

1. Prepare sewing machine by threading upper thread and bobbin.
2. Wind the bobbin by hand if the selected thread is too large to be wound on the machine.
3. Adjust the bobbin case tension using a small screwdriver. Loosen the screw until the thread easily moves through the bobbin. If it is too tight, the bobbin will not unwind properly and will jam the machine.

6.64 Adjust the tension using a small screwdriver to loosen the screw on the side of the bobbin until the thread glides easily through the bobbin case.

4. Transfer design to the back of the fabric.
5. Working from the back, place fabric in machine and begin stitching, using a straight stitch at the desired length. Back stitch at the beginning and end of each line.

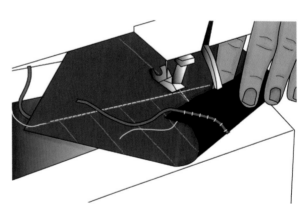

6.65 Work with the back side of the fabric facing up and stitch. The bobbin thread will create a design on the fabric.

6. Stitch along design until complete.
7. For curvy or flowing lines, a free-motion foot can be attached to the machine for easier movement (see Free-Motion Embroidery Instructions on pages 211–212).

Examples

Figures 6.66 and 6.67 show examples of bobbin work using a gold thread.

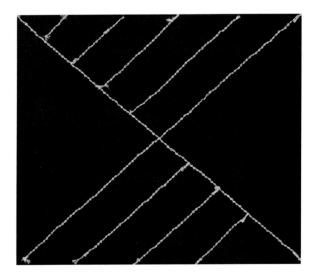

6.66 Geometric gold thread pattern created using a bobbin-work technique.

6.67 Curvy, random patterns can be created with a bobbin-work technique using a free-motion embroidery foot.

ENVIRONMENTAL IMPACT: EMBROIDERY

Embroidery has a relatively low environmental impact when done on a small scale. The only real implication lies in the dyeing of embroidery material. Even, consistent, colorfast color is required for threads, and because of that leveling agents (used to avoid speckling) and dye carriers are often introduced to large vats of water. Because thread, yarn, and ribbon have less surface area than fabric, there is more waste produced when the dye baths don't fully exhaust. Commercial dyeing companies have taken this into account and now produce products specifically for dyeing threads and yarns. These machines cut down tremendously on waste by using targeted heat and constant circulation to allow for even coverage using smaller quantities of dye.

As a designer, the best way to limit the environmental impact is avoid waste. Always prepare samples before beginning larger projects to avoid purchasing or disposing of unused threads or ribbon that will ultimately end up in a landfill.

Try to do some research before purchasing products. Look into the manufacturer of the materials and see what sort of precautions they take to limit the footprint of its products. Most larger companies will include this information on the website. Buying materials from smaller companies that only use natural dyes is another option, but remember, just because the dyes are natural doesn't mean that they are completely eco-friendly. Even natural dyes require carriers and fixers that can be harmful to the environment.

Additional Resources

Sourcing: Most local craft and fabric stores will have the materials needed for bobbin work. Nancy's Notions (www.nancysnotions.com), Kreinik (www.kreinik.com)

Inspiration: *Fine Embellishment Techniques* by Jane Conlon, Practical Thread Magic (www.practicalthreadmagic.blogspot.com)

STUDENT PROJECTS

1. *Self portrait*: Machine embroidery is a fun way to draw on fabric. Recall early days of art education when an instructor told you to draw without picking up the pencil. The same idea can apply to free-motion embroidery and bobbin work. On an 8" × 8" piece of stabilized fabric, draw a portrait of yourself using the fabric as the canvas and thread as the ink. Try to use as few continuous lines of thread as possible throughout the whole piece. Include shading and precise details.

2. *Recreate a scene from your favorite movie or book*: Embroidery has long been used as a form of communication and a way to express ideas. Select a scene from your favorite movie or book and recreate it as embroidery. The design you create doesn't have to be literal but should at least symbolically reference the scene. The final piece should be at least 8" × 8" and include at least one embroidery or machine technique and a minimum of five basic stitches. Present the final piece as if it were to be displayed in a gallery and be prepared to discuss and/or defend the material and design decisions.

3. *Repeat pattern*: Embroidery can be used in repeat patterns for dramatic effect. Design a small motif, symbol, or image to be repeated on a larger scale that uses at least five of the basic stitches demonstrated in this chapter. Make a pattern of the final design. Transfer the pattern to a 2" × 2" piece of stabilized fabric and create a small embroidered sample. Next, create a repeat pattern on a 10" × 10" piece of stabilized fabric by first transferring the design and then embroidering it using the predetermined stitches. Present your final piece professionally along with a sketch of how the sample could be used as a fine art piece, garment, or accessory for the home.

KEY TERMS

- battu
- blanket stitch
- bobbin work
- buttonhole stitch
- chain stitch
- couching
- cross stitch
- drawn work
- embroidery
- embroidery needle
- free-motion embroidery
- French knot
- ground fabric
- guipure
- leather embroidery
- metal-thread embroidery
- needle eye
- plunging method
- purl
- rapport
- satin stitch
- stumpwork
- tapestry needle
- trompe l'oeil

ENDNOTES

1. Clarke Simon. *Textile Design*. London: Laurence King Publishing, 2011.

2. Ibid.

3. Kamitsis, Lydia. *Lesage*. New York: Universe/Vendome Publishing, 2000.

4. The Embroiderers' Guild. *Embroidery Studio*. Newton Abbot, Devon, UK: David & Charles, 1996.

5. Best, Muriel, *Stumpwork: Historical and Contemporary Raised Embroidery*. London: B.T. Batsford Limited, 1987.

6. The Embroiderers' Guild. "Drawn Thread Work." Accessed April 14, 2012, http://www.embroiderers guildwa.org.au/Types%20of%20Embroidery/DrawnThread.htm.

7. The Editors of Creative Publishing. *Exploring Textile Arts*. Minnesota: Creative Publishing International, 2002.

chapter 7

EMBELLISHMENT

OBJECTIVES:

+ Attaching beads using basic stitches

+ Embellishing leather

+ Adding shine to fabric using foil or glitter

+ Using feathers as an embellishment, attached individually or as fringe

Embellishment is the art of adding three-dimensional objects to the surface of fabric to create shine, dimension, and drama. Embellishment can cover an entire garment like scales, known as **sequins,** or it can be applied sparingly by attaching each bead or feather deliberately using any beading stitch (Figure 7.1). Embellishment can also be added using **webbed fusing**, or glue webbing to attach foil for a flat, shiny effect. Like all surface design processes, there are some environmental implications to consider; see the box on page 222 for further discussion.

BEADING

Beading is the art of embellishing fabric by attaching beads. The methods are simple and are limited only by the designer's imagination. Most needlework techniques can be adapted to beading with the right bead, needle, and thread.

Beads are as varied as people and should be chosen specifically for each project. There are a few main categories of beads, distinguished by either the shape or material. Beads come in nearly any shape and size, but three of the most basic shapes include **bugle beads**, narrow oval-shaped beads; **seed beads**, tiny round beads sometimes used as a filler between larger beads; and **lentil beads**, or *sequins*, flat beads with a hole in the center, designed to be stacked or overlaid. Table 7.1 illustrates some basic bead shapes. The material used to make beads is another distinguishing factor. **Acrylic bead** refers to any bead made of synthetic materials. These beads are usually more consistent in color

7.1 Tsumori Chisato RTW Fall 2013 oceanic-inspired embellishment uses glass beads in a variety of shapes, colors, and sizes to achieve depth and intrigue. The placement against the black background creates a visual separation as well as a canvas for the embellishment to stand out.
Giannoni/WWD; ©Condé Nast

Table 7.1: Basic Bead Shapes

	bugle or barrel
	decorative (virtually any shape is available)
	dice
	double cone
	lentil, rondelle, sequins
	teardrop
	seed, rocaille (glass seed bead)

and shape than other beads. They are also some of the sturdiest beads and are good for less delicate projects. Bone and wood beads are made of either bone or wood and are usually inconsistent in size or shape; crystal bead refers to any bead made of a crystal—Swarovski is a good example; and finally metal beads, which, can come in any size or shape but are often heavy and reserved for use on sturdier fabrics like canvas or leather.

Needle choice depends on the size of the hole in the bead and the ground fabric. Try to use the smallest needle possible to avoid leaving puncture marks on the fabric. Needle length also depends on the bead choice; it should be long enough to fit through as many beads as are going to be applied at once. Shorter needles are generally easier to use, but longer needles can speed up the embellishing process.

Thread should also be chosen based on the size of the bead. Synthetic threads tend to be stronger, and there is nothing worse than watching hours of work unravel following a broken thread. Bonded beading threads are sold under a variety of brand names but are nothing more than very fine fishing wire, often used when the thread is intended to disappear into the bead and background fabric. However, choosing threads that are thicker or a different color can add dimension to the embellishment.

The human fascination with beads dates back to approximately 108,000 BC[1]; they were first made from objects like shells, pebbles, rocks, teeth, and clay and were used to create simple designs. The discovery of glass and metal led to further advances in embellishment designs and in how beads were made. Stones and glass were ground and drilled to produce interesting shapes that could easily be attached to garments. The first recorded glass bead was found in an Egyptian royal grave dating back to the 21st century BC.[2] This is also around the time that the first sequins were used: small gold disks were applied to burial garments. It is assumed that they were placed there to ensure the financial stability of the wearer in the after life.[3]

As the art form progressed, complex beadwork was used throughout the world in church vestments, clothing, and accessories. It was used to depict religious motifs and symbols that represented particular meanings to a mostly illiterate population. Examples include the spiral bead, which represented the symbol of knowing, and the eye bead, which represented spiritual perception. The bead color also contributed to the symbolism: white represented purity and green implied harmony, for example.[4]

Nearly every culture around the world developed and used their own traditions, tools, and skills when it came to bead making, and trade routes like the Silk Road introduced new techniques to other cultures. The Venetians were, and still are, particularly well known for detailed glass beads.[5]

As the art of beading commercialized, so did the organization of the industry. Haute couture embroidery houses called **paruriers**—adornment makers—opened in France. Their devotion to craftsmanship and experimentation was unparalleled around the world. It became common practice for one garment to require 400 to 2500 hours of intricate hand sewing to create (Figure 7.2).[6]

7.2 Lesage created lush textures for Balmain using a combination of beading, embroidery, and feathering. Notice the various sizes and shapes of beads used and how they add depth to the design. © TopFoto / The Image Works

There are two basic stitch categories when considering embellishments: beading and couching. *Beading* is when the beads are sewn directly through the fabric, while *couching* requires that beads are prestrung then laid on top of the fabric and secured using a couching stitch that is passed over the string of beads.

Stitches can be used alone or in a combination of ways. Variation in the beads is equally important, and nearly any object can be used for beading as long as it has a hole for thread to pass. Unconventional objects such as rocks, wood, and washers can be used (Figure 7.3). Beading can take any garment, handbag, or home good from ordinary to extraordinary.

A wide variety of beaded results can be achieved using the following basic stitches and a little imagination.

7.3 Jessica Trosman used rocks to embellish a top in her Spring 2004 collection.
© *Urko Suaya*

ENVIRONMENTAL IMPACT: EMBELLISHMENT

The production of beads used for embellishment has a significant environmental impact because they are often produced using plastic or other synthetic materials that are not biodegradable and release toxins during production. The disposal of beads has become an increasing concern because traditional recycling plants cannot process them (as Richard Fausset discusses in the *Los Angeles Times* article "Mardi Gras Beads Cause Environmental Hangover," on February 15, 2013) and they tend to make their way into waterways and are dangerous to wildlife that mistake them for food. Wooden and bone beads also pose significant environmental concerns in terms of harvesting. It most countries, it is illegal to poach animals for their tusks or bones, but some still make their way into the market. Always research a company before making a purchase to ensure that their products are produced legally and ethically. The same goes for any bead made from precious gems, as they can also be gathered illegally or by a labor force that is not fairly treated or compensated.

The use of foil and glitter involves the application of glues; most sold at local craft stores are nontoxic and can even be handled by children. Always read the labels and wear gloves to protect skin. Never dispose of remaining glue, glitter, or foil outside because, like humans, animals are attracted to shiny objects and could accidently ingest the materials.

Feathers can be produced synthetically or harvested from animals. Synthetic options are produced in large quantities and are not biodegradable but do offer consistency in size and color that is not available with natural feathers. When using animal feathers, be sure to research the source to see how they are harvested.

Materials

Figure 7.4 shows materials that could be used for embellishing with beads.

+ Beads or other objects for embellishing
+ Embroidery hoop
+ Fabric to embellish on
+ Needle
+ Stabilizer
+ Thread

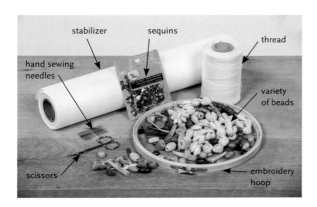

7.4 Materials needed for adding beads to fabric.

Instructions

1. Choose a needle that will easily slide through the beads that are to be attached.
2. Knot the thread before drawing it through the fabric, hiding the knot on the back side. Note that some slick threads will not hold knots well, so another option is to make a tiny back stitch on the back of the fabric where the first bead will be placed to secure the thread.

USING AN EMBROIDERY HOOP

Any beading stitch is created using an embroidery hoop to ensure proper tension of the fabric, making for easier beading.

The **back stitch** is a basic stitch used to attach individual beads in a continuous line across the fabric's surface.

VIDEO
Go to Chapter 7 Video Tutorial: Beading

Instructions

1. Bring the needle up through point #1 and through three beads. Slide the beads down to the fabric surface and insert the needle back through the fabric after the last bead (point #2).

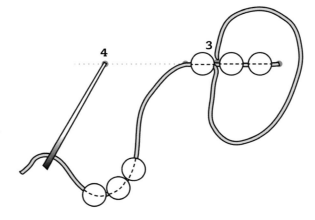

7.5b Bring the needle up between the second and third beads (#3) and pass the needle through the third bead. Add three more beads and pass the needle through #4.

Example

Figure 7.6 shows beads attached to fabric using a back stitch.

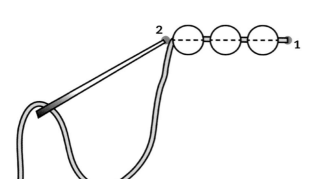

7.5a Bring the needle up through #1 and through three beads. Insert needle at the end of the beads through #2.

7.6 Wooden beads secured to fabric using a back stitch.

2. Bring the needle back up through the fabric between the second and third beads (point #3) and pass the needle back through the third bead. Add three more beads to the thread and bring the needle down through point #4. Repeat process until desired result is achieved.

Couching beads is the easiest way to attach prestrung beads to the surface of the fabric. The string of beads is laid onto the fabric and secured with a second thread using small stitches.

Instructions

1. Begin with prestrung beads, then remove some beads from one end, thread the needle, and pass the end of the prestrung beads to the back side of the fabric and knot.

2. Thread a second needle, knot the thread, and bring it up through the back side of the fabric very close to the first prestrung bead at point #1. Insert the needle at point #2, up through point #3, and down through point #4. Repeat as needed until the beads are secure.

Example

Figure 7.8 shows a couching stitch.

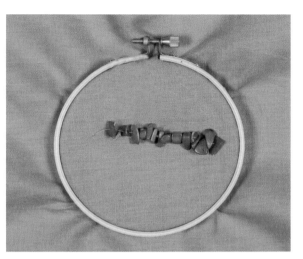

7.8 Small stones attached to fabric using a couching stitch.

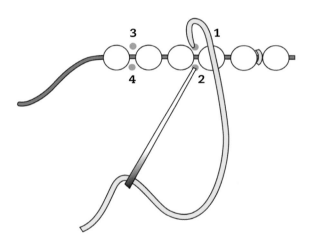

7.7 Using a second threaded needle, bring the thread through the back of the fabric at #1. Insert the needle at #2, up through #3, and down through #4.

The **dangle stitch** is used to attach beads that will hang independently from the fabric's surface, much like fringe.

VIDEO
*Go to Chapter 7
Video Tutorial:
Beading*

Instructions

1. Bring needle up through the fabric at point #1 and string several beads.

2. Thread a stop bead, pass the needle back through all of the beads EXCEPT the last (stop) bead to the back side of the fabric at point #2, and secure with a knot.

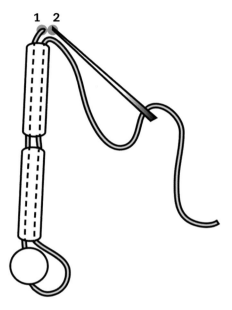

7.9b Thread a small stop bead and pass the needle back through the beads, avoiding the last bead. Insert the needle back through the fabric at #2 and secure.

Example

Figure 7.10 shows a dangle stitch.

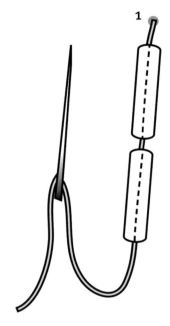

7.9a Bring needle up through the fabric at #1 and string several beads.

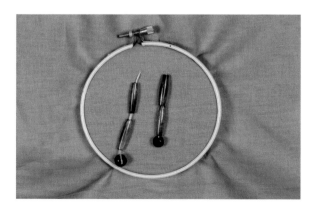

7.10 Long wooden beads attached to fabric using a dangle stitch.

The **filling stitch** is used to fill in shapes by stringing beads across the surface and securing into place. Most commonly, the end beads are secured with another stitch because filling stitch tends to be susceptible to snagging.

Instructions

1. Determine the shape and size of the area that is to be filled.
2. Bring the needle up through the fabric at one corner of the design (point #1) and string enough beads to fill in the width of the shape. Slide beads to the fabric's surface and insert the needle after the last bead (point #2).

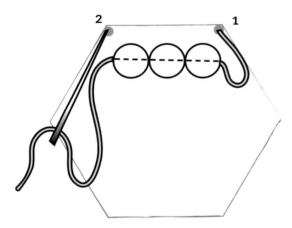

7.11a Bring the needle up through #1 at one corner of the shape. String enough beads to fill the width of the shape and insert the needle after the last bead at #2.

3. Bring the needle back up close to point #2 at point #3, string more beads, and insert needle at the end of the row of beads, close to point #1 at point #2. Continue until the shape is filled.

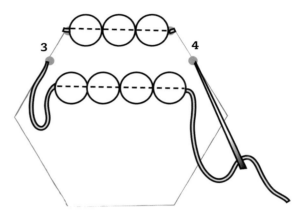

7.11b Bring the needle back up through the fabric close to #2 at #3, string more beads and insert needle at the end of the row, close to #1 at #4.

Example

Figure 7.12 shows a filling stitch.

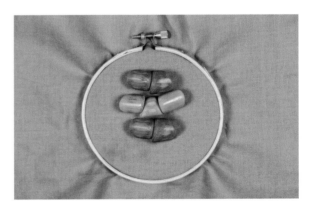

7.12 Wooden beads secured using a filling stitch.

The **stop stitch** is used to attach two beads, usually a single large bead or beads that will stand on end and a small bead (the stop) to help secure larger beads.

Instructions

1. Bring needle from the back side of fabric at point #1 through the first and larger bead. String smaller (stop) bead onto thread and pass needle back through the first larger bead (close to point #1) to the back side of the fabric and secure.

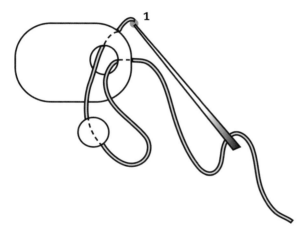

7.13 Bring needle from the back of the fabric at #1 and thread the first and largest bead. String the smaller bead and pass needle back through the first bead, avoiding the second bead. Pass needle back through fabric close to #1 and secure on the back side.

Example

Figure 7.14 shows stop stitches with various beads.

7.14 Stop stitch using combinations of glass and wooden beads.

Sequins are small, flat "beads" often applied in groups to add shine and drama. They are secured individually using a back stitch and worked from right to left.

STUDIO:

VIDEO
Go to Chapter 7 Video Tutorial: Beading

Instructions

1. Bring the needle up through the fabric at point #1. Slide the sequins down the needle and back stitch, bringing the needle back down at point #2, next to the right edge of the sequin.

2. Bring the needle back up at point #3—the distance between point #1 and point #3 is equal to the width of one sequin. Continue working toward the left until the desired length is achieved.

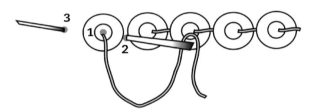

7.15 Bring the needle up at #1, slide on a sequin and back stitch, bringing the needle back down at #2 next to the right edge of the sequin. Bring the needle up at #3.

Example

Figure 7.16 shows sequin examples.

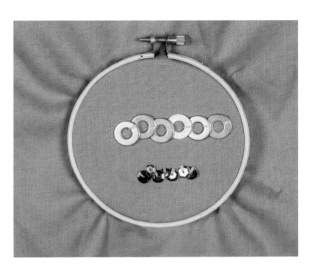

7.16 Any flat bead can be attached as sequins, including washers.

Leather embellishing is any of the above beading stitches on a piece of leather. Because needles cannot penetrate the leather cleanly, holes need to be made before stitching begins.

Materials

Figure 7.17 shows some of the materials needed to embroider on leather.

+ Awl or leather punch
+ Beads or other objects to use as an embellishment
+ Thick cork piece or cutting board
+ Mallet

7.17 Materials needed to puncture holes in leather for embellishing.

Instructions

1. Before beginning any stitches, create holes in the leather in a size that will allow the thread to easily pass through. Use an awl and a piece of cork to create small holes or a specially designed leather punch for larger holes.

2. Determine the placement of holes as appropriate to the desired stitch, and create the stitch following any of the instructions above.

Examples

Figure 7.18 shows an example of beading on leather.

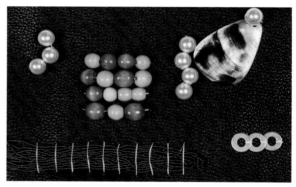

7.18 Top row, left to right: pearl dangle stitch, filling stitch using wooden beads, back stitch using pearls, stop stitch using abalone shell and a pearl. Bottom row, left to right: bundle of prestrung beads couched with wax thread, washers attached like sequins.

FOIL AND GLITTER

Foil and **glitter** are applied to the surface of fabric using a liquid glue, like Tulip or Jones Tones Glue, or a fusible web, like Bondaweb, to add shine to a larger area of fabric. Foil comes in a variety of colors and is fused to a sheet of cellophane. The sheet is laid upon the glue or web and pressed into place. The cellophane sheet is then peeled away, leaving the foil on the fabric. Foil can be applied all over a garment or used in random patches as an accent (Figure 7.19).

Glitter can be purchased as a powder to be mixed into paint or sprinkled onto glue or webbing, as a glitter stick, or as a spray. Each variety will require a slightly different application technique, but for the purposes of this text, a powder will be used and simply sprinkled onto the glue or web. It can be used sparingly to create a delicate shimmer or condensed to intensify an area.

7.19 Elie Saab Fall Couture 2012 uses a printed silk jacquard to resemble gold leafing/foiling. A similar look can be achieved with foil if it is applied randomly. Do not saturate an entire area with Bondaweb or glue—instead leave some areas free of adhesive so the foil will not stick. This is a useful technique when a worn and tattered look is desired. *Giannoni/WWD; ©Condé Nast*

Materials

Figure 7.20 shows some of the materials needed to foil fabric.

+ Fabric
+ Foam or paintbrush
+ Foil glue
+ Foil sheets

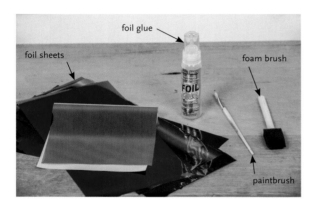

7.20 Materials needed to add foil to fabric.

Workspace

+ Any workspace is appropriate—just be sure to cover all surfaces to avoid cross contamination of projects.

Instructions

1. Secure fabric to work surface or iron onto freezer paper to keep it from shifting while working.
2. Apply glue designed for foil.

3. Use a foam brush to spread the glue into the desired pattern. Stamps or screens can also be used to apply glue in a controlled manner.

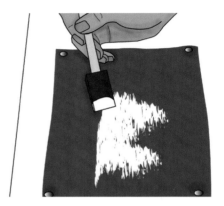

7.21 Apply glue to fabric using a foam brush, paintbrush, or stamp.

4. Allow the glue to dry until tacky and lay the foil sheet (color side up) over the glue and press firmly.
5. Slowly peel off foil sheet to reveal design.

7.22 Lay foil color side up on tacky glue. Press the foil into the glue and slowly remove.

Materials

Figure 7.23 shows some of the materials needed to add glitter to fabric.

+ Fabric
+ Foam or paintbrush
+ Glitter
+ Glitter glue

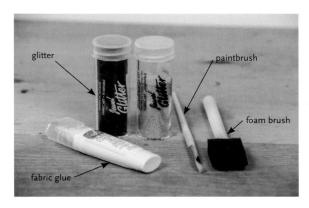

7.23 Materials needed to glitter fabric.

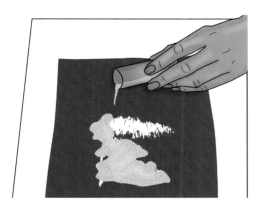

7.24 While the glue is still wet, apply glitter and allow to dry. Excess glitter is shaken off and can be reused.

Workspace

+ Any workspace is appropriate—just be sure to cover all surfaces to avoid cross contamination of projects.

Instructions

1. Secure fabric to work surface using pushpins, or iron onto a piece of freezer paper to avoid shifting during glitter application.
2. Apply glue designed for glitter application to the fabric using a foam brush or stamp (Figure 7.21).
3. Sprinkle glitter over wet glue and allow to dry before shaking off excess glitter.

Examples

Figures 7.25 through 7.27 show foil and glitter examples on fabric.

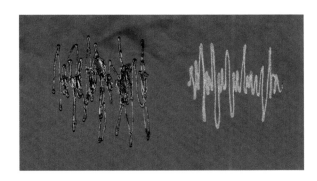

7.25 Foil and glitter applied with a squirt bottle to satin.

7.26 Foil and glitter applied to leather using a stamp.

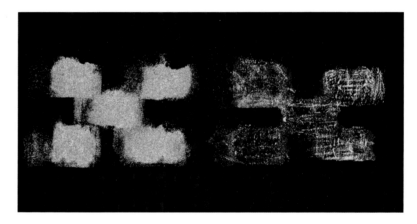

7.27 Foil and glitter applied to black linen with a wooden block.

Additional Resources

Sourcing: Dharma Trading Company (www.dharmatrading.com), Michael's (www.michaels.com), Hobby Lobby (www.hobbylobby.com), Hancock Fabrics (www.hancockfabrics.com), Joann Fabrics (www.joann.com)

Inspiration: FIDM Museum (www.fidmmuseum.org), The Metropolitan Museum of Art (www.metmuseum.org)

FEATHERING

Feathering is the use of feathers as an embellishment. It became popular in the 1960s when experimental embroidery was trendy.[1] It has remained a consistent embellishment technique since and can be seen on everything from homewares to shoes and hats (Figure 7.28).

Feathers can be attached individually using a couching stitch, or a hole can be punctured through the stem of the feather and it can be attached like any traditional bead. However, when an all-over look is required, feather fringe can be created using a sewing machine and applied in layers to the fabric (Figure 7.29).

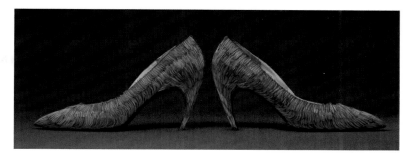

7.28 Roger Vivier for Christian Dior, Evening shoes, 1959, are created from kingfisher feathers and leather perched upon a sculpted heel that Vivier is so well known for. *Brian Sanderson/FIDM Museum and Library*

7.29 Giambattista Valli Fall Couture 2012 created a full feather skirt. Similar results can be achieved by creating feather fringe and attaching it in layers onto a woven fabric base. *Giannoni/WWD; ©Condé Nast*

Materials

Figure 7.30 shows some of the materials needed to create feather trim.

+ Embroidery hoop for hand stitching feathers
+ Feathers
+ Needles
+ Pins
+ Tear-away stabilizer
+ Thread
+ Twill tape—at least 1 inch wide (see Appendix B, Figure B.41)

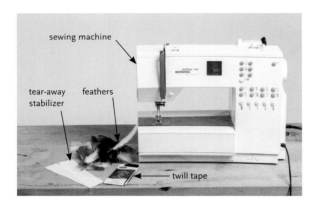

7.30 Materials needed to create feather fringe using a sewing machine.

Workspace

1. A sewing machine with a standard presser foot is needed to create fringe, while an embroidery hoop, needle, and thread are used to attach feathers by hand.

Instructions for Hand Stitching Feathers

1. Hand stitch a feather by passing the needle and thread through the shaft of the feather and then wrapping tightly around the feather shaft, penetrating the fabric on each pass.

7.31 Hand stitch feather by passing the needle through the shaft of the feather and then wrapping the thread around the feather and shaft, penetrating the fabric on each pass.

Instructions for Creating Feather Trim

1. Cut strips of tear-away stabilizer about 2 inches wide.
2. Lay feathers onto stabilizer, lining the tips up at one end.
3. Stitch at 3/8 inch from the feather tips. Stitch back and forth across the feathers a few times, making sure to back stitch at each end, until the feathers are secure.

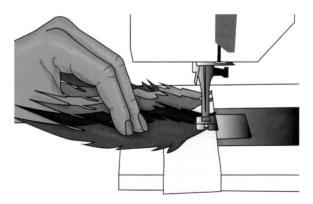

7.32 Line the tips of the feathers up along the edge of tear-away interfacing. Stitch at 3/8 inch back and forth until the feathers are secure.

4. Tear away stabilizer below the stitching line.

7.33 Tear away the stabilizer below the stitch line.

5. Wrap 1-inch twill tape around the tips of the feathers so that there is 1/2 inch on each side of the feathers.

7.34 Wrap 1-inch twill tape around the tips of the feathers so that there is 1/2 inch on each side.

6. Stitch 1/8 inch from the edge of twill tape to further secure the feathers and hide the feather tips.

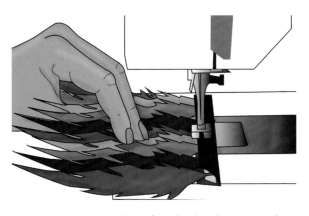

7.35 Stitch the twill tape 1/8 inch from the edge (the opposite edge of the fold) to secure.

7. Strips of feathers can be layered onto fabric to create an all-over feather look or can be used as trim.

Examples

Figures 7.36 and 7.37 show feather examples.

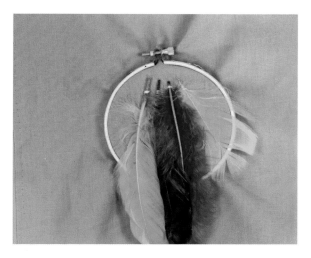

7.36 An example of hand-stitched feathers.

7.37 An example of feather trim.

Additional Resources

Sourcing: Most local craft and fabric stores carry the supplies needed to feather. Michael's (www.michaels.com), Hobby Lobby (www.hobbylobby.com), Hancock Fabrics (www.hancockfabrics.com), Joann Fabrics (www.joann.com)

Inspiration: FIDM Museum (www.fidmmuseum.org), The Metropolitan Museum of Art (www.metmuseum.org)

STUDENT PROJECTS

1. *Bead density*: The application of beads can have a dramatic effect when densely clustered and can add hints of shine when used sparingly. Create a collection of three beaded samples that utilize the same motif but applied sparingly, medium density, and high density. Make a sample for each measuring at least 4" × 4" using the same stitching and beads.

2. *Beads and symbolism*: Beads were often used to tell a symbolic story to a mostly illiterate population. Research how different shapes and colors of beads portrayed particular meanings in a culture or society of your choosing (Egyptian, Venetian, Chinese). Write a 700- to 800-word essay on the finding and create a reference chart that includes an example of the bead selected along with its meaning.

3. *Using embellishment to create a border pattern*: Embellishing along the edges of garments is time and cost effective and can produce dramatic results. Select foil, glitter, or feathers and combine that with at least two different beading stitches. Design a border pattern and embellish it along the edges of a 6" × 6" piece of fabric of your choosing. Create some repetition within the design and consider how it will wrap around corners and curves. Use a variety of bead sizes, materials, and textures to achieve depth in the design. Record the results and discuss at least three applications of the final border sample.

KEY TERMS

- acrylic beads
- back stitch
- beading
- bugle beads
- dangle stitch
- embellishment
- feathering
- filling stitch
- foiling
- glittering
- leather embellishing
- lentil bead
- paruriers
- seed beads
- sequins
- stop stitch
- webbed fusing

ENDNOTES

1. Dubin, Lois Sherr. *The History of Beads: From 100,000 B.C. to the Present.* New York: Abrams, 2009.

2. Coles, Janet, and Robert Budwig. *Beads: An Exploration of Bead Traditions around the World.* New York: Simon and Schuster, 1997.

3. Spivak, Emily. "A History of Sequins from King Tut to the King of Pop." *Smithsonian.com,* December 28, 2012. Accessed May 14, 2014, http://www.smithsonianmag.com/arts-culture/a-history-of-sequins-from-king-tut-to-the-king-of-pop-8035/?no-ist.

4. Tresidder, Jack. *Dictionary of Symbols: An Illustrated Guide to Traditional Images, Icons, and Emblems.* San Francisco: Chronicle Books, 1998.

5. Coles, Janet, and Robert Budwig. *Beads.* 1997.

6. Conlon, Jane. *Fine Embellishment Techniques.* Newtown, CT: The Taunton Press, 2001

7. Kamitsis, Lydia. *Lesage.* New York: Universe/Vendome Publishing, 2000.

chapter 8

COMBINING TECHNIQUES

Combining techniques allows the creation of truly beautiful and interesting surface design. It adds dimension and additional texture, but there are many factors to keep in mind: fabric choice, dye appropriateness, order of applications, iron temperature, and so on.

When combining and layering techniques, equal parts planning and experimentation are required. Start with an inspiration, which could be a painting, a garment, a room, a landscape, anything. Use that inspiration to guide the fabric selection (consider fiber content, too) and colorway, and then begin to experiment. Create samples using a variety of surface design techniques and decide which suit the needs of the final piece. Consider how the final piece will be used: Will it be in a gallery, in a home, or on a body? Who is the intended market? What are functionality and durability needs? It wouldn't be appropriate to bead a seat cushion; not only would it be uncomfortable to sit on but the beads' durability would be in question. However, an embellished headboard is a viable option because it won't see the wear that a cushion would.

Once the techniques are chosen, make a new set of samples and begin to layer techniques. Start with at least three layers and go on from there. Sometimes the results can be muddied and overworked, but that is ok: experimentation is necessary. Other times, the piece might feel flat and lifeless. In that case, add a few more layers until greater depth is achieved.

The experimentation process could and should go on forever, but eventually deadlines have to be met and decisions need to be made. Look at all of the samples and decide which works best for the project and why.

Once the final project has begun, don't be afraid to improvise. Often, working in a larger scale creates a host of problems that weren't foreseen in samples. Try to embrace the challenges that will inevitably arise and adapt to them while staying true to the original vision.

Consult Table 8.1 in this chapter to help guide the exploration of layered surface design and the box on page 246 for a discussion on ways to limit the environmental impact of layering and combining surface design techniques.

STUDiO:

VIDEO
*Chapter 8
Video Tutorial:
Combining
Techniques*

Table 8.1: Quick Guide to Determine the Order of Surface Design Techniques

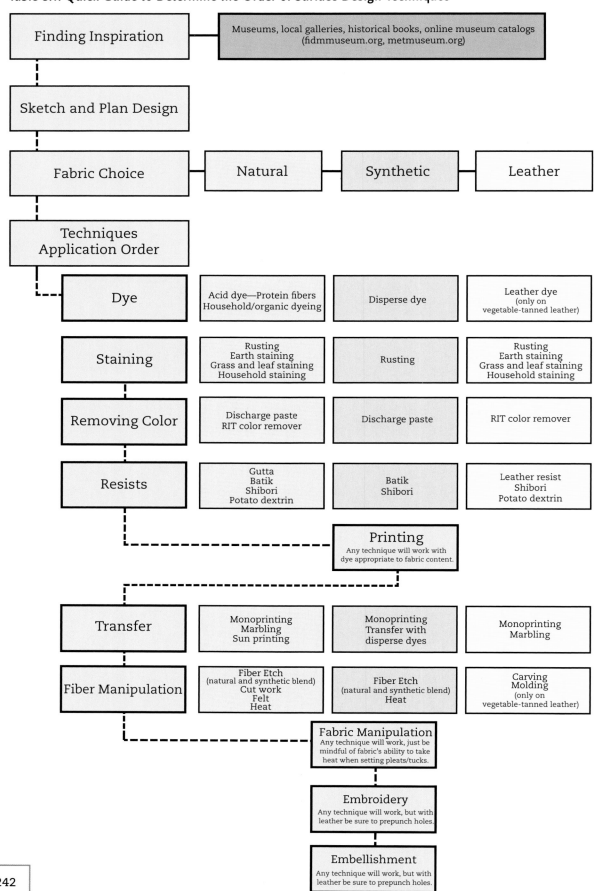

Finding Inspiration	Museums, local galleries, historical books, online museum catalogs (fidmmuseum.org, metmuseum.org)		
Sketch and Plan Design			
Fabric Choice	Natural	Synthetic	Leather
Techniques Application Order			
Dye	Acid dye—Protein fibers Household/organic dyeing	Disperse dye	Leather dye (only on vegetable-tanned leather)
Staining	Rusting Earth staining Grass and leaf staining Household staining	Rusting	Rusting Earth staining Grass and leaf staining Household staining
Removing Color	Discharge paste RIT color remover	Discharge paste	RIT color remover
Resists	Gutta Batik Shibori Potato dextrin	Batik Shibori	Leather resist Shibori Potato dextrin
Printing — Any technique will work with dye appropriate to fabric content.			
Transfer	Monoprinting Marbling Sun printing	Monoprinting Transfer with disperse dyes	Monoprinting Marbling
Fiber Manipulation	Fiber Etch (natural and synthetic blend) Cut work Felt Heat	Fiber Etch (natural and synthetic blend) Heat	Carving Molding (only on vegetable-tanned leather)
Fabric Manipulation — Any technique will work, just be mindful of fabric's ability to take heat when setting pleats/tucks.			
Embroidery — Any technique will work, but with leather be sure to prepunch holes.			
Embellishment — Any technique will work, but with leather be sure to prepunch holes.			

DESIGNER PROFILES

ThreeASFOUR is an avant garde fashion label founded in 1998 by four designers—Kai Kuhne, Gabriel Asfour, Adi Gil, and Angela Donhauser—who hail from Germany, Lebanon, Israel, and Tajikistan, respectively. The label is well known for its creative combinations of texture and color and theatrical displays. In 2005, one of the founding members, Kai Kuhne, left the group after some creative differences, but that did not slow down the others—they continued to be a force in the fashion industry. In 2007, the team received a CFDA fund nomination and gained mainstream prestige with a t-shirt collaboration with the Gap. The experimental nature of the label has gained the attention of The Metropolitan Museum of Art and The Victoria and Albert Museum, who have acquired pieces for exhibition. Most recently, threeASFOUR exhibited their spring/summer 2014 collection MER KA BA, at the Jewish Museum of New York. Every season, threeASFOUR embraces various surface design techniques to take simple silhouettes to the avant-garde, making them wearable and desirable to a sophisticated fashion consumer (Figures 8.1a–c).[1]

8.1a ThreeASFOUR's RTW Spring 2012 silk-de-chine-embellished dress is decorated with traditional Middle Eastern iconography. The winding blue and silver cords could have been couched on the surface of the fabric or applied as bobbin work. Small metal hamsa shapes are delicately placed within the wandering cords or condensed to create the effect of larger, metal-plated areas. The body stocking is likely screen printed, an undertaking possible in a small studio space if created in segments. Because the knit stretches around the body, the fabric should also be stretched when printing. If not, the pattern will appear worn and cracked when it is tightly wound around the body.
Centeno/WWD; ©Condé Nast

8.1b ThreeASFOUR's RTW Spring 2013 asymmetric jacket was made with a mismatch of fabrics including silks, leathers, and moiré. Each patch is sewn independently, and occasionally pieces are not fully tacked to the jacket, creating unexpected volume. The patches may seem random, but they are the result of careful planning.
Chinsee/WWD; ©Condé Nast

8.1c ThreeASFOUR's RTW Fall 2011 collection was inspired by string instruments and featured halter-neck dresses embroidered in Spirograph patterns to resemble the strings of a harp. This particular look is divided into six segments differentiated by a corded center front seam and angled pin tucks. The long red and white threads could be created with a hand running stitch, couched embroidery thread, or bobbin work. Even more interest is added when these threads are strung across a printed stripe pattern.
Aquino/WWD; ©Condé Nast

Susan Cianciolo is a New York City designer who uses thrift shop finds to piece together new garments. The addition of embellishments, pleats, twists, and prints to the garments transforms them from thrift shop finds to high-end garments found in exclusive New York department stores (Figure 8.2).

8.2 Susan Cianciolo created this look by combing a hand-printed dress with a crocheted sweater. The print on the dress could be achieved by hand or with a monoprinting technique. Black dye could be splattered across the surface of the fabric using a heavily saturated paintbrush, or dye could be laid onto a surface like freezer paper and manipulated until the desired pattern was achieved. At that time, the fabric can be carefully laid onto the dye and allowed to absorb. Some areas of the garment appeared to be printed in a more controlled manner, probably using a screen to stamp to get the consistent circles of dye seen throughout the garment.
Photograph by Rosalie Knox

Johan Ku is a Tokyo-based designer, born in Taipei, where he began his career as a graphic designer but eventually moved into fashion after receiving a master's degree from Central Saint Martins. He is known for sculpture-like silhouettes and innovative textiles. For his Fall 2013 collection, he used a variety of fabric manipulation techniques to create depth, texture, and drama in his ghostly collection (Figure 8.3).

8.3 For RTW Fall 2013 Ku created a garment that is lush in texture by combining patchwork with stitching. A similar look can be accomplished by overlapping, scrunching, and puckering fabric pieces, which are then secured using a free-motion technique. This technique creates subtle volume, and a wool-like fuzziness is achieved by exposing some raw edges. Further embroidery was added in splashes of red and white.
Giannoni/WWD;
©Condé Nast

Julie Shackson is a graduate of Howard Gardens in Cardiff, Wales, with a degree in fine arts. But Shackson has been creating fine art and textile design since she was small child. Her first love was knitting and then later photography and book arts. She draws inspiration from the natural elements of the English countryside and says, "My subject matter arises from the microcosm, to the macrocosm: patterns and flowing landscapes in biological and geological realms."[2] Shackson uses these inspirations to guide her work, which ranges from paintings to textiles to mixed media collages. She also has strong connection with interior design and has translated many of her works to murals and textiles for home furnishings (Figure 8.4).

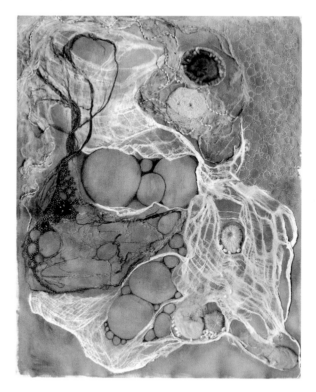

8.4 Textile artist Julie Shackson started this artwork by adding acrylic paints to canvas using the colors of a shoreline beach pool as inspiration. She then added soaked and stretched mulberry bark and dyed silk fibers. Embellishment was added in the form of beadwork, embroidered silk cocoons, and real pearls. Shackson then teased out shapes and forms with dyed scrim and velvet and then added both hand embroidery and free-motion machine embroidery to make bubbles in the water. Finally, she drew some pebbles with a fine pencil and darkened the shadows with an ink pen.
Courtesy Julie Shackson

ENVIRONMENTAL IMPACT: COMBINING SURFACE DESIGN TECHNIQUES

When it comes to combining techniques, the best way to limit the impact on the environment is to recycle and upcycle. Consider using salvaged yardage of fabric as a base or a piece of vintage lace as an appliqué. Deconstruct old garments or upholstery to create samples. Use a collection of buttons as embellishments or embroider using an old ball of yarn. Look around before making any purchases. Hidden treasures can be found everywhere and that includes reusing treasures of the past. Upcycling garments and upholstery can bring new life to old objects.

Search through fabric and swatch bins for fabric to use as samples. Experimenting on as many different kinds of fabric as possible is pivotal to the success of any technique. So, why not experiment on fabric that would have otherwise ended up in a landfill?

As a designer, be mindful of the materials that you consume and the effect that consumption has on the environment. Avoid waste with careful planning, and experiment on small samples of fabric before moving on to larger pieces. Not only will this save a lot of money, it will also help to protect our environment.

Karen Casper, a United Kingdom–based textile artist and designer, creates mixed media fine art pieces, garments, and headpieces. She does not focus on one technique in particular but enjoys combing techniques like devoré, quilting, print, fabric manipulation, and embellishment for the most unique and tactile results. Even though Casper uses traditional textile techniques, she stays true to her vintage esthetic and incorporates contemporary technology to produce "innovative futuristic pieces that ultimately create an art and fashion crossover"[3] (Figures 8.5a and b).

8.5a *Coraline*, created by Karen Casper, is an exploration of the environmental issues that threaten coral reefs and their habitats caused by pollution, destructive fishing practices, overfishing, careless tourism, and the subsequent effect this damage has on sea life. This garment represents the textures, colors, and contours of the underwater world, creating "preserved textiles." Casper wanted the bodice to reflect the growth and cultivation of the natural world. She did that by using traditional textile techniques and vintage materials injected with contemporary technology to create something otherworldly. This image shows the "day" colors of certain coral species; when the lights go out, the glow-in-the-dark "night" version representing the electric creatures of the Abyss emerges. The piece is constructed using Casper's signature 3D embroidery that includes antique/vintage lace. This piece also includes quilting, devoré, digital print, and lots of embellishment.
© *Ian McManus Photography, www.ianmcmanus.com*

8.5b A close-up of Karen Casper's piece *Coraline*.
© *Ian McManus Photography, www.ianmcmanus.com*

Karen Nicol is an embroidery and mixed-media textile artist who has created work for gallery, fashion, and interior design in her London-based design and production studio for over 25 years. She designs "demi-couture" custom embroidery for a ready-to-wear market with an inventive range of skills. Her materials, resources, and techniques are constantly changing and adapting to fashion needs. Clients like Chloé, Givenchy, and Chanel have taken advantage of her ability to create "painterly" fabric applications (Figures 8.6a and b).

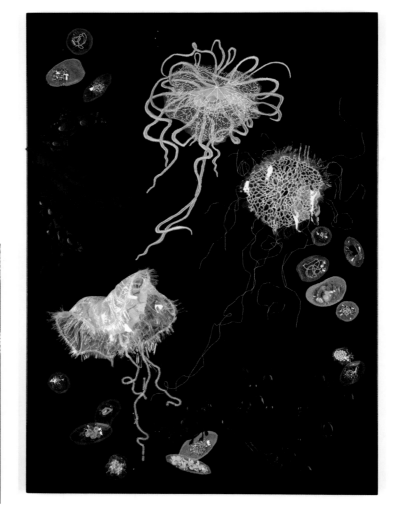

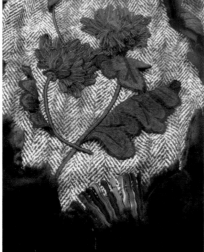

8.6a This is a dip-dyed vintage skirt with fur and sequin trim. It is embroidered with black and indigo viscose threads, and the leaves are machine embroidered on felt and partially sewn to the background.
© Karen Nicol

8.6b This is a piece by Nicol commissioned for Shell Oil London as part of an oceanography exhibit. Scoured clear sequined ribbons are used with glass, organza, indigo-dyed cloth, beads, and Irish embroidery. Tiny beads were placed inside organza pockets and appliquéd to the surface. Long embroidery stitches weave through sheer fabric circles to represent the jellyfish's body, and gossamer threads create the tentacles.
© Karen Nicol

Nava Lubelski works with accidents using stained or damaged textiles that she contrasts with very deliberate needlework to compare the chance nature of the stain with the tediousness of hand embroidery (Figures 8.7a and b). She says that her work "explores the contradictions between the impulse to destroy and the compulsion to mend."[4]

8.7a This is a piece by Neva Lubelski called *Structurally Sound*, created in 2010. Stains on fabric are highlighted with machine stitching around drips of color. What appears to be an impact splatter is a heavily embroidered cutwork circle that is held in place with a web of threads in turquoise and rose. Tight blanket stitches in white and black help to create the splatter effect, while bursts of yellow and orange add unexpected depth to the piece.
© *Nava Lubelski*

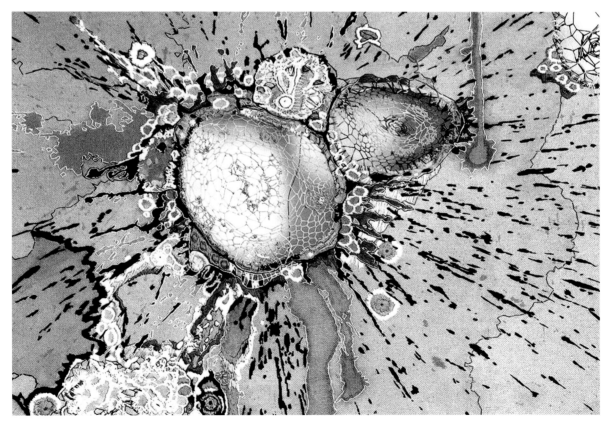

8.7b Detail of *Structurally Sound* by Nava Lubelski.
© *Nava Lubelski*

STUDENT PROJECTS

1. *Upcycling:* Adding techniques to an existing garment, home decoration, or furniture is a great way to breath new life into old objects. Select a product in your home (garment, curtains, throw pillows, slip covers, etc.) and give it an upgrade. Select a minimum of three techniques from this text and apply them to the chosen product. For example, using dark-colored cotton curtains, the techniques applied could be adding a print using discharge paste, overdyeing the entire piece so the discharged areas became a new color, and then foiling could be added sparingly to create a slight shimmer. Record the process and be prepared to discuss the results. Think about the market and potential price points.

2. *Create a Fine Art Piece:* Fine art isn't limited to paintings and sculptures; it also encompasses the field of textile design. Create a fine art piece. The dimensions are up to you, but it should be a minimum of 36" × 36". Use a least eight different techniques in the piece and consider basic principles of design such as balance, proportion, rhythm, scale, and color. Think about how the piece will be presented:, will it be hung on a wall or is it a three-dimensional piece? Then create samples and sketches to gather your ideas before starting the final piece. Record your process and be prepared to discuss/defend your material and technique choices.

3. *Varying Layered Combinations:* Create a collection of six samples measuring at least 6" × 6". Start by selecting an inspiration, color story, and fabric. Choose at least five techniques to layer on each sample. Use the same materials for each sample but layer them differently. Remember that some techniques have the best results when completed early in the process, but sometimes the "best" results aren't always the desired results. Start with small samples to experiment while recording your process thoroughly. Keeping records will help tremendously when completing the final six samples. Present your collection professionally and be prepared to discuss what worked and what didn't, both technically and aesthetically.

ENDNOTES

1. "threeASFOUR: Designer Biography," New York Magazine Fashion Shows, accessed June 6, 2012, http://nymag.com/fashion/fashionshows/designers/bios/asfour/.

2. "Julie Shackson Artist: Biography," accessed May 15, 2014, http://www.julieshackson.com.

3. "Tulle Candy and Floss: Karen Casper," accessed May 15, 2014, http://www.tulleandcandyfloss.co.uk.

4. "Nava Lubelski," Accessed June 6, 2012. http://www.navalubelski.com.

APPENDIX A
Tips, Workspace, and Preparation

BURN TEST

A burn test can be done to determine fiber content. Using tweezers, hold a small section of fabric and burn with a match or lighter. The way the fabric reacts to heat and flame will help to determine its fiber content. Always use caution and work near a water source.

Natural Fibers

Natural fibers such as cotton, hemp, and rayon will burn rapidly and produce an afterglow. The scent is similar to burning paper (Figure A.1).

A.1 When natural fibers like cotton, hemp, and rayon are burned, they produce a glow and a scent similar to burning paper.

Synthetic Fibers

Synthetic fibers such a polyester and nylon melt when they come into contact with the flame but quickly burn out, leaving a hard bead. The odor is similar to melting plastic (Figure A.2).

A.2 Synthetic fibers melt when in contact with a flame but burn out quickly, leaving a hard bead.

Wool and Silk Fibers

Wool and silk fibers burn slowly and tend to char. They leave a crushable ash and have a scent similar to burning hair (Figure A.3).

A.3 Wool and silk fibers char and crumble when burned, emitting a scent similar to burning hair.

STABILIZERS

Stabilizers are used to prevent puckering and distortion of fabric during stitching and printing techniques. Many products are available to suit almost any need. Be sure to read the manufacturer's instructions to determine if the product is right for the fabric and technique chosen.

The most common stabilizers are tear-away stabilizers for stitching on heavyweight to medium-weight fabrics. They can be torn easily from the back of the fabric after stitching. Water- or heat-soluble stabilizers are used on lightweight, delicate fabrics and lace and can be removed with water or an iron after stitching is complete.

Freezer paper is commonly used for printing and transfer techniques to keep the fabric flat during dye application and while drying. It is applied by ironing the shiny side of the paper to the back side of fabric (Figure A.4).

A.4 Various stabilizers. Back: cotton ironed to the shiny side of household freezer paper. Left to right: water-soluble stabilizer, heat-soluble stabilizer, tear-away stabilizer.

TRANSFER METHODS

Most decorative stitching techniques require designs to be marked onto the fabric's surface. A local craft or sewing store will have a variety of options useful for any stitching technique on any color fabric. Choose a product that is easy to use, highly visible, and can be removed based on the needs of the fabric. For example, water-soluble marking tools can only be used on washable fabrics and trims. Dark fabrics require the use of light-colored chalks or pens.

Transferring designs to the fabric's surface depends upon its color and density. For lightweight and light-colored fabrics a light box works well, while chalk paper and a tracing wheel work best on dark-colored, heavyweight fabric (Figure A.5).

A.5 Design transfer methods include, from left to right: lightbox, water-soluble white chalk pencil, tracing wheel used with tracing paper, disappearing pen in white, tailor's chalk, and colored wax-free tracing paper.

MAKING A STAMP

Stamps can be made with most household objects including washers, buttons, or rope. Objects such as these can be glued to wooden blocks or dowel rods. Complex patterns can be achieved by carving into a rubber pad using special carving tools (Figure A.6).

A.6 Left to right: stamps created by gluing household objects to wooden blocks, pins and nails pressed into a cork, and a rubber stamp carved with specialized tools.

CREATING A PADDED WORK SURFACE

A padded work surface is useful for many printing and transfer techniques. It creates a soft surface onto which fabric can easily be pinned to maintain a smooth, even printing surface. The batting used in a padded table is particularly useful for screen printing and stamping because it allows the screen or stamp to be pressed firmly and evenly onto the fabric's surface.

Materials

+ Muslin
+ Quilter batting (on a roll)
+ Sheet of plywood
+ Staple gun and staples

Instructions

1. Using a large piece of plywood, staple batting to the board using a staple gun. Be sure to wrap the batting tightly around the plywood to avoid lumps.
2. Wrap a piece of muslin around the padded board and on the back and staple into place.

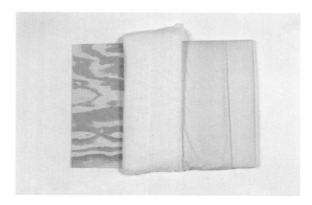

A.7 A padded work surface can be created by stapling sheet batting and muslin tightly around a plywood board.

STRETCHING FABRIC

Fabric is often stretched onto wooden frames before resists and dyes are applied. It keeps the fabric tight and free from puckering and pulling during resist and dye application and while drying.

Materials

Figure A.8 shows some of the the materials needed to stretch fabric.

+ Design to be transferred
+ Fabric to be stretched
+ Hammer
+ Masking tape
+ Pencil for transferring pattern
+ Pushpins
+ Stretcher bars appropriate to the size of the project

A.8 Materials needed to stretch fabric onto a wooden frame.

Instructions

1. Assemble wooden stretcher frame. Make sure to create a stretcher that is comparable to the size of the finished piece.
2. Lay fabric over the stretcher and secure four points, creating a "+" sign, with pushpins. Be sure that the fabric is tight, but not tight enough to pull it off-grain.

A.9 Start by placing pushpin in a + pattern. Pull fabric tight but not tight enough to pull it off-grain.

3. Next, secure the corners of the fabric with pushpins, keeping the fabric tight.

A.10 Secure the four corners with pushpins.

4. Continue pulling fabric tight and securing with pushpins. Always attach pushpins in pairs. Make sure that the pin on the opposite side of the frame is parallel to the first.

5. Apply masking tape around the edges to protect the fabric from fraying.

A.11 Apply masking tape around the frame, securing the ends of the fabric to keep it from fraying.

6. To transfer a design to stretched fabric, tape the paper pattern to the back side of the stretched fabric, inside the frame, so that it is flush against the fabric. The design will be visible from the right side when using a light-colored, lightweight fabric such as silk.

A.12 Tape paper, design facing down, to the back side of the screen so that it is flush against the screen mesh.

7. Using a pencil or water-soluble marker, lightly trace the pattern onto the fabric.

A.13 Trace the design onto the fabric using a light pencil line or a water-soluble marker.

CREATING A SCREEN

Screens are often used for printing because they allow an image to be reproduced consistently. Screen mesh is stretched across a wooden stretcher and secured with staples. Duct tape is applied next to protect the frame from water damage that can occur after repeated rinsing. After a design is transferred to the screen, Speedball Drawing Fluid is painted onto the surface of the mesh. This will be the part of the design that will be printed. Once dried, a Speedball Screen Filler is added to clog the unpainted portion of the screen and prohibit dye penetration in those areas. Once dry, the drawing fluid is washed away using warm water. After one last opportunity to dry, the screen is ready for use.

Materials

Figure A.14 shows some of the materials needed to create a screen for printing.

+ Design to be transferred
+ Duct tape
+ Hammer
+ Paintbrush
+ Pencil or water-soluble marker
+ Plastic spoon
+ Rubber gloves

+ Speedball Drawing Fluid (Figure A.15)
+ Speedball Screen Filler (Figure A.16)
+ Screen-printing mesh
+ Staple gun and staples
+ Squeegee (Figure A.17)
+ Wooden stretcher appropriate to the project size

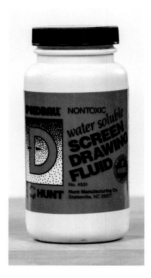 

A.15 Speedball Drawing Fluid.   **A.16** Speedball Screen Filler.

A.17 A squeegee used to draw Speedball Screen Filler across a mesh screen.

A.14 Materials needed to create a screen for printing.

Instructions

1. Lay screen mesh over assembled wooden frame and, with a staple gun, staple into place using the same procedure as in Stretching Fabric, Steps 1 through 4.

2. Hammer down any raised staples.

3. Apply duct tape to the top side of the screen covering the staples. The duct tape helps to keep water from collecting in the cracks of the screen and damaging the project.

5. Continue adding duct tape until the wooden frame is covered.

6. To transfer a design, tape the pattern to the back of the screen and use a pencil or water-soluble marker to trace it onto the fabric's surface.

7. Using Speedball Drawing Fluid and a paintbrush, apply drawing fluid to the front side of the screen, being sure that the design is thoroughly covered. Any gaps or areas of thin application will not block out the screen filler.

A.18 Apply duct tape onto wooden frame, covering staples.

A.20 Apply Speedball Drawing Fluid to the front of the screen using a paintbrush.

4. Flip the screen over and, using duct tape, create a lip that reaches from the edge of the stretcher and onto the screen. This will act as a well for the dye to be placed for printing.

8. Allow to dry completely.

9. Using a plastic spoon, apply Speedball Screen Filler to the lip created with duct tape on the backside of the screen.

A.19 Create a lip (dye well) on the back side of the screen using duct tape.

A.21 Using a plastic spoon, apply Speedball Screen Filler to the lip created with duct tape on the back side of the screen.

10. Using a squeegee, draw the screen filler across the screen in even strokes. Depending on the size of the screen and the squeegee, more than one pass may be necessary.

11. Allow screen filler to dry.

12. In a large sink, spray the screen until the drawing fluid dissolves. Sometimes an old toothbrush is necessary to get out any stubborn areas.

13. Allow to dry before use.

A.22 Use a squeegee to draw Speedball Screen Filler evenly across the mesh. More than one swipe may be necessary, depending on the size of the screen and squeegee.

A.23 A finished screen, dried and ready for printing.

SETTING UP A STEAMER

Materials

+ Bundled fabric
+ Metal colander (used only for steaming fabric) or aluminum foil punctured with small holes for lightweight bundles.
+ Metal pot with lid (used only for steaming or dyeing fabric)
+ Towel

Instructions

1. Select a metal colander that can fit upside down inside a large metal pot, or, for lightweight bundles, lay aluminum foil over the pot and press down to create a small bowl shape. Using a pencil puncture small holes in the aluminum.

2. Add a few inches of water to the pot, making sure that water level will not reach the fabric bundle.

3. Rest fabric bundle on top of the colander or aluminum foil.

4. Fold an old towel a few times so that it fits on top of the pot without touching the burner and cover with a lid. This helps to absorb any excess water and avoid droplet marks on the fabric.

5. Allow to steam for an appropriate time based upon the chosen technique.

A.24 Fabric steaming can be done with a large pot and an upside-down colander.

APPENDIX B
Visual Library of Materials

Throughout this text, many different supplies, products, and tools are used. Use this library of images as a reference for selecting appropriate materials.

COLOR REMOVER

B.25 Color remover—RIT brand, Chapter 2, Color Remover

B.26 Discharge paste—Jacquard brand, Chapter 2, Discharge Paste Technique

DYE

B.27 Acid dye—Jacquard brand, Chapter 1, Acid Dye

B.28 Disperse dye, Chapter 1, Disperse Dye

B.29 Leather dye—Fiebing's brand, Chapter 1, Leather Dye

B.30 Marbling dyes, Chapter 3, Marbling

B.31 Setacolor dyes, Chapter 3, Sun Printing

B.32 Silk dyes—Jacquard brand, Chapter 2, Gutta on Silk

DYE BINDERS, CARRIERS, AND DISSOLVING AGENTS

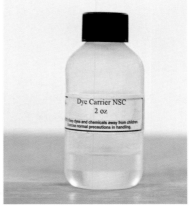

B.34 Calgon (water softener), Chapter 3, How to Thicken Disperse Dye

B.33 Alum, Chapter 1, Household/Organic Dye Methods

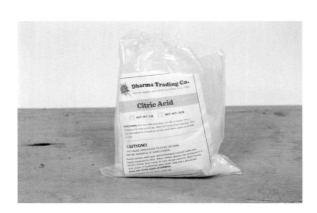

B.35 Citric acid, Chapter 1, Acid Dye

B.36 Dye carrier, Chapter 1, Disperse Dye

B.37 Methocel and alum, Chapter 3, Marbling

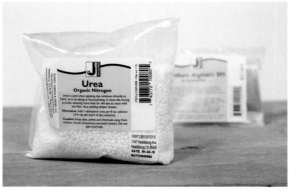

B.38 Urea, Chapter 3, How to Thicken Acid Dye

DYE SET

B.39 Dye set—Jacquard brand, Chapter 2, Gutta on Silk

DYE THICKENER

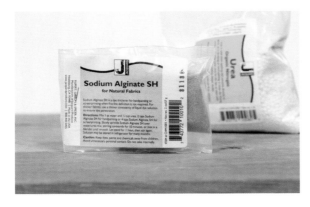

B.40 Sodium alginate, Chapter 3, How to Thicken Acid Dye

EMBELLISHMENT

B.41 Twill tape, Chapter 7, Feathering

EMBROIDERY

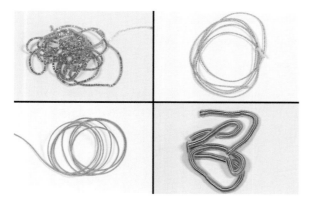

B.42 Gold threads. Clockwise: Gilt No. 4 bright check purl, fine Grecian twist, No. 6 wire bullion, No. 4 jaceron, Chapter 6, Gold Thread Embroidery

FELTING

B.43 Felting needles, Chapter 4, Needle Felting

B.44 Foam pad, Chapter 4, Needle Felting

FIBER REMOVER

B.45 Fiber Etch, Chapter 4, Fiber Removal Using Fiber Etch

LEATHER TOOLING

B.46 Compass, Chapter 4, Carving

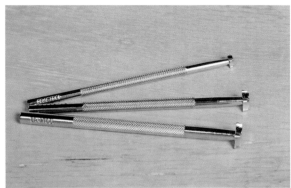

B.47 Leather stamps, Chapter 4, Carving

B.48 Modeling spoons, Chapter 4, Carving

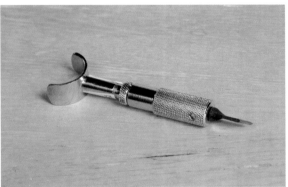

B.49 Swivel knife, Chapter 4, Carving

PRINTING

B.50 Freezer paper, Chapter 3, Monoprinting

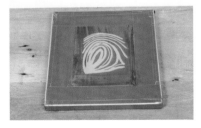

B.51 Screen used for screen printing, Chapter 3, Screen Printing

B.52 Squeegee, Chapter 3, Screen Printing

QUILTING MATERIALS

B.53 Cording, Chapter 5, Cording

B.54 HeatnBond, Chapter 5, Applique

B.55 Polyester batting, Chapter 5, Trapunto

B.56 Sheet batting, Chapter 5, Machine Quilting

RESISTS

B.57 Gutta and applicator bottle, Chapter 2, Gutta on Silk

B.58 Eco-Flo leather resist, Chapter 2, Leather Resist

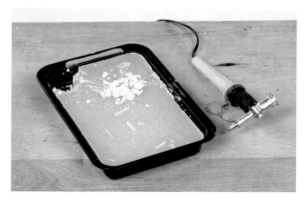

B.59 Tjanting and wax, Chapter 2, Batik

STABILIZERS

B.60 Sulky water-soluble stabilizer, Chapter 6, Free-Motion Embroidery

GLOSSARY

acid dyes Dyes used on animal protein fibers.

acrylic bead Refers to any bead made of synthetic materials.

alcohol-based leather dyes Leather dyes that are quickly absorbed into the surface of the leather and dry rapidly.

appliqué Stitching one fabric to another background fabric.

back stitch A basic stitch used to attach individual beads in a continuous line across the fabric's surface.

basic shirring Threads are stitched across the surface of the fabric in parallel lines. The fabric is then slowly scrunched up the threads until the desired amount of puckering has occurred.

bandhani An Indian word used to describe a shibori technique.

batik Applying hot wax to a fabric's surface to eliminate a dye's ability to penetrate that area.

batting Fiber filling used in quilting fabric.

battu Flat metal strips of gold used in gold work.

beading The art of embellishing fabric with beads.

bias cut Fabric cut at a 45-degree angle to allow the fabric to stretch.

blanket stitch A finishing stitch often used along the edge of blankets.

block printing, or *stamping* Using household objects or a specially designed carved block to apply dye to fabric.

bobbin work The use of a bobbin to sew threads to fabric that cannot easily feed into a standard sewing machine.

broderie chimique A term used to describe fabric that simulates machine embroidery.

bugle beads Narrow, oval shaped beads.

buttonhole stitch Tightly packed blanket stitches.

cellulose fibers Plant fibers.

chain stitch A series of looped stitches that resemble a chain once complete.

chrome tanning The most common type of leather tanning. It uses a mixture of chromium sulfate and other chemicals to permanently change the color of leather.

cochineal An insect, that when crushed provides a crimson color.

colorfastness A fabric's ability to retain a vibrant color.

cording Narrow, stitched channels of fabric filled with yarn or cord to create ridges.

couching An embroidery technique in which yarns or thick threads are laid onto the surface of a fabric and attached with small consistent stitches. Also refers to a beading technique in which prestrung beads are laid on top of fabric and secured using a stitch that is passed over the string of beads and into the fabric to keep them secure.

cross stitch X-shaped stitches that can be created singularly or worked in rows.

cutwork The removal of pieces of fabric using Fiber Etch or small embroidery scissors.

cyanotype/sun printing Images created using the sun to "develop" a transfer pattern onto fabric that has been treated with a specially designed dye.

dangle stitch Beads that are attached to hang independently from the fabric's surface, much like fringe.

devoré, or *burn out* The removal of fibers from a fabric's surface.

dimensional felting, or *inclusion felting* The practice of adding a third dimension to the surface of the felted fabric.

direct application Directly applying dye to the surface of the fabric using brushes, stamps, or screens.

direct smocking A hand-stitching technique that gathers fabric into small shapes as the threads are pulled tight.

discharge paste A paste used to remove, discharge, or extract color from a previously dyed fabric.

disperse dyes Dyes used on synthetic fibers.

drawn thread work Removing individual threads from a fabric.

drawn work, or *open work* The manipulation of threads within a fabric.

dye A chemical bath of a colorant dissolved into water used to permanently change the color of a fabric.

earth staining Using dirt, soil, or clay to create a pattern on fabric.

ebru Controlled method of marbling developed in Turkey.

elastic shirring The use of elastic to create a shirred fabric.

embellisher Commercial felting machine.

embellishment The art of adding three-dimensional objects to the surface of fabric to create shine, dimension, and drama.

embroidery A decorative pattern created by sewing threads through or onto fabric.

embroidery needle, or *crewel needle* Medium-length needle with a long eye.

English smocking Shirred fabric is stitched and bound into decorative patterns.

fabric manipulation The act of manipulating the surface of fabric to create a three-dimensional pattern through additional sewing, stuffing, or folding.

feathering The use of feathers as an embellishment.

felt A nonwoven cloth that's been pressed together and has no internal structure such as threads or an adhesive to maintain its stability.

fiber reactive dye Dye used on cellulose fibers.

filling stitch A stitch used to fill in shapes with beads.

fixed Making a design permanent on fabric.

foiling Using glue or fusible webbing to adhere foil to fabric.

free-motion embroidery A web-like pattern of stitches achieved using a sewing machine.

French knot Raised, knotted points of thread on the surface of the fabric.

glittering Using glue or fusible webbing to adhere glitter to fabric.

grass and leaf staining The use of grasses and leaves to stain fabric.

ground fabric The background fabric that embroidery is created on.

guipure Low-relief metal-thread embroidery.

gutta A thick latex resist used to create intricate details; used almost exclusively on silk.

hydrophobic fabrics Water-repellent fabrics.

immersion technique, or *tub dyeing method* Fabric is submersed and agitated until the color is sufficiently absorbed.

indigo Natural substance used to achieve blue dye colors.

leather carving Compressing parts of the leather surface to create a relief.

leather dyeing Application of a consistent color to the surface of leather.

leather embellishing The addition of beads to a piece of leather using prepunched holes.

leather embroidery Embroidery created on a piece of leather.

leather molding Creating a three-dimensional design by carefully stretching wet, vegetable-tanned leather over a waterproof form, securing it, and allowing it to dry thoroughly.

leather resists Applied to vegetable-tanned leather to eliminate the full penetration of water-based leather stains.

leather tooling The manipulation of the surface of leather with the use of knives, modeling spoons, or stamps to carve away material, creating a negative pattern, or molding wet leather over a form to create a positive effect.

lentil beads, or *sequins* Flat beads with a hole in the center and designed to be stacked or overlayed.

machine quilting Using a sewing machine to create straight, even, and consistent stitch lines across padded fabric.

madder Natural substance used to achieve reds, purples, violets, and browns in dyes.

Madeira embroidery A white needlework technique composed of patterns of small holes or eyelets.

marbling, or *Suminagashi* Technique created by placing dye upon a treated water bath. The Japanese word means "ink floating."

metal-thread embroidery Embroidery created with gold or silver metal threads.

monoprinting A combination of printmaking and painting that creates a single image that can be transferred onto fabric.

mordant, or *dye carrier* Helps dye adhere to fabric and provides colorfastness.

needle eye The loop at the top of the needle that the thread passes through.

needle felting, or *dry felting* The creation of felt using only wool and a barbed needle that is moved through the surface of the wool into a foam board until the fibers begin to bond and tangle.

nuno felting Felting with natural fibers.

oil-based leather dyes Leather dyes made of an oil base: they penetrate the leather and even soften the hand.

oil tanning, or *latigo* A process that creates a water-resistant, flexible, strong leather that is often used for laces or products such as shoes that are consistently exposed to the elements.

paruriers Haute couture embroidery houses.

passementerie The addition of ribbons, braids, or trim to the surface of fabric to resemble a woven or embroidered pattern.

patchwork The creation of fabric by sewing together smaller, often mismatched pieces to create a large piece of fabric, or attaching one fabric to another background fabric.

pattern tucks, or *pintucks* Tiny folds of raised fabric secured with stitching along the entire fold.

plangi A word used in Indonesia to describe a shibori technique.

pleats Folds of fabric are pulled from the surface and secured using stitches at one end to create fullness at the other.

plunging method A technique that uses a large needle to plunge the gold thread to the backside of the fabric.

potato dextrin An organic resist made with actual potatoes and used to create a crackled appearance on fabric.

printing The act of applying an easily repeatable pattern to fabric.

protein fibers Animal fibers.

Prussian blue Bright blue color traditionally associated with cyanotype.

purls Hollow metal threads used in metal thread embroidery.

quilting Stitching that fastens three layers of fabric together.

rapport A high-relief metal-thread pattern.

raw leather Leather with all fats and oils removed.

resists Used to block the penetration of dye, stain, or paint on a fabric's surface.

Richelieu cutwork Fabric made of distinctive buttonhole bars crossed through the cut-out areas of a fabric.

roving Precarded and predyed wool.

rusting The creation of a pattern on fabric or leather using any rusty metal object.

satin stitch A stitch often used to fill in large areas. It can be made at an angle or straight across and consists of side-by-side stitches.

scoured Fabric washed in very hot water (140 degrees) to remove any dirt, oil, or sizing.

screen printing A method of printing that allows for an exact repeat of a clean crisp image by pressing dye through a thin, painted mesh screen wrapped around a wooden frame.

seed beads Tiny round beads sometimes used as a filler between larger beads.

sequins Small, flat "beads" often applied in groups to add shine and drama. They are secured individually using a back stitch and worked from right to left.

Setacolor Sunlight-reactive dye.

shibori, or *tie-dying* Technique of binding or folding of fabric before it is placed into a dye bath.

shirring Fabric that is contracted to a smaller size when gathered along multiple parallel rows of straight stitching and is sometimes filled with cording.

Silk Road A trade route that connected Asia to the western civilizations of Europe.

sizing A chemical coating applied to fabric to repel stains or dirt.

smocking Finely pleated or folded fabric that is stitched and bound.

spirit- or water-based leather dye A nontoxic leather dye.

squeegee A tool used in screen printing that forces the dye over the screen and through the mesh.

staining Adding pattern to fabric using direct application by applying objects, dye, or paint directly to the surface of the fabric.

standard pleating The consistent folding of fabrics to create fullness.

standard tucks Controlled folds of fabric that are stitched along the entire fold.

stay A piece of fabric used to stabilize an area.

stop stitch A stitch used to attach two beads, usually a single large bead or beads that will stand on end and a small bead (the stop) to help secure larger beads.

stumpwork Raised or padded embroidery.

Synthrapol A commercial, concentrated cleaner used to scour fabric and to fix dye in a final dye bath.

tanning The process of permanently changing the color and hand of leather.

tapestry needle, or *chenille needle* Blunt, short needle with a large eye.

tjanting A penlike tool that keeps wax hot so that it slowly drains toward the tip during batik application.

transfer printing Applying a pattern to fabric or leather using dye, paint, or stain which is often not repeatable.

trapunto, or *Italian quilting* Traditionally created by stitching the outline of a shape or pattern through two layers of fabric—the top fabric and the lining—and then stuffed with batting.

trompe l'oeil Embroidery that simulates other techniques like quilting, passementerie, and bobbin work.

tucks Folds of fabric are pulled from the surface and stitched from one end of the fabric to the other.

vat discharging Removing color in a large tub or washing machine.

vegetable tanning Leather tanning technique with a combination of oak bark and other chemicals.

Venetian cutwork Characterized by a padded buttonhole stitch around open areas.

warp Horizontal thread within a fabric.

webbed fusing, or *glue webbing* Used to adhere foil or glitter to fabric.

weft Lengthwise thread within a fabric.

wet felt Created by layering roving. Each layer runs perpendicular to the one below to ensure that the fibers entangle. Heat, moisture, and an agitator are used to create a compact fabric.

BIBLIOGRAPHY

100 Fashion Designers: Cuttings from Contemporary Fashion. New York: Phaidon Press Inc., 2005.

Barton Jane, Mary Kellogg Rice, and Yoshiko Iwamoto Wada. *Shibori: The Inventive Art of Japanese Shaped Resist Dyeing*. Tokyo, Japan: Kodansha International Ltd., 1999.

Bednar, Nancy, and JoAnn Pugh-Gannon. *Encyclopedia of Sewing Machine Techniques*. New York: Sterling Publishing Co., Inc., 2001.

Belfer, Nancy. *Batik and Tie Dye Techniques*. New York: Dover Publications, 1992.

Best, Muriel. *Stumpwork: Historical and Contemporary Raised Embroidery*. London: B.T. Batsford Limited, 1987.

Blum, Diyls E. *Roberto Capucci: Art of Fashion*. Philadelphia, PA/New Haven, CT: Philadelphia Museum of Art in association with Yale University Press, 2011.

Bosence, Susan. *Hand Block Printing and Resist Dyeing*. Newton Abbot, UK: David & Charles, 1985.

Brackmann, Holly. *The Surface Designer's Handbook*. Loveland, CO: Interweave Press LLC, 2006.

Buck, J. Robert. *Leather: The New Frontier in Art*. Fort Worth, TX: Tandy Leather Company, 1992.

Calasibetta, Charlotte Mankey, and Phyllis Tortora. *Dictionary of Fashion*. New York: Fairchild Publications, 2003.

Chenoune, Farid. *Carried Away: All About Bags*. New York: Vendome Press, 2005.

Clarke, Simon. *Textile Design*. London: Laurence King Publishing, 2011.

Coles, Janet, and Robert Budwig. *Beads: An Exploration of Bead Traditions Around the World*. New York: Simon and Schuster, 1997.

Conlon, Jane. *Fine Embellishment Techniques*. Newtown, CT: The Taunton Press, 2001.

Crabtree, Amanda. "Time with Tinctory." *Bella Armoire*, September/October, 2010.

Crabtree, Caroline, and Christine Shaw. *Quilting, Patchwork & Applique*. London: Thames & Husdon, 2007.

"A Dash of Salt," *Alternative Photography*. Accessed March 30, 2012, http://www.alternativephotography .com/wp/processes/saltprints/a-dash-of-salt.

Deschodft, Anne-Marie, and Doretta Davanzo Poli. *Fortuny*. New York: Harry N. Abrams, Inc. Publishers, 2000.

"Did You Know . . . How Acid Dye Works." Accessed April 29, 2014, http://www.dharmatrading.com /home/did-you-know-how-acid-dye-works.html.

"Dionne Swift: Textile Artist." Accessed June 2, 2012, http://www.dionneswift.co.uk.

Dubin, Lois Sherr. *The History of Beads: From 100,000 B.C. to the Present*. New York: Abrams, 2009.

Duerr, Sasha. *The Handbook of Natural Plant Dyes*. Portland, OR: Timber Press, 2011.

Dunnewold, Jane. *Complex Cloth: A Comprehensive Guide to Surface Design*. Washington: Martingale & Company, 1996.

Elisha, Dorit. *Printmaking and Mixed Media*. Loveland, CO: Interweave Press LLC, 2009.

The Editors of Creative Publishing. *Exploring Textile Arts*. Minnetonka, MN: Creative Publishing International, 2002.

The Embroiderers' Guild. "Drawn Thread Work." Accessed April 14, 2012, http://www.embroiderersguildwa.org.au/Types%20of%20Embroidery/DrawnThread.htm.

The Embroiderers' Guild. *Embroidery Studio*. Newton Abbot, UK: David & Charles, 1996.

Fausset, Richard. "Mardi Gras Beads Cause Environmental Hangover." *Los Angeles Times*, February 15, 2013. Accessed May 14, 2013, http://articles.latimes.com/2012/feb/15/nation/la-na-mardi-gras-beads-20120216.

Ishii, Setsuko. *Dyes from Kitchen Produce*. Mulgrave, Vic., Australia: Images Publishing, 2010.

"Julie Shackson Artist: Biography." Accessed May 15, 2014, http://www.julieshackson.com.

Kamitsis, Lydia. *Lesage*. New York: Universe/Vendome Publishing, 2000.

Kerlogue, Fiona. *Batik: Design, Style, and History*. New York: Thames and Hudson, 2004.

Kosloff, Albert. *Textile/Garment Screen Printing*. Cincinnati, OH: ST Publications, 1987.

Lambert, Eva, and Tracy Kendell. *The Complete Guide to Natural Dyeing*. Loveland, CO: Interweave Press LLC, 2010.

Lane, Ruth. *The Complete Photo Guide to Felting*. Minneapolis: Creative Publishing International, Inc., 2012.

Llado i Riba, Maria Teresa, and Eva Pascual i Miro. *The Art and Craft of Leather: Leatherworking Tools and Techniques Explained in Detail*. New York: Barron's, 2006.

Maddox, William A., Dr. *Historical Carvings in Leather*. San Antonio, TX: The Naylor Company, 1940.

Maurer-Mathison, Diane. *The Ultimate Marbling Handbook*. New York: Watson-Guptill Publications, 1999.

McPherson, Di. "Mud and Dirt: Australian Soil as Self-Expression." *Textile Society of America Symposium Readings* 225 (2008). Accessed May 1, 2014, http://digitalcommons.enl.edu/tsaconf/255.

Merriam-Webster Dictionary. Online edition. Springfield, MA: Merriam-Webster, 2003. Also available at www.merriam-webster.com.

Mullins, Willow. *Felt*. New York: Berg, 2009.

"Nava Lubelski." Accessed June 6, 2012, http://www.navalubelski.com.

Nicol, Karen. *Embellished: New Vintage*. London: A&C Black Publishers, 2012.

Oelbaum, Zeva. *Blue Prints: The Natural World in Cyanotype Photographs*. New York: Rizzoli, 2002.

Packwood, Kimberly. *Rust and Clay Dyeing*. Iowa, 2006. E-edition.

Quinn, Bradley. *Textile Designer at the Cutting Edge*. London: Laurence King Publishing Ltd, 2009.

"Sabi Westoby: Artist Statement." Accessed May 7, 2014, http://www.sabiwestoby.com/artists-statement.html.

Sabi Westoby, email message to author, May 8, 2014.

Singer, Margo. *Textile Surface Decoration: Silk and Velvet*. Philadelphia: University of Pennsylvania Press, 2007.

Spivak, Emily. "A History of Sequins from King Tut to the King of Pop." *Smithsonian.com*, December 28, 2012. Accessed May 14, 2014, http://www.smithsonianmag.com/arts-culture/a-history-of-sequins-from-king-tut-to-the-king-of-pop-8035/?no-ist.

Tellier-Loumagne, Francoise. *The Art of Embroidery: Inspiration Stitches, Textures and Surfaces.* London: Thames and Hudson, 2006.

"Timeline of Fabric History." Threads in Tyme LTD. Accessed May 5, 2014, http://threadsintyme.tripod.com/timelineoffabrichistory.htm.

"threeASFOUR: Designer Biography," New York Magazine Fashion Shows. Accessed June 6, 2012, http://nymag.com/fashion/fashionshows/designers/bios/asfour/.

Tresidder, Jack. *Dictionary of Symbols: An Illustrated Guide to Traditional Images, Icons, and Emblems.* San Francisco: Chronicle Books, 1998.

"Tulle Candy and Floss: Karen Casper." Accessed May 15, 2014, http://www.tulleandcandyfloss.co.uk.

Wallis, Susanna. *Beginner's Guide to Needle Felting.* Tunbridge Wells, Kent, UK: Search Press Limited, 2008.

Ware, Mike. *Cyanotype: History, Science and Art of Photographic Printing in Prussian Blue.* London: Science Museum and National Museum of Photography, Film and Television, 1999.

White, Christine. *Uniquely Felt.* North Adams, MA: Storey Publishing, 2007.

White, Palmer. *Haute Couture Embroidery: The Art of Lesage.* New York: The Vendome Press, 1987.

Wolf, Colette. *The Art of Manipulating Fabric.* Iola, WI: Krause Publications, 1996.

INDEX